ORDER PKI TC

TAKE AWAY: PUB. INFO MUST BE
   IN THE MANDATE -
Q? DOES ANYONE KNOW THIS
   PERSON? PATRICIA LEWIS?
   GET HER TO SIT SOUTHCOM
STEELE: DO INFO AUDIT ON HAITI?

PEACEKEEPING AND PUBLIC INFORMATION

THE CASS SERIES ON PEACEKEEPING
ISSN 1367-9880
General Editor: Michael Pugh

This series examines all aspects of peacekeeping, from the political, operational and legal dimensions to the developmental and humanitarian issues that must be dealt with by all those involved with peacekeeping in the world today.

1. *Beyond the Emergency: Development within UN Peace Missions*
   edited by Jeremy Ginifer

2. *The UN, Peace and Force*
   edited by Michael Pugh

3. *Mediating in Cyprus: The Cypriot Communities and the United Nations*
   by Oliver P. Richmond

4. *Peacekeeping and the UN Specialized Agencies*
   edited by Jim Whitman

5. *Peacekeeping and Public Information: Caught in the Crossfire*
   by Ingrid A. Lehmann

Peacekeeping and Public Information

Caught in the Crossfire

INGRID A. LEHMANN

FRANK CASS
LONDON • PORTLAND, OR

First published in 1999 in Great Britain by
FRANK CASS PUBLISHERS
Newbury House, 900 Eastern Avenue
London, IG2 7HH

and in the United States of America by
FRANK CASS PUBLISHERS
c/o ISBS, 5804 N.E. Hassalo Street
Portland, Oregon, 97213-3644

Website http://www.frankcass.com

Copyright © 1999 Ingrid A. Lehmann

British Library Cataloguing in Publication Data

Lehmann, Ingrid A.
  Peacekeeping and public information: caught in the
  crossfire. – (Cass series on peacekeeping; no. 5)
  1. Peace movements 2. Reconciliation 3. Reconciliation – Case
  studies 4. International relations 5. Peace – Government
  policy
  I. Title
  327.1'72

ISBN 0-7146-4930-9 (cloth)
ISBN 0-7146-4490-0 (paper)
ISSN 1367 9880

Library of Congress Cataloging-in-Publication Data

Lehmann, Ingrid A., 1948–
  Peacekeeping and public information: caught in the crossfire /
  Ingrid A. Lehmann.
    p. cm. – (Cass series on peacekeeping, ISSN 1367-9880; 5)
  Includes bibliographical references and index.
  ISBN 0-7146-4930-9 (cloth). – ISBN 0-7146-4490-0 (pbk.)
  1. United Nations–Armed Forces. 2. Communication in
  international relations. I. Title. II. Series.
  JZ6374.L44 1999
  327.1'72–dc21   98-47853
                                                  CIP

Typeset by Vitaset, Paddock Wood, Kent
Printed in Great Britain by
Bookcraft Ltd, Midsomer Norton, Somerset

Contents

List of Maps

I have come across men of letters who have written history without taking part in public affairs, and politicians who have concerned themselves with producing events without thinking about them. I have observed that the first are always inclined to find general causes, whereas the second, living in the midst of disconnected daily facts, are prone to imagine that everything is attributable to particular incidents, and that the wires they pull are the same as those that move the world. It is to be presumed that both are equally deceived.

Alexis de Toqueville

Preface

In 1994, while on leave from the United Nations, I began to look anew at some of the external political factors affecting my field of work. My role had been, for a number of years, to inform the public about United Nations activities in the maintenance of peace.

The fact that the UN's image in western countries, following a period of shortlived euphoria between 1989 and 1992, was approaching another low point in 1994 encouraged my rethinking of the issues of communications for international organizations. It was, nevertheless, a shock to realize that my nearly two decades of service in the organization had left me with a tendency to overreact to bureaucratic inefficiency and an exaggerated sense of institutional myopia.

A year as a Fellow at the Center for International Affairs at Harvard University both afforded me new insight into my profession and led me to end that phase of it. This resulted in my writing this book, *Peacekeeping and Public Information*, which deals with the interface of two professional fields: international communications and conflict management by international organizations.

Over the last three years, I have been greatly assisted and stimulated by many who have worked in peacekeeping, and by those who care about the free flow of information and the potential that global communications technologies offer to practitioners of international affairs.

I cannot name all the fellows and faculty members at Harvard's Center for International Affairs and at the Fletcher School of Diplomacy who encouraged and propelled my initial thought processes. In 1996–97, my last year of research and writing, invaluable advice and support has come from colleagues at the Lester B. Pearson Canadian International Peacekeeping Training Centre, in particular Alex Morrison and Jamie Arbuckle. My special thanks go to Yale University's United Nations Studies Programme which provided me with a research base and an office. Bruce Russett, Jean Krasno and Jim Sutterlin gave very valuable professional advice during that crucial period.

Throughout, my thesis adviser at the Department of Political Science at the *Freie Universitaet Berlin*, Ulrich Albrecht, has been very supportive, albeit at long distance. Klaus Huefner of the Department of Sociology at the *Freie Universitaet Berlin* provided constructive criticism as second evaluator of the dissertation.

I would like to take this opportunity to thank the many colleagues at the United Nations who granted me interviews and assisted my requests for information in a most helpful manner: Jan Arnesen, Philip Arnold, Franz Baumann, Eric Berman, Derek Boothby, Gary Collins, Fred Eckhard, Ayman El-Amir, Eric Falt, Marrack Goulding, Kevin Kennedy, Hiroko Miyamura, Peter Schmitz, Fred Schottler, Mikhail Seliankin, Peter Swarbrick, Patricia Tome, Roy Thomas, Lena Yacoumopoulou, Wolfgang Weisbrod-Weber and Stephen Whitehouse. These colleagues provided factual details for the case studies which were not available in any other form than through the eyes and ears of practitioners.

Among journalists and other authors in the field, I received information and useful pointers from Frank Chalk, Cindy Collins, Doug Dearth, Trevor Findlay, Kristof Gosztonyi, Nik Gowing, Marc Gramberger, Ferdinand Klien, David Last, Steve Livingston, Johanna Neuman, James Schear, Jonathan Stromseth and Thomas Weiss. My friends Hana Lane and Marvin Surkin were helpful with early drafts of the manuscript. In the final editorial stages, my greatest debt is to Jamie Arbuckle who never tired of critiquing, editing and urging me on.

All of these individuals volunteered their help in response to my seemingly endless requests for information and advice. Any mistakes and errors in judgment are nevertheless entirely my own. The views expressed herein are those of the author and do not necessarily reflect those of the United Nations; I am, however, unaware of any contradictions between what I have said here and official policies of the United Nations.

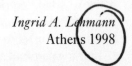

Ingrid A. Lehmann
Athens 1998

Foreword

Frank Cass Publishers are to be congratulated on this series of books which are teasing out the lessons to be learnt from the rise and decline of the United Nations' peacekeeping activities since the end of the Cold War.

The present volume is particularly stimulating and instructive. Dr Ingrid Lehmann is a public information specialist who has held key responsibilities both for policymaking in New York and for the public relations of several peacekeeping operations in the field. In New York she consistently argued that there should be a properly planned and funded information component in each mission. Unfortunately this good advice was not always heeded; and even when it was, the antiquated financial and procurement procedures of the United Nations usually caused months to pass before an effective information presence was established.

The five carefully researched case studies in this book show how high a price was paid for these shortcomings. They also show how much could be achieved when the mission's leadership was dynamic and information-conscious. These are important lessons, for, as Dr Lehmann convincingly demonstrates, there is a mutually reinforcing relationship between public perceptions of a crisis and the international response to it.

Technology now provides us with 'instant news' from zones of conflict. Unfortunately it does not provide us with greater accuracy; indeed the editor's demand for immediacy leaves even less time for the research on which accuracy depends. Nor can a peacekeeping operation rely on the parties to the conflict to give their supporters an accurate account of what it is trying to do. On the contrary, deliberate misrepresentation of UN activities can be an instrument of war, as happened in Rwanda and Yugoslavia.

A peacekeeping operation therefore has to get its own message across. And it has to do so both within its area of operations, so as to win the cooperation of the local people, and outside it, so as to retain the political and financial support of the international community at large. What is so compelling about Dr Lehmann's book is the empirical evidence it presents that several recent peacekeeping missions were not given the means of doing this, even when the staff concerned had clearly identified the need. The delay in providing the mission in Cambodia with an effective radio station is a particularly glaring object lesson.

Dr Lehmann's analysis leads inexorably to the conclusion that no one other than the peacekeeping operation itself can be relied upon to report accurately about its purposes and activities. It must therefore have the capacity, from the first day of its arrival on the scene, to convey its own story, to combat disinformation and to keep the record straight. As one who wishes that this lesson had been better learnt when he was in charge of UN peacekeeping, I hope that Dr Lehmann's work will be read widely by all those who need to know this truth – diplomats, soldiers, NGO's, academics and the media themselves.

MARRACK GOULDING
UN Under Secretary-General for Peacekeeping, 1986–93
Oxford, April 1998

Acronyms and abbreviations

ANC	African National Congress
CDR	Coalition pour la Défense de la République
CMAC	Cambodian Mine Action Centre
CPP	Cambodian People's Party
DPKO	UN Department of Peacekeeping Operations
DPI	UN Department of Public Information
FUNCINPEC	United National Front for an Independent, Neutral, Peaceful and Cooperative Cambodia
IFOR	Implementation Force
KPNLF	Khmer People's National Liberation Front
MIST	Military Information Support Teams
MISTF	Military Information Task Force
MNF	Multinational Force
MPIO	Military Public Information Officer
MRND	Mouvement Republicain National pour le developpement
OAS	Organization of American States
OAU	Organization of African Unity
OSCE	Organization for Security and Cooperation in Europe
PDK	Party of Democratic Kampuchea
RPF	Rwandese Patriotic Front
RSK	Republic of Serb Krajina
RTML	Radio-Télévision Libres Milles Collines
SFOR	Stabilization Force
SNC	Supreme National Council
SOC	State of Cambodia
SOFA	Status of Forces Agreement
SWABC	South-West African Broadcasting Corporation
SWAPO	South-West African People's Organization
TDT	Tactical Dissemination Team
UNAMIC	UN Advance Mission in Cambodia

UNAMIR	UN Assistance Mission for Rwanda
UNCIVPOL	UN Civilian Police
UNCRO	UN Confidence Restoration Operation in Croatia
UNMIH	UN Mission in Haiti
UNMOP	UN Military Observers in Prevlaka
UNOSOM	UN Operation in Somalia
UNPREDEP	UN Preventive Deployment
UNPROFOR	Un Protection Force
UNREO	UN Rwanda Emergency Office
UNSMIH	UN Support Mission in Haiti
UNTAC	UN Transitional Authority in Cambodia
UNTAES	UN Transitional Administration in Eastern Slavonia
UNTAG	UN Transition Assistance Group

Introduction

United Nations peacekeeping operations in the early 1990s underwent significant changes. These changes occurred in response to acute crises in, among other places, Somalia, the former Yugoslavia, Rwanda, Angola, Cambodia and Haiti. UN missions deployed in these countries manifested not only a tenfold increase in numbers of peacekeepers between 1992 and 1994, but also changes in the very concept of peacekeeping itself.[1] The classical model of interpositioning of military forces was, if not replaced, at least substantially widened by the inclusion of enforcement missions and by the involvement of civilian organizations for humanitarian aid, resettlement of refugees, human rights monitoring and electoral supervision. The complexity of these situations was compounded by weakened or failed state structures in those countries.

A parallel – and seemingly unrelated – development occurred in the field of information and communication technology, which propelled the electronic media into a position of increased significance in international relations. The arrival of the satellite dish, portable computer and cellular telephone changed the way in which conflicts were reported and received by worldwide audiences. 'Instant news' and 'real-time television' became the catchwords of the 1990s, making the media, in the eyes of some, a 'driving force' in international relations.[2] While the actual role of media coverage of conflicts is still debated by policymakers and journalists, what has become increasingly clear is that public perceptions, as forged by a variety of media, locally, nationally and globally, can no longer be ignored.

In previous decades, with the Cold War and other, not-so-cold, wars dominating the opinion foreground, public opinion was little concerned with peacekeeping missions. The 'Information Age' of the 1990s both coincides with and characterizes the post-Cold War era in which peace operations have expanded so rapidly. Or, as Shashi Tharoor has aptly put it:

> the new transcendence of the global media added a sense of urgency to these crises: it is a striking coincidence that the reach

and impact of CNN and its imitators peaked precisely at this time of post-Cold War concordance. Television showed that action was needed, and the end of the Cold War meant that action was possible.[3]

This also means that public perceptions of UN field operations are rapidly formed by instant television images generated in the area of conflict. The international and the local public view of an operation have a measurable influence on its perceived effectiveness.[4] Furthermore, as experiences of UN operations in Somalia, Bosnia and Rwanda have shown, media images of a humanitarian emergency and their (often negative) effect on the perceptions of the conflict among public and policymakers alike, can impact the entire peace process.[5]

This new and important dynamic and its ramifications for the international policymaking processes are not yet fully appreciated. Real-time television reporting enables growing numbers of people in different parts of the world to follow emerging situations and conflicts, notwithstanding the often superficial nature of international news reports.[6] While media reports of crises such as Somalia have inspired politicians in various countries to undertake considerable relief efforts, responses to other similar cases, such as Sudan, have been tardy or inadequate. Media images of peace operations in which casualties have been incurred have caused some countries to withdraw their military contingents, as did the United States from Somalia, and the Belgians from Rwanda. Similar reporting of such tragedies did not affect the 'staying-power' of others, such as Pakistan, which did not withdraw when over 20 of its soldiers were killed in Somalia.

At the outset of most humanitarian crises the reaction of the leaders of the international community, as reflected in action by members of the UN Security Council, tends to be cautious and prudent. Consequently, Security Council resolutions are often symbolic measures, which are in language and substance designed to satisfy the need 'to do something'. They often are carefully crafted compromises, arranged among diplomats representing the interests of governments and their domestic political considerations. These resolutions are thus not necessarily designed to ameliorate the catastrophe, let alone to address its causes. When the crisis recurs at a later stage, repeated media coverage tends to exacerbate the phenomenon known among humanitarian agencies as 'donor fatigue'.

It is one of the main tenets of this book that the combined effect of the exponential growth in peacekeeping operations between 1988 and 1994 on the one hand, and the rapid change in communications technology on the other, was not recognized by the leadership of the United Nations. It is suggested here that the absence of a corporate appreciation of the importance of public perceptions has been a major factor in the erosion of support for the United Nations and its peacekeeping missions on the part of several of its member states.[7]

Negative images of operations in Bosnia, Somalia and Rwanda no doubt affected public perceptions of these missions worldwide, subsequently lowering the level of support in key contributing member states, as well as in the public-at-large. Senior UN officials have recognized this and, on occasion, complained that 'world public opinion's perception of the UN's worth depends to an exaggerated extent on how well its peacekeeping operations are faring'; or, as Secretary-General Kofi Annan remarked at his first press conference at UN headquarters in February 1997, the UN 'does quite a bit of work in the economic and social field, but it doesn't get the publicity peacekeeping gets'.[8]

Unfortunately, at the high point of UN peacekeeping in the mid-1990s, when the number of peacekeepers peaked and its operations were the most visible internationally due to worldwide instant news coverage, the UN's public information efforts were hampered by the absence of a directing body of doctrine or consistent management principles regarding public affairs in peacekeeping missions. As this book will show, effective management of the public dimension of some of these missions did occur, but it was accidental rather than planned.[9]

To shed light on the complex information requirements of UN peace-keeping operations, this study focuses on four primary research questions:

- Under which conditions have UN peacekeeping operations developed effective communication strategies and information programmes?
- What were the consequences of having or not having an effective information programme, for the running of the operation and for the peace process in general?
- What are the bureaucratic constraints for international organizations in developing effective information programmes?
- Which are the most important factors that can help overcome such bureaucratic hurdles?

SOME DEFINITIONS

Peacekeeping is used in this book as the concept which has been evolved over 50 years by the United Nations, namely as the use of principally military multinational forces, authorized by the Security Council and under the command of the Secretary-General, operating with the consent of the parties to the conflict, 'to seek a solution by negotiation, enquiry, mediation, conciliation, arbitration, judicial settlement...' in accordance with Chapter VI of the UN Charter.

The issue of consent, which, in the peacekeeping context usually connotes agreement by the parties to the mandate and the composition of the force, is currently being widely debated among peacekeeping experts.[10] In this study it is used in the sense developed by Charles Dobbie, who has postulated a 'consent divide' which, doctrinally, is the most significant distinguishing factor between peacekeeping and peace enforcement.[11]

Expanding on Dobbie's concept, consent is utilized in this study in the sense of popular support or, at a minimum, acquiescence, which must be maintained and nurtured by the peacekeeping mission. If weak or waning, it is argued here, public support (which is itself a vital aspect of consent) in the area of operations and internationally, should be built by using creative and professional information campaigns in the field.[12] It is thus important to distinguish, doctrinally and practically, between the consent of the parties (meaning governments or warring factions) and the consent of the population. In fact, gaining the consent of the latter can help to maintain the consent by the former.

Public Information refers to the policy and practices of the United Nations and other international organizations to disseminate their information materials (print, audio, visual) worldwide, through media contacts, direct mailing and a system of information centres in key capitals, as well as the field headquarters of peacekeeping missions. The information products are usually couched in neutral, objective language, which meet the strict UN criteria of impartiality. The term *public affairs* has also been employed by some recent missions, as well as *education*, in particular in reference to voter education and human rights education.

Public Relations refers to the efforts of governments, companies and individuals to communicate their point of view with the intention of persuading and influencing attitudes and behaviour. Particularly useful is the concept of 'corporate image-making', which has been successfully used by some governmental agencies, including, for a brief period, by the United Nations.[13] It often employs opinion surveys, target audience analysis, campaign plans and other professional public relations strategies.[14]

Military information campaigns, or 'psychological operations', are used routinely by the US military and others to 'promote specific opinions, emotions, attitudes and/or behaviour of a foreign audience ...'[15] It is generally seen by military planners as a 'force multiplier', but for non-military audiences it often connotes propaganda and manipulation. Following the

Gulf War, there has been an extensive debate as to the nature of the relationship between the media and the military, particularly in the United States.[16] There is, following the experiences in Bosnia and Rwanda, a need to analyse further how the propagation of ethnic hatred and racist incitement to violence by one or more of the parties can be effectively countered in a peacekeeping mission.

The processing of information which produces 'intelligence' has been anathema to traditional UN peacekeeping operations. However, the difficulties which were encountered in Somalia and Bosnia showed that the absence of reliable intelligence impeded the ability of the UN to counteract propaganda directed at itself. In Rwanda, the absence of an intelligence response capability exacerbated the dangers of the situation for the peacekeepers. As a result, the concept is now being given more positive consideration for future operations,[17] but it is, as such, outside the scope of this book.

Political Communication is defined as the exchange of symbols and messages that have been shaped by and have consequences for international organizations and their field operations. Thus, the type of communication we are concerned with in this study is by definition transnational in its effects, even if the symbols and messages are locally generated. Typically, communication in and by a peacekeeping operation originates in the theatre of operations, but it has regional and international political consequences: in neighbouring countries, troop contributing and other donor nations, as in the countries which are members of the Security Council and have a direct impact on the peacekeeping operation's mandate.

The levels of management, command and control of peace operations are commonly referred to and differentiated by use of terminology which was originally military, but is now widely used by civilian organizations as well. These are:

> *The strategic level*: This generally refers to the diplomatic and political level. As used in this book, the strategic level includes the United Nations (Security Council, General Assembly and Secretariat), as well as the member states, plus other comparable international bodies such as the Organization for Security and Cooperation in Europe (OSCE), the Organization of American States (OAS) or the Organization of African Unity (OAU).
> *The operational level*: This refers to the field mission in a given theatre of operations or country. The operational level is led by a head of mission, usually either a Special Representative of the Secretary General or a Force Commander.

The tactical level: All of the mission field components subordinate
to the head of mission, be they civilian or military, are collectively
referred to as the tactical level.

THE SELECTION OF CASE STUDIES

This book examines five case studies which have been chosen for a variety
of reasons, including: the accessibility of primary documentation, the
availability for interviews of officials who were directly involved in the
planning and operational phases of the mission, the quality of secondary
source materials, and the suitability of the case study for testing and
evaluating the operational principles or working hypotheses outlined in the
next Chapter.

It will be noted that the five case studies span four continents and a period
of eight years, from 1989 to 1997. All the case studies except one are of United
Nations peacekeeping missions in developing countries; all of them had weak
or disintegrating state structures.

Two of them, Namibia and Cambodia, concluded on notes of 'success' in
the time frame envisaged for them in comprehensive peace agreements. One,
the UN Assistance Mission for Rwanda (UNAMIR), was withdrawn in 1996
following a request from the government. Another, the UN mission in Haiti,
(UNMIH) went through three distinct phases, which are described in turn
in that Chapter; that operation was concluded as this book was being written.
The final case study, of the UN operation in Eastern Slavonia, was ongoing
as this book was written, but ended its mandate on 15 January 1998. A review
of this operation will demonstrate the extent to which the UN learned, or
failed to learn, from its prior experiences in the former Yugoslavia.

In the case of Namibia, I worked in that mission area for one year, first as
the head of a UN Transition Assistance Group (UNTAG) District Centre
(Khomasdal) and then, for the second half of that year I was, in addition, the
District Supervisor of the Windhoek Electoral District, which was the second
largest in the country. In the case of Cambodia, I travelled to the area of
operations for a week in September 1992 as part of a delegation of the UN
Association of the United States which visited a total of six peacekeeping
missions. I visited the mission area of UNMIH in October–November 1995
and again in May 1996, as a member of the faculty of the Lester B. Pearson
Canadian International Peacekeeping Training Centre. In September 1996,
I conducted a research visit to Eastern Slavonia and the UN Transitional
Administration in Eastern Slavonia (UNTAES) with a colleague from the
Pearson Centre. The only one of these missions I have not visited is Rwanda.

Case Study One: Namibia – UNTAG

The Namibia operation demonstrated the results of the creation of a very positive image for a peacekeeping mission. It made effective use of external and internal information programmes. A voter education campaign was the *sine qua non* for registration of voters and the conduct of the election in a country without any democratic experience. Cultural sensitivity was central to the effectiveness of the operation in all phases and at all levels.

Case Study Two: Cambodia – UNTAC

The early recognition of the strategic importance of communications was vital for the Cambodia operation, which was the largest and most complex in the history of the United Nations. The UN Transitional Authority in Cambodia (UNTAC) set up the largest information/education programme of any UN peacekeeping mission to date, including its own radio station. UNTAC made an impact on Cambodian society through its human rights education programmes and through assisting in the creation of an open media environment.

Case Study Three: Rwanda – UNAMIR

This case study demonstrates, sadly by omission, the importance of public perceptions and the need for an education campaign in the face of ethnically-motivated hate campaigns by one or more of the belligerents. That large numbers of Rwandans and several peacekeepers lost their lives was due in no small part to the absence of an effective information capacity during the crucial early phase of the mission.

Case Study Four: Haiti – UNMIH

The Haiti case study shows, as in Namibia and in Cambodia, the vital role of education programmes in a post-conflict environment. It was also the first time that military information techniques ('psychological operations') were applied in a peacekeeping environment. The case study traces the information campaigns through three distinct phases of the mission.

Case Study Five: Eastern Slavonia – UNTAES

This operation in the former Yugoslavia took place in a United Nations-administered post-conflict environment. It was characterized by a bold and imaginative civil affairs programme and charismatic leadership. It used information programmes effectively to promote stability in a very volatile region and among a chronically unstable population. Curiously, this apparently highly successful operation has been since its inception very little covered by the media. Its programme of public affairs will be analysed against the backdrop of the largely negative experience of the UN Protection Force (UNPROFOR), the first UN mission in the former Yugoslavia, to determine if the UN is capable of learning lessons from one operation, and subsequently applying them to another.

This book is intended to make a contribution to the continuing discussion of better management and effectiveness of information programmes of the United Nations. It is hoped that it will help current managers and policy-makers in the UN Secretariat and some key members states concerned with priorities, policies and leadership issues for peacekeeping missions, to understand the modalities of the missions' interaction with the countries in which they are deployed.

Secretary-General Kofi Annan's 1997 reform proposals *Renewing the United Nations* speaks of the need 'to instil a culture of communications' in the United Nations. This book underlines the vital importance of communications as a strategic management function, which, in order to be effective, has to extend to its most visible field missions, the peacekeeping operations.

NOTES

1. For an overview of these developments, see *Supplement to An Agenda for Peace: Position Paper of the Secretary-General on the Occasion of the Fiftieth Anniversary of the United Nations*, United Nations Document A/50/60 and S/1995/1, 3 Jan. 1995 and *The Blue Helmets – A Review of United Nations Peacekeeping* (3rd edn) New York: United Nations, 1996, Part I: Introduction.

2. Among the growing literature on this subject, I was guided, in particular, by two articles by Nik Gowing, 'Real-Time Television Coverage of Armed Conflicts and Diplomatic Crises: Does it Pressure or Distort Foreign Policy Decisions?', *Working Paper*, Shorenstein Barone Center, Harvard University, June 1994 and Gowing, 'Media Coverage: Help or Hindrance for Conflict Prevention?' *Diagnostic Paper*, Carnegie Commission on Preventing Deadly Conflict, New York, 1996 and Johanna Neuman, *Lights, Camera, War – Is Media Technology Driving International Politics?* New York: St. Martin's Press, 1996.

3. Shashi Tharoor, 'The Future of Peacekeeping', in Jim Whitman and David Pocock (eds), *After Rwanda – The Coordination of United Nations Humanitarian Assistance*, London: Macmillan, 1996, p.20.

4. See Ingrid Lehmann, 'Public Perceptions of UN Peacekeeping: A Factor in the Resolution of International Conflicts', *The Fletcher Forum of World Affairs*, 19/1, Winter/Spring 1995.

5. Neuman (n.2 above), p.228, states: 'Conventional wisdom holds that pictures got the United States in, and pictures forced the United States out ... Those who held this view often cited public opinion as forcing the hands of policymakers.' She disagrees, and so do other observers. Steven Livingston and Todd Eachus, 'Humanitarian Crises and US Foreign Policy: Somalia and the CNN Effect Reconsidered', *Political Communication*, 12, 1995, p.427, come to the conclusion that, in the case of Somalia, 'media content came in response to official initiatives, not the other way around', and that 'the media serve as instruments of those officials who are most adept at using news to further their policy goals'. In another article, 'Beyond the "CNN-Effect": Clarifying the Media-Foreign Policy Dynamic', Steven Livingston argues that media reports on international crises can both accelerate and impede the policy process and that they serve as 'agenda-setting agents'. (Manuscript made available by the author, Washington, 1996.)

6. See Garrick Utley, 'The Shrinking of Foreign News – From Broadcast to Narrowcast', *Foreign Affairs*, 76/2, March/April 1997.

7. This policy of neglect of the public dimension can also be noted in regional organizations, in particular the European Union. For a comparison of the information policies of the United Nations and the European Union see Marc R. Gramberger and Ingrid Lehmann, 'UN und EU: Machtlos im Kreuzfeuer der Kritik? Informationspolitk zweier internationaler Organisationen im Vergleich', *Publizistik*, 40, 1, 1995. Marc Gramberger in 1997 published his doctoral dissertation in German which is a very thorough, historically documented and systematic approach to the EC/EU's information policies and practices: Marc Gramberger, *Die Oeffentlichkeitsarbeit der Europaeischen Kommission, 1952–1996 – PR zur Legitimation von Integration*, Baden-Baden: Nomos Verlagsgesellschaft, 1997.

8. Marrack Goulding (then) UN Under Secretary-General for Political Affairs, to the author, 29 May 1996; Secretary-General Kofi Annan, transcript of his press conference in New York on 13 Feb. 1997, p.6.

9. This situation changed drastically at the strategic level in July 1997 when the Secretary-General's report (A/51/950) entitled *Renewing the United Nations: A Programme for Reform* appeared, which will guide the Secretariat's work henceforth. It refers, in paragraph 61, to the Report of the 'Task Force on the Reorientation of United Nations Public Information Activities' which was issued in August 1997 under the title, *Global Vision, Local Voice – A Strategic Communications Programme for the United Nations*. The Secretary-General in his report, supports the central tenet that 'the communications functions be placed at the heart of the strategic management of the United Nations' (p.17).

10. This debate, while intrinsic to peacekeeping, has in recent years been heightened following the UN experiences in Somalia and Bosnia, both of which were, at least for some time, operating under the enforcement provisions of Chapter VII of the UN Charter. The UN Secretariat's own definition of 'consent' as a main characteristic of peacekeeping operations has varied over the years. While up to 1992 'consent of the parties' was an integral element of UN peacekeeping doctrine, Secretary-General Boutros-Ghali, in *An Agenda for Peace, United Nations, New York, 1992*, p.11, added 'hitherto with the consent of all the parties concerned' to the definition. However, his subsequent report to the 48th General Assembly revised the definition by omitting the word 'hitherto'.

11. Charles Dobbie, 'A Concept for Post-Cold War Peacekeeping', *Survival*, 36/3, Autumn, 1995 draws the following lesson: 'In order to protect, sustain, promote and transmit consent, psychologically-oriented techniques, by addressing perceptions and attitudes,

have the greatest potential in peacekeeping'.

12. This argument was previously put forward by Ingrid Lehmann, 'Peacekeeping, Public Perceptions and the Need for Consent', *Canadian Defence Quarterly*, 25/2, Dec. 1995. Ambassador Walter Stadtler, in an address at the Lester B. Pearson International Peacekeeping Training Centre in Oct. 1995, stated that one of the main failures of the UN in Somalia was that it 'did not tell its own story'.

13. This refers to an attempt in the late 1980s by the UN Under Secretary-General for Public Information, Therese Paquet-Sevigny, to forge a global image campaign for the United Nations which is described in greater detail in Chapter 2.

14. See Charles T. Salmon (ed.), *Information Campaigns: Balancing Social Values and Social Change*, Newbury Park, CA: Sage, 1989 and James Grunig (ed.), *Excellence in Public Relations and Communication Management*, Hillsdale, 1992.

15. US 4th Psychological Operations Group (Airborne), *Capabilities Handbook* (July 1993). The United Nations Institute for Disarmament Research in Geneva has recently published a very thoughtful study by Andrei Raevsky, *Managing Arms in Peace Processes: Aspects of Psychological Operations and Intelligence*, New York and Geneva: United Nations, 1996.

16. For a critique of US press policies in the Gulf War, see John R. MacArthur, *Second Front, Censorship and Propaganda in the Gulf War*, New York: Hill & Wang, 1992; Johanna Neuman (n.2 above), Chapter 13: The Persian Gulf War; Everette Dennis (ed.), *The Media at War: The Press and the Persian Gulf Conflict*, New York: Gannett Foundation Media Center, 1991; Jacqueline E. Sharkey, *Under Fire – US Military Restrictions on the Media From Grenada to the Persian Gulf*, Washington, DC: The Center for Public Integrity, 1991 and Frank Aukofer and William P. Lawrence (eds), *America's Team – A Report on the Relationship Between the Media and the Military*, Nashville, TN: The Freedom Forum First Amendment Center, 1995.

17. Doug Dearth of the US Defense Intelligence Agency argues that there is a need for the UN to 'demystify intelligence information', that it is not 'the UN spying on its member states', but a meaningful activity. Doug Dearth, presentation 'Information and Intelligence – the UN Conundrum' at the Pearson Peacekeeping Centre on 6 May 1996. Thomas Weiss, from a different vantage point, argues that 'UN field operations have not systematically made use of information-gathering possibilities that result from having eyes and ears on the ground'. Thomas Weiss, *The United Nations and Civil Wars*, Boulder, CO: Lynne Rienner, 1995, p.202. See also the UNIDIR study referred to in n.15 (above).

ONE

Towards a Theory of Political Communication for International Organizations

COMMUNICATION AS A STRATEGIC MANAGEMENT FUNCTION

It is a central tenet of this book that effective communication has become a *sine qua non* for intergovernmental organizations and their field operations, albeit one not yet fully recognized by the politicians, diplomats and their senior managers.

At a time when revolutionary developments in information technology had left their imprint on the way the war in the Persian Gulf was perceived by worldwide television audiences, intergovernmental organizations, foremost the United Nations, continued to disseminate brochures and films by diplomatic pouch, following time-consuming translation into the 'official languages'. Daily press releases were still often sent by fax, and electronic mail was introduced only slowly in the late 1990s. There were, as many analysts and critics of the UN have maintained, frequent time delays in information received by the staff in the field. There were as well communication disconnects between the political decisionmakers in the Security Council and the Secretariat, and those attempting to carry out the mandates in the theatre of operations.[1]

Largely unbidden and as often unrecognized, communications have become a strategic command and management function. While this has been well recognized by corporations and by most governments – who consider advertising and public relations to be essential functions – it has continued to be undervalued and, in some instances, actively discouraged as a legitimate activity of the United Nations Secretariat.[2] Paradoxically, as the case studies in the following chapters will show, this has not necessarily prevented resourceful UN managers at the operational level from designing and implementing effective measures, given only sufficient leeway and resources. This book examines how, when, and under what conditions effective communication strategies and information programmes were implemented by United Nations civilian and military managers of peacekeeping operations, at the operational and tactical levels. It also portrays the consequences of the absence of effective information programmes, at the strategic level.

INTERNATIONAL COMMUNICATIONS THEORY

A general review of the relevant international relations literature[3] revealed that, with the exception of James Rosenau's more recent writings, scholars on the UN's role in international conflict resolution have not dealt adequately with the growing importance of public perceptions. There appears to be a near dearth of scholarly studies on the UN's information components in the political field. Following controversies in the 1970s and 1980s about a 'New World Information Order' and the difficulties encountered by UNESCO in some politically-motivated attempts at media control, the subject of 'public information' has not attracted the serious attention it deserves.

This being so, my subsequent theoretical exploration of the inter-relationship between, on the one hand, peacekeeping as a tool of international conflict resolution and, on the other hand, information dissemination as a vehicle to communicate with various publics about this activity, led me to study literature in the following, related fields covering a variety of disciplines. Some of these are:

- International communications theory, beginning with Harold Innis and Marshall McLuhan, postulating that perceptions are part of reality;
- Conflict resolution theories, in particular the characterization of the 'ripeness' of conflicts, and thus the timing of conflict resolution efforts;
- Analyses of bureaucratic decisionmaking and their applicability to international organizations;
- Perception studies;
- Management theories which focus on communication strategies, corporate image-making and other public relations concepts;
- New approaches to the public dimensions of foreign policy which have been developed by journalists and policy analysts;
- The role of media reporting in wars and humanitarian emergencies;
- Propaganda analysis;
- Military concepts of psychological operations in their application to peacekeeping and to 'operations-other-than-war'.

These approaches from a variety of disciplines and professions have influenced my research and contributed to my conceptualization of a strategy to communicate better with wider audiences, and to be more effective in peacekeeping and conflict resolution.

Alexander George distinguishes between 'substantive theory' and 'process theory' which has also guided my own analysis of the United Nations role in peacekeeping:

> Substantive theory provides knowledge of standard foreign policy undertakings, instruments of policy, and strategies. Process theory focuses on how to structure and manage the policymaking process to increase the likelihood of producing more effective policies. Of course, substantive knowledge and process intersect as policy specialists analyse a problem and consider alternative options for dealing with it. And of course various political and organizational factors and situational constraints come into play that may limit the impact of substantive knowledge.[4]

Following George's distinction, I divided the relevant approaches to the subject of peacekeeping and public information into 'substantive' theories, and theories related to bureaucratic 'processes'. In this manner, I began to develop a strategy for effective political communication for and by international organizations, which allowed me to design a set of principles of communication for peacekeeping operations.

SUBSTANTIVE THEORIES

1. The Concept of Political Communication

This concept has received continuous attention from communications theorists beginning with Harold Innis's seminal work *Empire and Communications* (1950); Marshall McLuhan later coined the idea of a 'global village', which may seem today to have been optimistic and simplistic, in view of the widening technological gaps between developed and developing countries.

With the exception of some recent studies in the field of public opinion and international governance,[5] the impact of public perceptions on international politics is not yet analytically well developed.[6] While in Europe statistical data exist about public opinion on various issues confronting the European Union (the 'Eurobarometer'), no reliable worldwide data on perceptions and attitudes of people in the 185 member states of the United Nations exist.[7] This situation led Philip Everts in 1995 to conclude:

> In summarizing the findings on attitudes towards the United Nations, the point to be emphasized is the inadequacy of available data ... In terms of substance of attitudes all we know is that there is a high level of awareness of the United Nations, a low level of knowledge about some of its component elements, a high degree of interest in several of the key problems it tackles, and an overall positive evaluation of the institution itself.[8]

However, there is a growing body of literature about the role of media in conflicts and humanitarian crises. Following the Somalia and Rwanda emergencies, aid agencies, concerned journalists and academic institutes such as the International Centre for Humanitarian Reporting, the Thomas Watson Institute for International Studies and the World Peace Foundation have held a series of symposia and have published their reports on the interrelationship between the media and policy in international humanitarian crises.[9] These have influenced, in particular, the development of the case study on Rwanda in Chapter 5 of this book. But many of the writers and analysts from the humanitarian perspective see the United Nations, and in particular its military operations, too often as only a 'bureaucratic hindrance' to their own efforts, and not as a vital component in a joint response to humanitarian emergencies.[10]

2. Analysis of the International Political Environment

Bruce Russett has called this the 'macroscopic view of world politics', namely that 'the menu of choice in foreign policy' is set by the prevailing political environment.[11] Some political theorists have analysed 'environmental constraints', which, in the case of United Nations politics, would largely fall under the category of 'political will'. This notion refers to the political will of member states of the United Nations, as expressed in Security Council measures and General Assembly resolutions, indicating a willingness to expend effort and resources to make a mandate workable. Often, as we have seen in the cases of the UN operations in the former Yugoslavia and Rwanda, these efforts are half-hearted, 'too little too late', or simply ill-conceived and underfunded.

The concept of 'political will' has not yet been sufficiently instrumentalized by political scientists. It is furthermore muddled by the fact that it has, at times, been used as a convenient excuse for inaction or bureaucratic inefficiency on the part of some United Nations officials. It is vitally important for the purpose of this study that political communication by a UN operation must be seen in the larger international political context. It cannot function in isolation from the political environment in which it operates, either in the theatre of operations or at the international strategic (macro) level.

To better analyse each of the five case studies below in their macroscopic context, this study utilizes some recently developed theories from the field of conflict analysis, in particular, the concepts of conflict ripeness and the timing of an international intervention, as developed by Louis Kriesberg, William Zartman and others.[12]

Important insights have also been gained from analyses of successful peace settlements in Southern Africa, Central America and Cambodia. Particularly the studies by Chester Crocker, Fen Osler Hampson and James Schear have identified some of the vital factors that have made some peace agreements more readily implemented than others.[13] These generally agree that a workable peace settlement is a precondition for successful peacekeeping. Their writings are applied in the five case studies analysed in this book when assessing the political viability of peace agreements. In Namibia, Cambodia and Eastern Slavonia, the issue of 'ripeness' is viewed from the vantage point of 'consent', ie the extent of public support for the peace process as a whole and for the implementing peacekeeping operation in particular. In the case of Rwanda, the Arusha peace accords were not a workable basis for the UN operation in that country; in Haiti, the main issue initially was the return of the elected President.

The concept of 'political ripeness' is thereby expanded in this book. The issue is no longer just – as in classical peacekeeping operations – whether the hostile parties agree to a particular peace agreement and participate constructively in its implementation. By looking at public perceptions in the area of conflict, we are including the non-governmental dimensions of a peace process. The need for peacekeeping operations to be credible in the eyes of significant parts of the population(s) in question thus becomes a factor of strategic importance in implementing peace accords. Peace building requires, for obvious reasons, the willing participation of the people concerned.

Another element in all the case studies analysed below is the nature of the media environment in the area of operations. Obviously, the open flow of information, media diversity and the extent of governmental control are factors that make a difference in the ability of the peacekeepers to communicate with the population concerned. Furthermore, it is argued here, that those UN operations which had independent means of communication in the form of radio stations, information offices and mobile dissemination teams at their disposal, were in a better position to affect the communication process than those which did not have them. It is important to look at the whole spectrum of communication channels that were available, or, as has been argued about the operation in Rwanda, should have been made available to the peacekeepers to reach large population groups with their messages.

PROCESS THEORIES

Theories about the decisionmaking process in political bureaucracies are plentiful, even though they relate mostly to the national context, or the foreign policies of individual countries. The studies developed by Graham Allison in his book *Essence of Decision* (1966) and later expanded by Irving Janis, *Crucial Decisions* (1989) analyse decisionmaking in American foreign policy at critical moments. The process described by Allison as well as the indicators used to assess decisionmaking in the Cuban missile crisis can be applied to international organizations. Janis's 'constraints-model' of the foreign policy process can also be transposed to help understand decision-making in the United Nations. However, given the multitude of actors in the international sphere and the non-governmental, 'public' aspects of this study, they are of limited use.[14]

In looking at the bureaucratic decisionmaking processes in the United Nations with respect to its peacekeeping operations and their information components, I have identified the following elements, which will guide me in assessing the five operations analysed below:

- Leadership
- Implementation of mandates
- Information-processing by UN officials
- Resource allocation for the mission
- Institutional learning and training

The main thrust of this book is an analysis of the communication process between the United Nations Secretariat and its peacekeeping missions. Three levels of communication, which are interrelated, can be identified. These are:

- The international (the UN headquarters);
- The theatre of operations (local/host communications infrastructure);
- Mission-internal communication

The link between the first and second, ie the theatre of operations and how the international community views the area of conflict and the operation deployed there, is primarily established through media reporting – 'instant news' – from the theatre. To some extent UN headquarters can seek to influence these perceptions created by media images from the field, through its own press briefings and information disseminated through its own channels. However, once reporting from the theatre becomes predominantly negative, the UN's own statements countering the reporting are most likely belated attempts at damage control, and tend to have little impact.

The media-opinion-policy link depicted in *Figure 1* below is therefore one that affects all UN information efforts in the peacekeeping field:

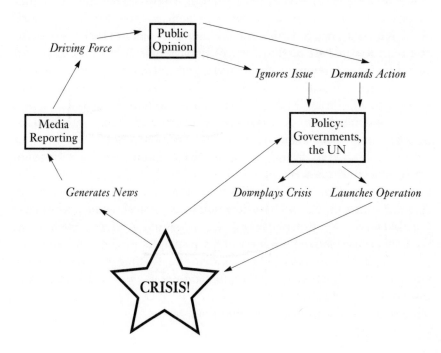

Figure 1

A vital aspect of the communications process in peacekeeping missions is the interaction between peacekeepers on the one hand, and the host country on the other. Formally speaking, this relationship is often regulated by a Status of Forces Agreement (SOFA), which codifies the legal position of the mission and of its members. However, as was outlined in the Introduction above, consent is a far broader concept; it cannot be created solely by legal agreements, it involves the attitudes of the population which may, as we shall see in the following case studies, shift over time. Consent must be built and maintained, as part of the larger process of peacebuilding.

Communication difficulties are often exacerbated by the fact that the new generation of peacekeeping operations impose their – or the international community's – values in the area in which they are deployed. This is particularly true when they have mandates dealing with human rights, democratic governance, freedom of the press and the imposition of legal norms. For peacekeeping operations with such wide-ranging mandates, communication with the population over the introduction (or imposition) of these goals is absolutely vital.

In most areas of recent conflict there are usually disagreements over values which may threaten the power of dominant political groups or factions, such as the Khmer Rouge in Cambodia, the military junta in Haiti or extremist Hutus in Rwanda. It is, therefore, of great importance to international peacekeepers to develop and maintain independent means of communication with the local population. This may require access to printing presses and broadcasting facilities, ie independent communication channels.

It is also important that the peacekeepers' own behaviour is above reproach. Issues such as impartiality and impeccable conduct can, when not scrupulously observed by members of the Force, become areas of contention. Misconduct by the peacekeepers, real or perceived, can be exploited by those who wish to undermine the peace process. This is why the mission-internal communication process is a vital function in any peacekeeping operation.

Based on my own experience and the analysis of the relevant literature in the field, I have worked out a set of six principles of communication for peacekeeping operations. They guided the further inquiry into the interrelationship between peacekeeping and public information in the five case studies and will be used as benchmarks for measuring the effectiveness of those operations from a communications perspective.

Principle 1

Public perceptions are a strategic factor which affects conflict resolution and peacekeeping operations at all levels.

Principle 2

International public opinion and local public concerns interact in creating images of United Nations peacekeeping operations that, once established, become inseparable from, and exercise continuing influence on, the political process.

\ *Principle 3*

To be effective in implementing their mandates, field missions must, from the outset, include external (public) and mission-internal information programmes as a strategic and operational-level management function.

\ *Principle 4*

In the peacekeeping environment of the 1990s, education campaigns on specific issues, such as human rights, electoral processes and the rule of law are likely to be important components of peacekeeping operations.

\ *Principle 5*

Information campaigns in peacekeeping missions must be culturally sensitive to the host country's information environment, without compromising principles such as freedom of the press and human rights.

\ *Principle 6*

Peacekeeping operations are conducted in an open environment in which transparency of policy and objectives is a principal characteristic of the management of the mission.

This study's main tenet, as outlined so far, is that communication is a strategic management function for international organizations, particularly when they operate in a peacekeeping mode. The application of these six principles will be scrutinized in each of the following case studies. It is surmised that, while the observance of the six principles of communication will not guarantee success for a peacekeeping operation, their contravention will, sooner or later, produce major difficulties for the operation as its public image deteriorates, its message gets lost and its internal communications wither.

NOTES

1. The complaints about serious deficiencies in the information flow are most prevalent at the tactical level. A senior colleague at the Pearson Peacekeeping Training Centre, having returned from an extended tour of duty with both UNPROFOR and IFOR in 1996, told a group of students in an introductory presentation that his greatest problems encountered during his peacekeeping duty was the lack of communication with UN headquarters. Major General Lewis MacKenzie, the first Force Commander of the UN Protection Force in the Former Yugoslavia, said memorably: 'If you are a commander of

a UN mission, don't get into trouble after five p.m. or on the weekend. There is no one in the UN to answer the phone!' Lewis MacKenzie, *Peacekeeper – The Road to Sarajevo*, Toronto: Harper Collins, 1994, p.510.

2. Similar problems exist in other intergovernmental organizations. For a comparison of the United Nations and the European Union and their information policies see Marc Gramberger and Ingrid Lehmann, 'UN and EU: Machtlos im Kreuzfeuer der Kritik? Informations politik zweier internationaler Organisationen im Vergleich', *Publizistik*, 40.1, 1995, and Marc Gramberger, *Die Oeffentlichkeitsarbeit der Europaeischen Kommission, 1952–1996* – PR zur Legitimation von Integration, Baden-Baden: Nomos Verlagsgesellschaft, 1997.

3. Among the publications of a more general nature surveyed I made particular use of the following: Ken Booth and Steve Smith (eds), *International Relations Theory Today*, Philadelphia, PA: Pennsylvania State University Press, 1995, James Der Derian (ed.), *International Theory – Critical Investigations*, New York: New York University Press, 1995, Lori Fisler Damrosch (ed.), *Enforcing Restraint – Collective Intervention in Internal Conflicts*, New York: Council on Foreign Relations, 1993, Judith Goldstein and Robert Keohane (eds), *Ideas and Foreign Policy – Beliefs, Institutions and Political Change*, Ithaca, NY: Cornell University Press, 1993, Robert E. Riggs and Jack C. Plano, *The United Nations–International Organization and World Politics*, Belmont, CA: Wadsworth, 1994, Adam Roberts and Benedict Kingsbury, *United Nations, Divided World – The UN's Roles in International Relations*, Oxford: Clarendon Press, 1993 and James N. Rosenau, *Turbulence in World Politics – A Theory of Change and Continuity*, Princeton NJ: Princeton University Press, 1990.

4. Alexander George, *Bridging the Gap – Theory & Practice in Foreign Policy*, Washington, DC: US Institute of Peace Press, 1993, p.20.

5. James Rosenau, *The United Nations in a Turbulent World*, Boulder, CO and London: International Peace Academy Occasional Paper Series, 1992; Oscar Niedermayer and Richard Sinnott (eds), *Public Opinion and International Governance*, Oxford: Oxford University Press, 1995.

6. For example, the *Handbook of Political Communication* edited by Dan D. Nimmo and Keith R. Sanders, Beverly Hills, CA and London: Sage, 1981 refers exclusively to 'political communication settings' which are national.

7. Between 1989 and 1993 the Department of Public Information carried out public opinion polls of attitudes to the UN in 38 member states. They were considered expensive and, in some instances, politically sensitive, and were discontinued. These polls showed that UNICEF and UNESCO had more impact on public opinion than the Security Council, the General Assembly or the Secretary-General. In general, the comment by Philip Everts, in his article 'NATO, the European Community, and the United Nations' (1995) is still accurate: 'Public Opinion data on the United Nations and its activities are almost non-existent. While a search of available sources yielded more than 1,300 questions on NATO as an international institution, less than 150 questions were asked about the UN, including many which are hardly useful', in Oscar Niedermayer and Richard Sinnott (n.5 above), pp.403–28.

8. Everts (n.7 above), pp.422–3. The latter point is corroborated by opinion polls in the United States conducted by the United Nations Association of the USA in 1995 'US Public Support for UN Grows' which stated that 54 per cent of Americans polled thought the UN was doing 'a good job' and in April 1996: 'New Poll Shows US Voters Prefer Pro-UN Candidates – Americans overwhelmingly support full US payment of UN dues'

(press releases issued by the UNA/USA).

9. Of particular value is the publication *Crosslines Global Report, The Independent News-journal on Humanitarian Action, Development and World Trends* issued in Geneva in cooperation with the International Centre for Humanitarian Reporting in Boston, USA. See, for example, its Special Report on the international symposium 'Weapons of War, Tools of Peace' in *Crosslines* 3(4), Dec. 1995/Jan. 1996. See also the collection of essays in Robert I. Rotberg and Thomas G. Weiss (eds), *From Massacres to Genocide – The Media, Public Policy, and the Humanitarian Crises*, Harrisonburg, VA: Donnelley, 1996.

10. John C. Hammock and Joel R. Charny, for example, describe the tendency to see UN bureaucrats as easy targets, as villains, along with the local military authorities. In Rotberg and Weiss (n.9 above), p.116. This station has inspired initiatives such as the one launched in 1995 by the Lester B. Pearson Canadian International Peacekeeping Training Centre for a 'New Peacekeeping Partnership' which includes a number of military and civilian partners in joint training exercises to better prepare for the new demands of humanitarian crises and peacekeeping operations. See Alex Morrison (ed.), *The New Peacekeeping Partnership*, Clementsport, NS: Pearson Peacekeeping Press, 1995).

11. Bruce Russett, *Power and Community in World Politics*, San Francisco: Freeman, 1974, pp.36–7.

12. Louis Kriesberg and Stuart J. Thorn (eds), *Timing the De-escalation of International Conflicts*, New York: Syracuse University Press, 1991, I. William Zartman (ed.), *Elusive Peace – Negotiating an End to Civil Wars*, Washington, DC: The Brookings Institution, 1995.

13. Chester Crocker, *High Noon in Southern Africa – Making Peace in a Rough Neighborhood*, New York and London: W.W. Norton, 1992; Chester Crocker and Fen Osler Hampson, 'Making Peace Settlements Work', *Foreign Policy*, Fall 1996, No.104; Fen Osler Hampson, *Nurturing Peace – Why Peace Settlements Succeed or Fail*, Washington, DC: US Institute of Peace Press, 1996; and James Schear, 'Riding the Tiger: The United Nations and Cambodia's Struggle for Peace', in William Durch (ed.) *UN Peacekeeping – American Policy and the Uncivil Wars of the 1990's*, New York: St Martin's Press, 1996 and James Schear, 'Bosnia's Post-Dayton Traumas', *Foreign Policy*, No.104, Fall 1996.

14. Recent works on the interrelationship between public opinion and foreign policy have also not been very helpful to further understanding of the international decision-making processes. For example, David D. Newsom, *The Public Dimension of Foreign Policy*, Bloomington and Indianapolis: Indiana University Press, 1996 lists the various players in the American foreign policy process, such as think tanks, lobbies and academic institutes, but does not go beyond the national perspective.

TWO

—◄○►—

Public Information Management in UN Peacekeeping

During the period under review, that is, from 1989 to 1996, there were principally two Departments of the United Nations Secretariat which were responsible for information dissemination within and about peacekeeping operations. These were the Department of Public Information (DPI) and the Department of Peacekeeping Operations (DPKO).[1]

DEPARTMENT OF PUBLIC INFORMATION

This Department was created in 1946 by the General Assembly, which, in one of its first resolutions (13, I) mandated the Department to 'promote to the greatest possible extent an informed understanding of the work and purposes of the United Nations among the peoples of the world'. The General Assembly stated that the United Nations 'cannot achieve its purposes unless the peoples of the world are fully informed of its aims and activities'.[2] This resolution developed further the notion contained in the Preamble of the United Nations Charter that 'WE THE PEOPLES OF THE UNITED NATIONS DETERMINED to save succeeding generations from the scourge of war ...'

The history of DPI over the next five decades reflected the inherent contradictions between these lofty aspirations and the shifting interests of member states. The Department's primary mandate throughout was to disseminate information on issues, as determined by the General Assembly. From time to time, the General Assembly felt the need to exercise oversight over DPI, and to restrain it from overstepping its information mandate.

This continuing and persistent conflict of interest between the UN Secretariat and the member states was described by Leon Gordenker in an article published in 1968, in which he analysed various attempts at reforming the functions of the (then) Office of Public Information in the late 1950s. Gordenker's description of this process can easily be applied to subsequent years:

> As a whole, the outcome demonstrates once more both the durable force of an attractive idea and the truth of the maxim that secretariats have great weight in the policy process of inter-national, as of other, organizations. For despite repeated debate and attack OPI has proved enduring and resilient.
>
> During the last 15 years the many-faceted programme of the agency has shrunk somewhat, to be sure, under the economizer's knife. In particular, it was under unusually severe criticism in 1957, when the General Assembly established an expert com-mittee to investigate UN public information activities, and also in 1958, when the results of the inquiry were discussed.[3]

In addition to Gordenker's conclusion about the resilience and staying power of UN Secretariat units, his analysis of the discussions in 1957–58 about OPI's functions also reflected the debates, which continue to this day, over the value of 'a public relations approach' and the dangers of 'propaganda'.[4]

As has been argued elsewhere,[5] it is in my view unlikely that the UN, in the peacekeeping mode, would get caught up in an effort at one-sided manipulation or propaganda for which individual states have, especially during wartime, been severely criticized.[6] On the contrary, UN Secretariat officials, at Headquarters and in the field, are usually under close scrutiny from member states, NGOs and other 'UN watchers'. The tendency has been for Secretariat officials dealing with the press or public to err on the side of caution. Self-imposed restraints often give UN publications the blandness which similarly characterizes 'institutional' information efforts of other intergovernmental organizations such as the EU.[7]

DPI is in essence a department of the UN that services constituents, in particular the media, with accredited correspondents at UN headquarters and at its regional offices. It also maintains a close relationship with non-governmental organizations: 1,500 of them were associated with DPI world-wide in 1996, as well as some educational institutions (although that latter area of activity is primarily handled by UNESCO). DPI has, over the years, produced thousands of publications of varying length, as well as its own films, videos and radio programmes in the official UN languages. It also maintains a chain of over 63 Information Centres around the world which, in cooperation with the field offices of the UN Development Programme, seek to spread the UN's message in many countries.[8]

Throughout the more than five decades of DPI's existence, it has been one of the most frequently criticized departments of the Secretariat. Calls for the reform of DPI were again part of the restructuring efforts of the late 1980s. The most ambitious attempt to overhaul DPI was probably by the Canadian Under Secretary-General Therese Paquet-Sevigny who, in 1987–88, with a group of management consultants from her own country, sought to 'revitalize' the Department by a thorough review of all its functions.[9] The resulting restructuring took over two years to implement, and faced a number of unforeseen political hurdles. Tapio Kanninen described some of the problems Mrs Sevigny faced:

> In her consultations with the governments, delegates, media, public and private sector, NGOs and UN officials she found, however, a lot of scepticism and confusion about the UN, although expectations and curiosity were high. It was not easy to fulfil these expectations. There was first of all a multiplicity of mandates that Member States expected DPI to fulfil. This involved over 30 themes, more than 1,000 different activities and requires an average of close to 4,000 hours of coverage of meetings per year, 1,000 hours of video coverage, etc. However, in the communications industry the proportion of resources allocated to inform the public is much higher than that provided for DPI, although the latter has more mandates. In fact, in the course of 40 years, the annual proportion of the budget of the Department to the total United Nations net budget has decreased from 12.7 per cent to 5.3 per cent.[10]

As one of the consequences of this restructuring of DPI in the late 1980s, a 'Communications and Project Management Service' was created, which included a 'Peace and Security Programmes Section'. The mandate of this Section was, *inter alia*, to publicize the peacekeeping and peacemaking activities of the United Nations.[11]

The structure of the Department adopted as a consequence of this major reorganization was in effect throughout the period under review in this book. However, in March 1997 Secretary-General Kofi Annan announced that further changes in the management of public information would be made following a thorough review. He appointed a 'Task Force on the Reorientation of United Nations Public Information Activities' under the chairmanship of Mark Malloch Brown of the World Bank which included several journalists, among them Peter Arnett of CNN. This reorientation effort was still under way when this book was written. Its main goal is to strengthen the UN's institutional capacity to communicate, without making specific recommendations for UN field missions or peacekeeping operations.[12]

DEPARTMENT OF PEACEKEEPING OPERATIONS

This Department was formally created on 1 March 1992. Its predecessor was the Office for Special Political Affairs, which was headed for years by (now) Sir Brian Urquhart and, as of 1985, by (now) Sir Marrack Goulding. Information as a function of peacekeeping operations has only been formally recognized since 1988, when the UN, and its peacekeepers, were collectively awarded the Nobel Peace Prize. Prior to that, press and information work was considered incidental to peacekeeping operations. While a spokesperson was usually attached to each peacekeeping operation, his or her function was primarily to service journalists reporting from the mission area. The first time a comprehensive information strategy was worked out for a UN peacekeeping operation was at the end of 1988, as the UN prepared for the Namibia mission.

When the 'Peace and Security Programmes Section' of DPI was established following that Department's restructuring, it began to cooperate closely with the Department for Special Political Affairs under Marrack Goulding. All major information products, ie new publications and films, were sent to him for clearance. This close cooperation continues today in the production of information materials for worldwide use.[13]

However, differences between DPKO and DPI continue to exist, in particular with regard to the appointment of mission spokespersons and other information staff in the field. There is also the issue as to whom these staff primarily report, DPKO or DPI, and whose budget their posts are charged against. In practice, mission information staff members have to maintain good relations with both Departments and, should have both political experience and information skills. According to Fred Eckhard, the current spokesman for Secretary-General Kofi Annan, information issues in peacekeeping missions 'straddle the line' between the two Departments.[14] The disagreement as to which Department should handle information issues related to the setting up and running of peacekeeping missions came to a head in 1994 and 1995 when, following consideration by the General Assembly, it was decided to establish an information unit within the Department of Peacekeeping Operations. This was quite naturally opposed by DPI. The new unit was headed by Fred Eckhard until his appointment as spokesman of the Secretary-General in December 1996.[15]

DPI OPPOSES DPKO INFO UNIT BUT WON'T DO DECISION SPM

INTERDEPARTMENTAL COOPERATION

Notwithstanding these interdepartmental tensions, which in fact reflect major, recurrent policy disagreements between substantive departments (ie DPKO) and 'service' departments (such as DPI) in the United Nations Secretariat, several attempts were made by the two Departments to standardize procedures for information components in peacekeeping operations. They were, *inter alia*:

- The elaboration of a set of 'Media Strategies for Peacekeeping and other Field Operations';[16]
- 'Guidelines for Public Information Components in United Nations Peacekeeping and other Field Missions': (a draft Manual which has been circulating since 1996 and is being refined for use by the mission information personnel); and
- A Seminar on Public Information Policies and Practices for Field Missions, held in Glen Cove, New York, from 5–6 March 1997 at which 60 former Information Officers of peacekeeping missions, journalists and other information specialists participated.

While these discussions are continuing and will likely result in more formalized interdepartmental arrangements for the launching of new peacekeeping missions in the future, the following analyses of the information components of the UN operations in Namibia, Cambodia, Rwanda, Haiti and Eastern Slavonia, seek to contribute to a deeper understanding of the political and practical issues involved in communicating in and about peacekeeping operations.

NOTES

1. DPKO was established in March 1992; prior to that, its functions were performed by the Department of Special Political Affairs.
2. A/13(I).
3. Leon Gordenker, 'Policy Making and Secretariat Influence in the UN General Assembly: The Case of Public Information', in Robert W. Gregg and Michael Barkun, *The United Nations System and Its Functions*, Princeton, NJ: Van Nostrand, 1968, p.136.
4. Ibid., pp.149–54.
5. Ingrid Lehmann, 'Public Perceptions of UN Peacekeeping: A Factor in the Resolution of International Conflicts', *The Fletcher Forum of World Affairs*, 19/1, Winter/Spring 1995, p.112.
6. See Marvin Kalb, 'The Dangers of Patriotic Journalism' (unpublished manuscript, Harvard University, 1993) and John R. MacArthur, *Second Front, Censorship and*

Propaganda in the Gulf War, New York: Hill & Wang, 1992. It has, however been argued, that the United Nations information efforts on the issues of Apartheid and Palestine have been, and in the case of the latter, continue to be one-sided.

7. See Marc Gramberger, *Die Oeffentlichkeitsarbeit der Europaeischen Kommission*, Baden-Baden: Nomos Verlagsgesellschaft, 1997.

8. For a good description see the brochure *This is DPI - The United Nations Department of Public Information and How It Works*, New York: United Nations, 1984. This glossy brochure by DPI about itself was criticized by some states and not reissued.

9. See 'A Plan to Revitalize the Department of Public Information', presented to DPI staff on 23 Oct. 1987 (unpublished document). This attempt at restructuring followed a set of recommendations made by the 'Group of 18', who had been appointed to review all Secretariat offices in 1986.

10. Tapio Kanninen, *Organizational Retrenchment and Reorganization: The Case of the United Nations' Response to the Financial Crisis of the Mid-1980s*, doctoral book, City University of New York, 1990, p.104.

11. I was the first Chief of this Section from 1989 until 1991. In May 1997 the Section was functioning with five professionals and one general service staff member.

12. Interviews with members of the Task Force in May 1997.

13. The most notable products are the publications in the *Blue Book Series*, which have proven very useful, comprehensive compendia covering individual peacekeeping operations. For the five case studies analysed below, for example, a 'Blue Book' exists for the missions in Cambodia, Rwanda and Haiti (the latter only in French). There is also the overall historical account of all peacekeeping operations, *The Blue Helmets*, which is now in its third (1996) edition.

14. Fred Eckhard to the author on 30 April 1997.

15. At the time this book was completed, the position was vacant and the future of this information unit within DPKO was uncertain.

16. This draft was prepared by the PSPS of DPI in 1995 and updated and revised in 1996 and 1997.

THREE

————◄◦►————

The Information Programme of UNTAG
in Namibia, 1989–90

INTRODUCTION

In a number of ways, the UN Transition Assistance Group in Namibia (UNTAG) can be seen as a model for the large multilayered peacekeeping operations the UN undertook in the early 1990s. It was the first of the 'second-generation' of peacekeeping operations and exemplified the concept of 'wider peacekeeping'. As the publication *The Blue Helmets* asserts:

> The United Nations Transition Assistance Group (UNTAG) was a political operation, in which the tasks of each element – civilian, police, military – were bonded together in the field under the Special Representative, with a view to achieving a structural change in society by means of a democratic process, in accordance with an agreed timetable. Though it had elements reminiscent of other United Nations field operations, ... it had numerous novel aspects. It did not fit into the traditional mould of peacekeeping operations nor did it follow the pattern of the United Nations previous endeavours in the decolonization process. UNTAG was, in effect, in charge of the process ...[1]

It took just under one year for UNTAG to complete its main task, namely to supervise Namibia's transition to independence from South Africa. At its peak, more than 8,000 men and women from more than 120 countries were working from 200 locations in this vast, tropical and beautiful country. With the exception of a few days of crisis at the beginning of the operation in April 1989, UNTAG was able to function with the consent of the parties to the conflict, principally South Africa and the South-West African People's Organization (SWAPO). Most importantly, it mustered widespread support

NAMIBIA

UNTAG civilian deployment as of November 1989 (map no. 3952.15 (UNTAG) reproduced with the permission of the Cartographic Section, Department of Public Information, United Nations)

in the international community which, especially on the part of the UN, felt a historical responsibility towards Namibia.[2]

HISTORICAL BACKGROUND

The former German colony South-West Africa, a territory the size of half of Western Europe, had been administered by South Africa under a 'League of Nations' mandate. This mandate had been terminated by the UN General Assembly in 1966 and, in the following years, the country occupied much attention at the United Nations. The UN General Assembly, *inter alia*, created the post of 'Commissioner for Namibia', established a 'Council for Namibia', and founded a Training Institute for Namibia in Lusaka, Zambia; all of these were expressions of the UN's legal responsibility for and continuing interest in the territory.

Negotiations to resolve the Namibia issue began to bear fruit in 1976 when a 'Western Contact Group' of Diplomats from Canada, France, the Federal Republic of Germany, the United Kingdom and the United States worked out a framework for a settlement. Two years later, on 29 September 1978, the United Nations Security Council adopted Resolution 435, which approved the settlement plan. This resolution, although it could not be implemented until 1989, provided the basic blueprint for the country's transition to independence under UN supervision. '435' in the intervening years became a shorthand formula and rallying point for independence.

In August 1978, the Secretary-General of the United Nations, having appointed Mr Martti Ahtisaari of Finland as his Special Representative for Namibia, dispatched a survey mission to the territory. That mission prepared a preliminary assessment of the requirements for a UN peacekeeping mission.[3] It was fortuitous for the planning and operational cohesiveness of UNTAG, when it finally was deployed in 1989, that Mr Ahtisaari and several of his closest aides had continued their involvement in the peace process during that interim period. This continuity of senior staff proved a major asset in the eventual implementation of Resolution 435.

It took those 11 years to resolve several crucial outstanding military and political issues, foremost among them the absence of a cease-fire along the Angolan-Namibian border, exacerbated by an increased involvement of Cuban and South African forces in the Angolan civil war. Related to that, disagreement persisted in the 1980s about details of the implementation of Resolution 435, such as the size of the UNTAG military contingent, the monitoring of SWAPO bases, and issues related to Namibia's electoral system and its constitution.[4]

One interesting aspect of this protracted regional crisis in Southern Africa eventually worked in favour of the United Nations operation in Namibia. While the military power balance between the various combatants in Angola was constantly shifting throughout the 1980s,[5] the situation in South-West Africa remained relatively unchanged during those years. Thus the information about the territory which the UN had gathered in the course of the survey mission in 1978 was essentially unaltered by the time UNTAG was launched in March–April 1989. As Virginia Page Fortna put it: 'UNTAG went into Namibia with plenty of good information. The staff was particularly aware of political sensitivities and was therefore able to manoeuvre through them successfully.'[6]

MANDATE

The settlement plan contained in UN Security Council Resolution 435 prescribed a timetable for the operation, and listed various functions related to the electoral process. One of the essential provisions of the plan was the requirement that the UN Special Representative 'will have to satisfy himself at each stage as to the fairness and appropriateness of all measures affecting the political process at all levels of administration', and that he 'may himself make proposals in regard to any aspect of the political process'.[7] As will be seen below, Mr Ahtisaari was able to develop this mandate of control and supervision of the South African Administrators in 1989 to UNTAG's advantage. It effectively gave him a veto over all actions undertaken by the Administrators of the territory where this might be essential 'to enable the people of Namibia to freely and fairly determine their own future'.[8]

The 435 plan of 1978 also stipulated that the Special Representative of the Secretary-General would 'have at his disposal a substantial civilian section of the United Nations Transition Assistance Group, sufficient to carry out his duties satisfactorily'.[9] Ahtisaari and his senior team again took this point literally, when they set up an extensive and unprecedented network of UNTAG District Centres that largely mirrored the South African administrative divisions of the territory.

Furthermore, the settlement plan specified that 'all political parties and interested persons, without regard to their political views', be given 'a full and fair opportunity to organize and participate in the electoral process'. It then stated: 'Full freedom of speech, assembly, movement and press shall be guaranteed'.[10] The latter sentence became, in 1989, an important tool in decontrolling the biased media in South-West Africa, such as the South-West African Broadcasting Corporation (SWABC).

Also of significance for the political settlement was paragraph 10 of the plan which stated: 'The United Nations Special Representative will take steps to guarantee against the possibility of intimidation or interference with the electoral process from whatever quarter.'[11] This provision allowed the Special Representative, in response to incidents of violence and intimidation in several parts of the country in 1989, to work out a 'Code of Conduct for Political Parties'. All heads of the registered political parties were signatories to this Code and could be held responsible to observe its provisions.

Following the signing of the Tripartite Agreements by Angola, Cuba and South Africa at United Nations headquarters in New York on 22 December 1988, which provided for the phased withdrawal of South African and Cuban troops and led to the implementation of Resolution 435, the Secretary-General was asked, *inter alia*, to prepare a report on the implementation of Resolution 435, detailing specific requirements for implementation by the United Nations Secretariat. Major difficulties continued to be the size and cost of UNTAG's military contingent, difficulties that were to last into March 1989, when political disagreements in the General Assembly over UNTAG's budget were finally resolved.[12]

The Secretary-General's report (S/20412) recommended the necessary steps for the implementation of the peace plan which was to commence on 1 April 1989. This document contained no reference to an information mandate for UNTAG; the only reference to any of the future extensive UNTAG activities in informing and educating the Namibian population about the transition process is in paragraph 38 of that report, in referring to the 435 settlement plan: 'It makes provision for secret ballot and for full freedom of speech, assembly, movement and the press'.[13]

The important conclusion therefore is that UNTAG, as the first of the new generation of UN peacekeeping operations, did not have a specific information component or explicit information function as part of its mandate. Nevertheless, UNTAG did succeed, in the field, in executing one of the model information programmes of any UN field mission. How was this possible?

SURVEY AND PREPARATION

As part of the revitalization of the United Nations Department of Public Information which was begun in 1987 (see Chapter 2), a new unit was set up, the 'Peace and Security Programmes Section'. That Section had already organized, earlier in 1988, information and communication plans for the award of the Nobel Peace Prize to United Nations peacekeepers, as well as the 'identity programme' for the UN's humanitarian operation in Afghanistan.[14]

There existed, therefore, in 1988 in the Department of Public Information, a small nucleus of staff who were familiar with peacekeeping issues and/or had served in other peacekeeping operations. These, together with a group of dedicated unpaid interns, generated new and creative projects. The UNTAG information programme was destined to be a good example of their efforts.

A very important preliminary step in preparing a public information programme for the Namibia operation in advance of its actually being launched in the field, was that the Department of Public Information was asked by Mr Ahtisaari to provide a draft proposal for an 'identity programme' for UNTAG. This draft proposal, which was submitted in time to be included in the preliminary budget for the operation in January 1989, was worked out by a small team, after hours,[15] signed off by the Head of the Department in January and included in the planning process for the operation. This, in hindsight, had the very important result of having the information component budgeted for, and thus legitimized, several months prior to the launching of the operation. Thus the omission of the information component from the mandate was largely overcome by eleventh hour improvisation.

When an internal UN Secretariat survey mission left for Namibia in February 1989 I, as the Chief of the Peace and Security Programmes Section, was included in the team. This was another novel development, and allowed me to assess at first hand the Namibian communications infrastructure. I was thus able to determine precisely what information, production and distribution facilities would be available to the UN there. Following our return to UN Headquarters in New York in mid-February, budgetary assessments were revised, and preparations were set in motion to recruit staff for the various information functions in UNTAG. Also, arrangements for feedback were made with New York and other United Nations offices around the world.

Mr Ahtisaari designated Mr Fred Eckhard as his Spokesman and Mr Anwar Cherif as his Chief of Information. Back-up at UN Headquarters was provided by the remaining staff of the Peace and Security Programmes Section[16] of the Communications and Project Management Service in DPI, together with the Spokesman's Office of the Secretary-General.

TRAINING

The UN's Office of Human Resource Management organized two training sessions for Secretariat staff who had volunteered to be members of UNTAG's District Centres and other civilian functions. These were two-day sessions, held in March 1989 in New York and Geneva.[17] They were intensive training seminars geared to preparing staff for the political, military, environmental, health and administrative issues that would be facing them on the ground in Namibia.

The session in New York included role-playing exercises, simulations which allowed participants to project themselves into likely situations of conflict in the mission area. This type of training session was also a novelty for the UN Secretariat, and had very good results. As a consequence, staff who participated in these sessions, nearly all of whom became part of the 'first wave' of UN people in the transition group in Namibia, encountered very few problems in their field postings. The same can, unfortunately, not be said for the second, and much larger, group of Secretariat staff which arrived in May for the registration of voters. Many in the second wave received training only after they arrived in the area. They were, in many cases, ill-prepared for such simple tasks as operating four-wheel drive vehicles on the left of unpaved roads.[18]

A third round of training sessions for civilians was the vital electoral training given to about 1,000 election monitors. These were national officials with prior experience in election monitoring, who came to Namibia from all over the world for a two-week period for the election in November 1989. In the Windhoek electoral district alone, 180 election monitors were briefed in a one-day session, which comprised election- and district-specific training.

POLITICAL ENVIRONMENT IN NAMIBIA

Under Secretary-General for Special Political Affairs Marrack Goulding[19] was at the time the senior Secretariat official in charge of peacekeeping operations. In that function, he also served as focal point and chairman of the Secretary-General's task force for UNTAG in New York. In 1991, Mr Goulding offered this post-mission assessment of the context in which UNTAG operated:

> The task thus given to the United Nations was a difficult one for a variety of reasons. First, there had been a long and cruel war between the South African authorities and the South-West Africa People's Organization (SWAPO), the national liberation move- ment in Namibia, recognized as such by the United Nations. Second, that long and cruel war had brought about a profound distrust between the two sides. Third, the South African Administration in Namibia was essentially an apartheid-type

administration. Some of the features of what is called 'petty apartheid' had been lifted by the time the UN operation began, but the administrative structure of the country was one in which there was a separate administration for each racial group. The fourth problem that we had to face was that the South African security forces, again because of the war, had a dominant position in the government of Namibia. A large section of the northern, most populous part of the territory was a military area effectively under military administration. Finally, because of the long years of colonial rule, there was absolutely no tradition in Namibia of free and fair elections. There was thus a great deal of education that had to be done of the electorate itself about what a free and fair election amounted to and how it was done.[20]

The apartheid system, which had been in effect in South-West Africa for many decades, was still influencing attitudes and behaviour of the local population, black and white. It became clear to some of the UN personnel involved in the transition process that UNTAG itself was perceived as an actor on the political scene, and that its staff was scrutinized and observed and tested continuously for its impartiality and general approach to the country. Suspicions ran high, particularly among the white population, just as rising expectations led to an overestimation of the speed of the transition process among some blacks in the country. Most UNTAG staff were not prepared for this intensity of feeling, for and against the United Nations in Namibia.

The critical period occurred right at the beginning of the mission: on 1 April 1989, the date of the cease-fire and the beginning of the transitional period, a major incursion of more than 1,000 SWAPO combatants in the northern part of the country led to fighting with South African police forces. Intense battles continued for about ten days during which 300–400 combatants were killed. This led to an escalation in distrust between the two main warring parties in the territory, and ' to a discreditation of the United Nations at the very beginning of the operation'.[21] It took at least six weeks to straighten out this situation and get the operation back on its timetable. This could not have been achieved without the assistance of outside powers, namely high-level diplomacy from the United States, the Soviet Union, Cuba, Angola and other African states. According to Marrack Goulding, who himself travelled to Angola, Namibia and South Africa to assist in the negotiations, it was 'an example of how the successful conduct of these operations does require that the Secretary-General be supported by the Member States of the Organization'.[22]

Those first six weeks showed the volatility of the cease-fire arrangements, and the inability of the UNTAG military component to respond to serious violations of them at that time. More importantly, it also showed that a strong consensus existed in the international community for the Namibian peace process to continue as planned. Setbacks such as the one experienced in April/May 1989 could have derailed the plan in which so much political and negotiating effort had been invested by Western and other powers for so many years. Namibia and the United Nations operation there thus benefited from what Fen Osler Hampson has termed 'the staying power by third parties' in a difficult situation.[23]

Nevertheless, the events on and following 1 April 1989 produced a major credibility problem for the United Nations operation on the ground. While the peace plan was eventually rescued, mistrust of the United Nations, particularly among whites, increased drastically. This manifested itself in open hostility against UN personnel, which in some instances took the form of violence to UNTAG vehicles, such as tyre-slashing and defacing the vehicles with graffiti such as: 'UNTAG = United Nations Terrorist Assistance Group'.

In the District Centre in Khomasdal, a mixed-race suburb of Windhoek, which I was tasked to set up with a colleague and an interpreter, in May 1989, the population was initially quite taciturn towards the United Nations. Patience plus good public relations, which included visits to all local businesses, meetings with schoolteachers and pupils, church visits and the setting up of town meetings, helped eventually to overcome this. A great tool for gaining the sympathy of schoolchildren was to hand out UNTAG blue-and-white stickers and buttons, which were available by May: UNTAG's identity was being formed.[24]

A major development for the country was the return of refugees, an operation which was organized by the United Nations High Commissioner for Refugees. The original estimates for refugees (75,000)[25] were obviously exaggerated, and the eventual total figure of Namibian returnees was just under 43,000. However, in a country with a total population of just over a million, this was a substantial group. 'The great majority of returning Namibians came back from Angola, with smaller but significant numbers from Zambia. Altogether, returnees came from 46 countries, requiring a coordinated effort by UNHCR offices worldwide.'[26] This meant an influx of people who, in their many years of exile, had often received an excellent education which their relatives who remained at home sometimes resented. Those of the returnees who had been active in SWAPO and its military wing were, for obvious reasons, viewed with great suspicion by others who had stayed behind in the territory.

A similar situation was experienced by black and by white South African exiles several years later. This experience is portrayed by André Brink in his novel *Imaginings of Sand*. The returnee, Kristien Muller, who has worked for the African National Congress (ANC) abroad, visits South Africa just before the elections in 1994. When she ventures cautious criticism, she provokes this outburst from her own sister: 'When things became too hard to handle, you turned tail and ran away, expecting us to sort out the mess. And now that you're safe and far away you think you can gloat. But to us it's life or death, in case you haven't noticed.'[27]

A different problem related to Namibian returnees is described by Franz Ansprenger:

> The return of the refugees, in addition to its social effects, laid open a deep festering political wound which became a central theme of the election campaign. This theme probably cost SWAPO the two-thirds majority countrywide. Several hundred Namibians returned from exile not as SWAPO supporters but ex-prisoners of SWAPO and as bitter political opponents of the organization to which they had fled abroad in the past.[28]

It was also strongly suspected that the South African Bureau of Information was engaged in efforts to undermine the Namibian transition process. As late as September 1989, the killing of Anton Lubowski, a Windhoek lawyer of German origin who was one of the leading whites in SWAPO, served to fuel these suspicions and led to a near hysterical situation in the Namibian capital at the time. A few weeks prior to the elections, in late October 1989, the daily newspaper *The Namibian* printed a story, having uncovered a campaign by South Africa 'to discredit SWAPO and the UN' with a budget of 3.5 million South African rand.[29]

MEDIA ENVIRONMENT

Namibia, although sparsely populated, has 11 different population groups.[30] There are numerous languages spoken in the country: Afrikaans, English, Kwanyama, Ndonga, Herero, Nama, German and Bushman; and there are dialects within each language.[31] At the time of UNTAG's arrival in the territory, Afrikaans was still the *lingua franca*, but English was rapidly becoming the major language spoken throughout the territory. In the early 1980s, there was only one English-language daily newspaper, two Afrikaans papers and one German. In the course of 1989, several other daily and weekly organs came into existence,[32] thus rapidly expanding and diversifying the media landscape. In hindsight, this expansion of the media infrastructure looks like a logical and necessary by-product of the political transition process. This opening up of the media system in the country was encouraged by UNTAG in the spring of 1989. However, in the case of the government-controlled South-West African Broadcasting Corporation, some corrective measures had to be taken.[33]

SWABC provided radio broadcasts 'to the entire country through its nine radio services, broadcasting in 13 languages on FM, backed up by MW and SW'. A single television channel had been established in 1981 and produced '442 news bulletins per week in 12 languages'.[34] As far as the content of these broadcasts was concerned, the UN publication, *Blue Helmets* reports: 'As a result of many years of colonialism and apartheid, Namibia had a public information system which was geared to maintain this situation, with deeply partisan newspapers and a public broadcasting system prone to disinformation.'[35]

A driving force of the anti-435 and anti-UN sentiments among the predominantly German businessmen and farmers in Namibia during the first months of UNTAG's deployment was the daily newspaper *Allgemeine Zeitung* which, with its editor Hans Feddersen in the lead, helped to reconfirm old prejudices and to create new stereotypes among the influential German population.[36] This made working in Namibia in the transitional period particularly difficult for UN staff of German nationality. The weekly paper *Namibia Nachrichten* became more influential among the German-speakers as the independence process progressed and, following the elections in November 1989, the general tone of reporting in English, German and Afrikaans became much more positive and forward looking.

However, as some international correspondents, who were in Namibia prior to independence, also testified, the living and working environment for journalists remained difficult throughout the transition period. One, the German radio correspondent, Ferdinand Klien, relayed to the author that there had been various attempts to intimidate foreign correspondents[37] which made working conditions on the ground difficult and hazardous.

UNTAG'S INFORMATION FUNCTIONS

Blue Helmets summarizes the overall task thus:

> Above all, UNTAG had the political task of ensuring that a major change in political atmosphere took place so that there could be a free and fair campaign in a fully democratic climate. Numerous

changes in law, attitude and society had to take place. But Namibia had had no tradition of political democracy and had been subjected to a harsh and discriminatory system of administration for a hundred years. UNTAG's task was to ensure that, despite this, the people of the country could feel sufficiently confident, free from intimidation from any quarter, and adequately informed, to exercize a free choice as regards their political future.[38]

It was decided by the Special Representative of the Secretary-General that UNTAG would need an effective public information campaign if it were to succeed in its task of creating a free and open environment to allow Namibian self-determination. Three main functions stand out in achieving this vital goal: a) the creation of a positive identity for the mission itself; b) the use of a combination of print, radio and television to get its messages across; and c) the use of a network of political information centres all over the country. These three functional activities overlapped to a certain extent, but, in the following three sections they will be examined separately.

The Identity Programme

In retrospect, the most important innovation undertaken by UNTAG was its 'identity system'. This is a concept commonly applied by corporate management to create a 'brand identity' or 'corporate image'.[39] As was discussed in the previous Chapter, the United Nations Department of Public Information had already, in 1987, begun to apply creatively such public relations techniques as seemed suitable for an international organization. The aim of the UNTAG identity system was to present a consistent, uniform, positive image of UNTAG in Namibia and beyond, and to avoid a confused perception of the operation among the local population and in the international community at large.

Once it was decided by the political leadership of the mission to establish such an identity programme – a decision which was taken by Mr Thornberry and Mr Ahtisaari in January 1989 – a graphic designer, Jan Arnesen, was assigned at UN headquarters in New York to begin work on establishing UNTAG's identity in visual terms, by creating symbols, graphics and a typography which were then consistently applied on all of UNTAG's print products throughout the mission area. This system was seen as so important and successful in the Namibia context that Ms Arnesen was again assigned, in 1992–93 to produce an identity programme for the UN's Cambodia mission (which will be described in the next Chapter).

The identity system in Namibia was applied in lettering for UNTAG's vehicles and buildings, its stationery and business correspondence, all publications and internal memoranda, on business cards of UNTAG's staff, on bumper stickers, posters, decals and clothing items available for sale.[40] The identity system became such an all-encompassing activity that the Chief of Administration of UNTAG, Abdou Cisse, was seized with its implementation, thus ensuring overall mission-internal consistency.[41]

In launching this innovative and ambitious programme there was support in a number of important departments at UN headquarters, including the office of the Controller.[42] There was also continuing back-up support from the Department of Public Information for the UNTAG information programme. DPI seconded numerous staff to the mission, and sent both still photographers and film crews on several shortterm trips to the area of operation. This allowed the use of up-to-date film clips and photographs in the production of DPI's world worldwide information products. This senior level support for the UNTAG information programme at various levels of the UN Secretariat appears in retrospect to have been another factor in its effectiveness.[43]

Jan Arnesen estimates that the production of print materials in Namibia alone cost US$220,000, which is consistent with official secretariat accounting to the General Assembly.[44] The total number of information items produced during UNTAG's period of deployment was, according to *The Blue Helmets*, 590,000.[45] In the initial phase of the operation all items were printed in English and Afrikaans. Later on, as translation and production capacities allowed, print materials were also issued and distributed in Herero, Damara/Nama, Kavango, Owambo, Caprivi and German (the latter being used only for newspaper campaign advertisements).

An important element in the identity programme was its consistent use of slogans designed to communicate UNTAG's main message in a succinct form. The slogans proposed initially related to Namibian independence but later the slogan which was to become UNTAG's trademark for the transitional period focused on the election as the key event: *UNTAG – Free and Fair Elections in Namibia*. This choice was made by the Special Representative, Mr Ahtisaari, prior to the launching of UNTAG. It proved a wise choice, as it focused from the outset on the defining event in the transitional period – the elections.

In the period after June 1989, beginning with the three months voter registration phase, the slogans used on UNTAG print materials became even more election-specific, such as:

Free and Fair Elections mean ... Your Vote is Secret ... and Your Ballot is Safe

It's Your Time to Choose for Namibia
UNTAG Supervises and Controls the Voting Process
UNTAG Supervises and Controls the Counting Process

By October 1989, the messages conveyed in UNTAG's print products were almost exclusively related to electoral issues, giving detailed instructions about the technicalities of voting. By then, the Information Office of the Administrator-General of Namibia had also begun to issue colourful election education materials with the main slogans *Vote without Fear* and *Our Vote brings Peace*. This made clear that UNTAG's message had been received by all sides.

Multimedia Information Campaign

When assessing, in 1996, UNTAG's information campaign, Lena Yacoumopoulou, a United Nations radio information officer with experience in three peacekeeping missions, linked the implementation of UNTAG's political mandate to the information effort in the following words: 'The existence of a multifunctional mandate and the success of its implementation provided the information team with ample and positive material to work with, without having to resort to defensive damage control'.[46] The latter comment refers to Ms Yacoumopoulou's experience with the UN mission in the Former Yugoslavia.

UNTAG indeed produced ample material for UN information officers to work with: the registration of voters, the work of many different nationalities in over 40 UNTAG District Centres, the country's great variation of indigenous tribal groups, against the backdrop of a beautiful and interesting landscape, all provided excellent visual and aural material for the information officers.

The UNTAG Spokesman, Fred Eckhard, held a daily press briefing, attended regularly by the Windhoek-based press corps[47] and open to UNTAG staff on an 'as required' basis. The Spokesman's Office additionally produced a variety of press releases and fact sheets about the deployment of UNTAG military, figures about voter registration and other information related to electoral issues, as well as pronouncements by the Special Representative and news from New York (the Security Council, the Secretary-General and other officials and agencies of the United Nations).

By June 1989, a daily radio programme was produced which was broadcast twice a day in English, once a day in Afrikaans, Damara/Nama, German, Herero, Caprivi, Kavango and Owambo, and once a week in Tswana. The South-West African Broadcasting Corporation made its facilities and airtime

available to the UN free of charge. Its weekly ten-minute television programme, which was aired Saturday night and Sunday afternoon, was also
free of charge to the UN. For its visual production needs internally and internationally, UNTAG hired a local cameraman and freelance photographer for
the duration of the mission.

As far as censorship was concerned, Lena Yacoumopoulou reports that
'the South African administration did not ban or censor any of the
information programmes, with the exception of two phrases in the radio
programmes considered politically and commercially inappropriate at the
time'.[48] Ms Yacoumopoulou stresses the importance of the regular political
guidance received by the UNTAG information team from the Special
Representative's Office, which gave them considerable support, financially
and otherwise. Weekly meetings were held where the team was updated on
events and briefed on issues to be emphasized.[49] This allowed the information
officers to stay on top of political developments and to reinforce UNTAG's
political message in their work.

While there was a certain amount of staff competition and rivalry as in
any other international bureaucracy, the UNTAG information team is
remembered by those who worked in it as one of their most memorable experiences of their career. Jan Arnesen drew the following overall conclusions from
her experience when assessing UNTAG's identity programme in 1997:

> When planning for information programmes throughout the
> world, and for peacekeeping missions in particular, the United
> Nations understandably places the most emphasis on television
> and radio in an effort to reach a greater number of viewers or
> listeners. The problem with this approach is that, as experience
> has taught us, it can take several months to set up a radio station
> or to produce television programmes in areas where the
> infrastructure is not already in place to accommodate a rapid
> production schedule.
>   And in some regions, the remote rural areas are so remote that
> many people do not have access to television at all, and radio may
> be limited to one 'state' radio or the radio of one 'political party'.
> While it may be possible eventually to set up an independent radio
> station or television channel, it can be a lengthy process and
> though it has proven to be very successful in some key situations
> – notably for the Cambodia elections – it is important to look at
> an overall strategy for UN information programmes that
> encompasses all three media working together to enhance the
> UN's message and image in the 'field'.[50]

The Network of District Centres

The network of District Centres set up by the Special Representative throughout the country was, as is now well recognized, one of the crucial novel functions in this second generation peacekeeping mission. There were 42 UNTAG District Centres, not counting civilian police stations. The latter were, depending on circumstances, either collocated with the District Centres or, when in separate locations, cooperated with each other at the district level. There was, superimposed over the District Centres, a structure of Regional District Offices which were intended to undertake such coordinating functions. District Centre heads reported through their Regional Directors to the Special Representative on a weekly basis – or more frequently, if circumstances called for it. They provided assessments of the political and security situation in the districts and reported about their own political liaison work and public information outreach.

The tools for the information work of the Centres were provided by the UNTAG identity programme: posters, wall sheets, information sheets about registration procedures and voting instructions, bumper stickers, decals and T-shirts.[51] The Centres, in turn, provided UNTAG headquarters with the kind of feedback they needed to adjust their overall communication strategy. The Centre staff were the 'eyes and ears' of the mission, and naturally were also the most active users of UNTAG's information products.

The Centres thus had a dual information function: reporting, in the sense of information gathering and public relations. Both functions went hand-in-glove for the duration of the mission. In the later phases of the mission, in particular from September to November 1989, UNTAG Centres further-more assisted 'in the much-needed process of internal reconciliation'.[52] This process was closely related to the adoption of the 'Code of Conduct' for all political parties during the election campaign. The Code prescribed 16 points to which the nine heads of political parties had agreed in writing, which were, *inter alia*: forbidding intimidation, banning of weapons at political rallies, avoiding language that might incite to violence, respect for each others' symbols and campaign materials, bringing allegations of violations to the attention of UNTAG personnel.

In addition to publicizing this code widely throughout the country, UNTAG also implemented paragraph 12 which stated: 'Parties will meet on a fortnightly basis under the chairmanship of UNTAG regional directors or centre heads to discuss all matters of concern relating to the election campaign.'[53] Meetings were held in most District Centres which, in many cases, brought face-to-face political antagonists who had fought each other during the war. These UNTAG District Centre meetings discussed issues ranging from allegations of the intimidation of party campaign workers, to violence at party rallies and a multitude of other grievances, most of which were worked out peacefully at these meetings.[54]

The District Centres, while strictly speaking a part of the political set-up of UNTAG, thus performed a combination of political information functions in a manner which led subsequent peacekeeping missions to attempt to emulate the idea.

POLITICAL LEADERSHIP

The most important factor for the success of the UNTAG information programme was probably the significance attached to it by the leadership of the mission. UNTAG was the first of the new generation of peacekeeping operations and was very clearly and very openly political in its task and functions. The UN military played a secondary role in this mission, particularly after its main task, supervising the withdrawal of South African troops from the territory, had been achieved.

Mr Ahtisaari, the Special Representative of the Secretary-General, was closely involved in the formulation of the UNTAG identity programme at its inception in New York in late 1988. According to one of his longstanding associates who was to become the head of his office in Namibia, Cedric Thornberry, Ahtisaari 'understood the needs very well and was closely involved from the start'. Thornberry stressed in a letter to the author that Ahtisaari's 'backing was essential'.[55] It was also highly important that the information programme was 'under the direct supervision of the Special Representative',[56] ie that the Spokesman and the Chief of Information received daily guidance from both Thornberry and Ahtisaari.

Thornberry dates his own recognition of the importance of public information in Namibia back to 1974, when he first visited the country as a delegate of Amnesty International and 'began to learn about the savage undermining of a whole people practised in the name of ethnic separateness', an experience which 'impelled me into the conviction that only by reaching the people on the widest possible basis could we help them lose their fear and thus have the courage to reach out for a real act of self-determination'.[57]

The importance of political leadership for the information programme was also confirmed by Marrack Goulding, the New York-based Chairman of the UNTAG Task Force, in an interview with the author. Mr Goulding said that the UNTAG programme succeeded 'because its leadership understood from the beginning the necessity of a comprehensive information strategy, especially for local consumption, and was able to exploit its predeployment jobs to ensure that the necessary ideas and resources would be available'.[58]

CONCLUSION

UNTAG had the honour, albeit at that time unwittingly, to have ushered in the 'second generation' of peacekeeping operations. Seldom had a mission's mandate been so heavily and overtly political. Never before in the UN's history was there an operation implemented at all levels of society, principally through a network of civilian district offices. UNTAG's sizeable military contingent soon became part of the larger political task, ie assisting the country's transition to democracy and independence.

This was by no means clear to those who planned and executed the mission. Indeed, the *second* edition of *The Blue Helmets*, which went to press at the time of Namibia's independence, still advised its readers that 'a peacekeeping operation has come to be defined as an operation involving military personnel ...'[59] Nevertheless, the military and civilian relationship in UNTAG had already undergone major changes, and would evolve further along these lines in the Cambodia operation which will be analysed in the next Chapter.

It is noteworthy that the information requirements were not explicit in the original mandate of UNTAG, and might have been forgotten altogether but for some inspired last-minute improvization on the part of middle-level staff at United Nations Headquarters. The point is that the need for a strong information component was appreciated in time by the political leadership of the mission and was given adequate support by the UN Secretariat. The first 'principle' identified in Chapter I, that of recognizing the importance of public perceptions, was thus not overlooked for long, and provision was made, organizationally and financially, for what was only then emerging as a vital operational function.

The critical nature of cultural sensitivities was not recognized by the planners of UNTAG's information programme, even though they had to cope with an environment composed of 11 population and language groups. This situation was further complicated by deeply ingrained racial prejudices among the local population, as well as ambiguous attitudes of and towards the large numbers of returnees, black and white.

The open media environment so important to this mission here posed additional complications which would be encountered again on future missions, where controlled media suddenly are decontrolled, but are not necessarily therefore rendered reliable or responsible. In this case, the UN was put to some difficulty to avoid having merely unleashed a media which, if not outright harmful, had to be closely monitored for accuracy and objectivity. As will be seen, this issue has by no means since always been resolved as satisfactorily as it was in the case of the SWABC.

International and local opinion, and the need for mission-internal information dissemination, were simultaneously and quite effectively addressed by the identification programme. This programme was flexible enough to adapt as the mission progressed, eventually producing election-specific educational materials that helped Namibians transcend the racial boundaries and vote for their first democratic government.

Cedric Thornberry was by no means the architect of the UNTAG Information Programme, but he was one of its mentors. Upon reflection, he has termed it 'pioneering' and 'radical by the UN's standards' but, in reality, 'quite minimalist and conservative by those of the real world of publicity'.[60] In fact, in my view, it was probably the best that the United Nations is capable of mustering in the field. When put into the larger political context, the two issues identified by Fen Osler Hampson as having been essential in the success of the ambitious Namibia Plan – the 'staying power of third parties' and the 'ability of the United Nations to overcome the suspicion and hostility it faced at the beginning of the implementation period' – worked together. The 'staying power' of third parties interested in achieving a settlement of the Namibia issue was largely outside the control of the UN Secretariat; creating an information and communication capacity that satisfied the needs of international media and the various local constituencies was not.

NOTES

1. *The Blue Helmets – A Review of United Nations Peace-keeping* (3rd edn) New York: United Nations, 1996, pp.203–4.
2. The UN's historic responsibility for Namibia has been declared on numerous occasions. See, for example, the *Report of the Secretary-General* dated 19 May 1983 (contained in S/15776) in which he stated: 'I regard the problem of Namibia as a special responsibility of the Secretary-General in view of the unique relationship between the United Nations and the people of Namibia. I believe that the settlement of the Namibian question is of overriding importance for the future peace and prosperity of the entire region.' (para.20).
3. The author was a member of this 30-member survey team that went to Namibia in August 1978 and participated in both military and civilian briefings and meetings arranged by the South African administrators for this purpose. My (unpublished) diary of this trip is a principal source for this Chapter.
4. Several excellent accounts of the protracted negotiations about Southern Africa between 1978 and 1988 now exist. Foremost among them is the book by Chester Crocker, the top US negotiator, *High Noon in Southern Africa – Making Peace in a Rough Neighborhood*, New York: Norton, 1992. The South African military perspective on the last years of war

along the Angolan/Namibian border is recounted by Fred Bridgland, *The War for Africa – Twelve Months That Transformed A Continent*, Gibraltar: Ashanti, 1990. An excellent analytical perspective on the 'ripeness' of the conflict in Namibia is also contained in Chapter 3 of Fen Osler Hampson, *Nurturing Peace – Why Peace Settlements Succeed or Fail*, Washington DC: US Institute of Peace Press, 1996.

5. See Bridgland (n.4 above), who points out that, while in 1987 the Cubans had no more than 2,000 soldiers stationed in southwest Angola, by June 1988, 'more than 11,000 Cuban infantrymen were stationed in the southwest and some were patrolling to within 20 km of the border'. The South Africans, according to Bridgland, had detected three integrated Cuban/SWAPO battalions, which 'meant war, as far as the SAD was concerned'. (pp.347–8).
6. Virginia Page Fortha, 'United Nations Transition Assistance Group', in William J. Durch (ed.), *The Evolution of UN Peacekeeping – Case Studies and Comparative Analysis*, New York: St Martin's Press, 1993, pp.353–87.
7. S/12636 (10 April 1978), *Proposal for a settlement of the Namibian situation*, para.5.
8. Ibid.
9. Ibid.
10. Ibid, para.6.
11. Ibid, para.10.
12. The United Nations Secretariat assigns responsibility for the delay in procurement and shipping of vital logistical items for UNTAG to the political wrangling in the General Assembly over UNTAG's budget in February 1989. (*The Blue Helmets* (n.1 above), p.209).
13. S/20412, para.38.
14. At that time, the author headed the Peace and Security Programmes Section, which was, however, neither fully staffed nor budgeted. It was run parallel to (ie using the staff of) the Non-Governmental Organization Section of the Department, which the author also headed.
15. Due to the shortness of time, the people principally involved worked over the Christmas holidays 1988, at home and in their offices. They were: Francois Giuliani, the Acting Department Head, Armand Duqué, then head of the Executive Office of the Department of Public Information and Ingrid Lehmann, as Project Manager.
16. I was deployed to Namibia as Head of an UNTAG District Center in the Windhoek region on 31 March 1989 as part of the 'first wave' of Mr Ahtisaari's team.
17. I participated as a trainer in both the New York and the Geneva training sessions.
18. This second group of staff unfortunately had a very high rate of traffic accidents which led to the loss of life by several civilians, as well as members of the military contingents, working in the mission.
19. This function was, in 1992, renamed as Under Secretary-General for Peacekeeping Operations.
20. Marrack Goulding, 'Case-Study: The United Nations Operation in Namibia', in *The Singapore Symposium – The Changing Role of the United Nations in Conflict Resolution and Peace-Keeping, 13–15 March 1991*, New York: United Nations, 1991, p.33.
21. Ibid., p.35. A full account of the events around 1 April 1989 from the UN Secretariat's point of view is contained in *The Blue Helmets* (n.1 above), pp.216–19 which states: 'It had been a nightmare beginning to an operation which had been launched with so much hope'. For another perspective see Page Fortna, (n.6 above), pp.369–70 who speculates whether UNTAG could have prevented the infiltration by SWAPO had it been fully deployed: 'If UNTAG had tried to intervene militarily between SWAPO and SADF

during the April crisis, the results could have been disastrous. If they had been in place during that event, according to one source, they would have been withdrawn rather than become caught in the crossfire. On the other hand, if UNTAG forces had been in northern Namibia before 1 April, SWAPO might never have attempted the border crossing.' Another perspective was that of Alexander Cockburn who commented in the *Wall Street Journal* of 13 April 1989: 'Here then is the conspiracy mounted by South Africa, with the complicity of the UN ... Mr Ahtisaari and Mr Perez de Cuellar agreed first to unleash Battalion 101 and then five other South African battalions. Thus SWAPO men and civilians were mowed down under UN auspices. Emboldened by this coup, South Africa will continue to sabotage the possibility that a Namibia freed of its malign and illegal domination can finally emerge'.

22. Goulding (n.20 above), p.35.
23. Hampson (n.4 above), p.54. It should, however, be kept in mind that the information available to historians of the Namibia conflict writing after 1990 was not available to those working on the ground or in behind-the-scenes negotiations in various capitals. It is much easier for Page Fortna and Osler Hampson to write in 1993 or 1996 that Namibia 'was ripe for resolution' in 1989, than it was for the staff with UNTAG in Windhoek who kept their bags packed in April 1989 in anticipation of a possible evacuation of the mission area, as South Africa threatened to eject UNTAG and renege on its agreement to 435. See, for example, *The Namibian*, 7 April 1989, which reported (p.2): 'The Director of the Office of the Special Representative, Mr Cedric Thornberry, yesterday admitted that the United Nations were presented with an ultimatum to either allow the deployment of South African troops or have UNTAG kicked out of the country.'
24. While the political sympathies of the approximately 30,000 residents of Khomasdal were with the DTA (Democratic Turnhalle Alliance, see below), the inhabitants, even though shy, were generally well-disposed towards the United Nations presence. This could not be said of the majority of whites, in particular the businessmen and farmers of German origin. I encountered them at the beginning of June at the Windhoek Carnival when nasty racially-based vignettes about UNTAG and other foreigners prompted our leaving the festivities early in the evening. Ingrid Lehmann, 'Public Perceptions of UN Peacekeeping', *The Fletcher Forum of World Affairs*, 19/1, Winter/Spring 1995, p.5.
25. This section is based on information contained in Franz Ansprenger, *Freie Wahlen in Namibia*, Berliner Studien zur Politik in Afrika, No.10, Frankfurt: Lang, 1991 and *The Blue Helmets* (n.1 above), p.225.
26. *The Blue Helmets* (n.1 above), p.225.
27. André Brink, *Imaginings of Sand*, New York: Harcourt Brace and Jovanovich, 1996, p.49.
28. Ansprenger (n.25 above), p.51. Ansprenger gives a vivid description of the internal politics of SWAPO during and following exile. The problem of SWAPO prisoners continued to be of concern to UNTAG, as well. In September 1989, Mr Ahtisaari sent a nine-member UNTAG delegation to Angola to investigate allegations that Namibians continued to be detained by SWAPO at locations in Southern Angola.
29. 'SA's Covert Team', *The Namibian*, 20 Oct. 1989. This story was based on allegations of Ms Sue Dobson, an ANC operative who claimed she was part of a covert operations team of the S.A. 'Bureau of Information'.
30. Joachim Puetz, Heidi von Egidy and Perri Caplan (eds), *Namibia Handbook and Political Who's Who*, Windhoek: Magus, 1989, p.16, lists the following population groups: Owambo, Kavango, Herero, Damara, Whites, Nama, Coloureds, Caprivians, Bushmen, Rehoboth Baster and Tswana. More detailed information about the population groups and their distribution is contained in J.H. van der Merwe (ed.), *National Atlas of South*

West Africa (Namibia), Capetown: National Bookprinters, 1983, Tables 42–9.

31. Puetz, von Egidy and Caplan (n.30 above), p.16.

32. The *National Atlas* (n.30 above), lists four daily newspapers in 1983: *Die Republikein, Die Suidwester, The Windhoek Advertizer* and *Allgemeine Zeitung*. The *Namibia Handbook* of 1989 list, in addition to the above, the following 'advertising and news media': *Bricks, Africa, Namibia Times, Namibia Nachrichten, Namibia Today, NPF Bulletin, The Namibian, The Namibian Worker, The Worker, The Times of Namibia*. (pp.351–3).

33. *The Blue Helmets*, in hindsight, describes this UNTAG's task as 'neutralizing' the bias by providing Namibians 'with relevant and objective information'. (p.220). Cedric Thornberry, in a letter to the author dated 3 Jan. 1996, suggests a more active process of decontrolling the media. See also 'An Investigation into the Extent of Impartiality of the South West African Broadcasting Corporation', informal study by the *Namibia Peace Plan Study and Contact Group* circulated in Windhoek in July 1989 which calculated that the South African Administrator General was given approximately three times as much air-time as UNTAG on SWABC-TV (p.9), and which recommended 'that the SWABC immediately begin airing different perspectives on the same issues' (p.10).

34. Puetz, von Egidy and Caplan (n.30 above), p.354. To show the variation in the major languages used for broadcasting purposes, the *National Atlas* (n.30 above), Table 77, lists broadcasts only in seven languages.

35. *The Blue Helmets* (n.1 above), p.220. The German-language paper *Namibia Nachrichten*, 7 April 1989, criticized the inability of the German-language service of SWABC radio to cover events in Namibia in an objective fashion in an article '"Volksverdummung" – Radio hoer'n? – Nein danke!'.

36. See, for example, Hans Feddersen, 'Hilflose UNTAG', *Allgemeine Zeitung*, 12 April 1989; some more open-minded members of the German community in Windhoek dismissed the *AZ* as typically negative, parochial, and jokingly renamed it 'Die Gemeine', which can be interpreted as both 'mean' and 'common'.

37. Ferdinand Klien, freelance correspondent for *Rias Berlin*, based in Windhoek in 1989/90, in a letter dated 21 Dec. 1997, referred to attempts at physical intimidation against the representatives of AFP and Reuters, a freelance photographer and a radio reporter.

38. *The Blue Helmets* (n.1 above), p.210.

39. See, for example, James R. Gregory, *Marketing Corporate Image – The Company as our Number One Product*, Lincolnwood, IL: NTC Publishing, 1993.

40. Jan Arnesen, now Chief of the United Nations Exhibit Service, sent a detailed report on both her Namibia and Cambodia experiences to the author on 25 Jan. 1997. The following discussion of the UNTAG print programme is based on Arnesen's report and the author's own files.

41. A note for the file by Ingrid Lehmann addressed to Mr Joe Sills, dated 14 Feb. 1989 refers to Mr Cisse's early involvement in the establishment of the identity programme. Once UNTAG was deployed in the field, it became a routine activity of administrative staff reporting to Mr Cisse to implement the programme consistently.

42. Ibid. At that time, the Controller was Mr Luiz Maria Gomez. When presented with a draft information programme by the Department of Public Information in early Feb. 1989, Mr Gomez wrote a personal note to Mr Ahtisaari in which he described it as 'an excellent showcase of a full-blown, thought-through information programme'.

43. However, this perspective was not shared by all UNTAG-staff posted in the mission era. Cedric Thornberry, for example, called UN Headquarters' cooperation with UNTAG 'minimal'. Thornberry's letter to the author of 3 Jan. 1996.

44. Arnesen (n.40 above), p.4. and A/45/997, *Financing of the UN Transition Assistance Group*,

16 April 1991, which lists, under 'miscellaneous supplies and services' $23,000 for
contractual and other services, as well as $283,000 for 'various supplies and materials for
public information activities'. In reality, the total cost of the identity programme and the
print, radio and television programmes was probably much higher. The most common
estimate made by UN staff involved in the campaign was that it must have cost at least
one million US Dollars, and probably more when all activities of DPI's Information
Centres and various other UN offices such as the High Commissioner for Refugees are
taken into account.

45. *The Blue Helmets* (n.1 above), p.220.
46. Lena Yacoumopoulou, 'Information Campaigns in Peace-Keeping Missions', (unpub-
    lished manuscript, rev. Aug. 1996, draft).
47. There was a regular attendance of approximately 50 to 100 members of the press and
    staff at these daily briefings, although the total number of accredited journalists was
    probably close to 1,000. Not all of them either stayed in Windhoek permanently or, for
    that matter, attended UNTAG press briefings on a daily basis. Many of them were of the
    'parachute' correspondent type who would fly in for coverage of special events, such as
    the elections or independence of the country.
48. Yacoumopoulou (n.46 above), p.3. The two objectionable phrases referred to the mention
    of the death penalty which was about to be abolished, and to the naming of a commercial
    brand of vehicle.
49. Ibid.
50. Arnesen (n.40 above), p.1.
51. Arnesen (n.40 above), writes that she got very positive feed back from UN 'community
    outreach workers' both in Namibia and Cambodia on her products, as 'in many areas this
    was the only physical evidence, other than the white UN vehicles marked with black
    "UN", that these "outsiders" had come to their country, town or village for a more broad-
    reaching purpose other than to impose a foreign military presence'.
52. Alan James, *Peacekeeping in International Politics*, New York: St Martin's Press, 1990,
    p.260.
53. 'Code of Conduct for Political Parties during Present Election Campaign', UNTAG
    poster dated 12 Sept. 1989, and reprinted in *The Blue Helmets – Review of United Nations
    Peace-Keeping*, 2nd edn, United Nations, New York, pp.386–7.
54. This was the case in Khomasdal, where the UNTAG District Centre held a total of five
    meetings with the political leaders. At the final meeting on 1 November 1989, according
    the Centre's report to UNTAG headquarters, the political party leaders requested that
    UNTAG continue the weekly meetings after the election. The report states: 'They
    believed that we, in the District Centre in Khomasdal, had opened an avenue of
    communication which is vital to everyone's survival'. (Memorandum dated 3 Nov. 1989
    from I. Lehmann to Mr Ahtisaari).
55. Cedric Thornberry, in a letter to the author dated 3 Jan. 1996 following his retirement
    from the UN.
56. *The Blue Helmets* (n.1 above), p.210.
57. Thornberry (n.56 above).
58. Marrack Goulding to the author, 29 May 1996.
59. *The Blue Helmets: A Review of United Nations Peacekeeping*, Second Edition, New York,
    1990, p.4.
60. Thornberry to the author, 3 Jan. 1996.
61. Hampson (n.4 above), p.54.

◄⟨○⟩►

FOUR

The Information and Education Programmes of UNTAC in Cambodia, 1992–93

HISTORICAL BACKGROUND

United Nations involvement in the Cambodian peace process dates from 1979 when, following Vietnam's intervention in late 1978, the Security Council first considered the issue. At that time, however, the Council lacked the unanimity necessary to take action. In July 1981, following an International Conference on Kampuchea convened by the General Assembly, the Secretary-General's offer of 'good offices' was accepted by the parties to the conflict. Over the next four years, the Secretary-General's Representative for Humanitarian Affairs in Southeast Asia, Mr Rafeeuddin Ahmed, visited the area many times and had, by 1985, identified a set of objectives which were to be achieved by subsequent negotiations.

Intense diplomatic activity throughout the 1980s culminated, by the end of 1990, in a set of draft peace agreements which were accepted by all 12 members of the Supreme National Council of Cambodia. In April 1991, a ceasefire went into effect and the Secretary-General recommended the deployment of a United Nations Advance Mission in Cambodia (UNAMIC), to sustain the peace process and monitor the ceasefire.

A few weeks after the Paris Peace Accords on Cambodia were signed in October 1991, UNAMIC was deployed. It was clear that the United Nations would play a major role in implementing the peace agreements: the UN was to organize and conduct free elections, coordinate the repatriation of Cambodian refugees and displaced persons, coordinate the programme of economic rehabilitation and reconstruction, monitor and verify the withdrawal of foreign forces, monitor the demobilization of at least 70 per cent of the military forces of the Cambodian factions, foster an environment in which human rights and freedoms would be respected and, most importantly, supervise and control the existing administrative structures in Cambodia to these ends.

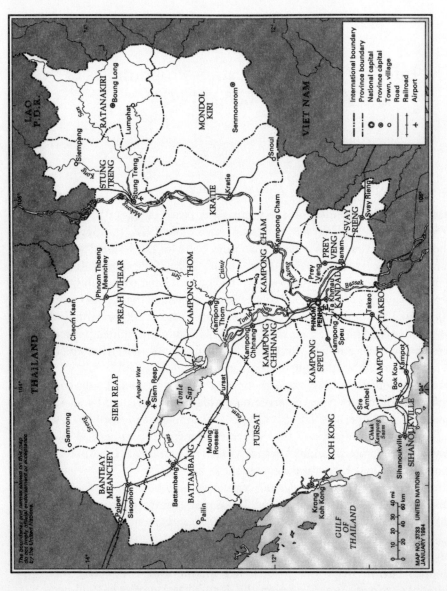

CAMBODIA

(map no. 3733 (Cambodia) reproduced with the permission of the Cartographic Section, Department of Public Information, United Nations)

The United Nations Transitional Authority in Cambodia (UNTAC) was to become one of the largest and most expensive operations in the history of UN peacekeeping up to that time. At its peak, UNTAC military personnel numbered close to 16,000; in addition there were 3,500 civilian police and over 1,000 international civilian staff. During the electoral period, more than 50,000 Cambodians served as electoral staff, and some 900 international polling station officers were seconded from 44 countries.[1] Cambodians elected a Constituent Assembly in 'free and fair elections' at the end of May 1993, which led to a new, democratic phase in the history of Cambodia.[2]

The overall cost of the operation was US$1.6 billion.[3] UNTAC was a prime example of a post-Cold War UN peacekeeping operation: large, composite, civil-military operations which served to implement international peace agreements. As in the case of Namibia, the UN's Cambodia operation benefited from a large measure of international support which helped to carry the peace process forward in times of crisis. The stark fact that the international community had failed to come to the aid of the country in the turmoil of the mid-1970s when hundreds of thousands of Cambodians lost their lives, now worked in favour of a visible and effective international presence there.[4]

ECONOMIC AND POLITICAL SITUATION AT THE TIME OF UNTAC DEPLOYMENT

Judging the 'ripeness' of the Cambodian conflict for settlement at the point of the deployment of the peace operation, many observers at the time expressed severe doubts as to whether conditions for a lasting settlement existed in Cambodia in 1992–93.[5]

A major hindrance to the operation was that one faction, the Khmer Rouge, even though it had signed the Paris Peace Accords, was by June 1992 essentially in non-compliance with the agreements and did not participate in the elections. As UN Secretary-General Boutros-Ghali admitted, 'this defiance and refusal to work towards reconciliation disrupted the work of UNTAC at nearly every turn, and forced the abandonment of a major component of the peace plan: demobilization of the four Cambodian armies'.[6] However, there were signs that all internal Cambodian parties experienced forms of war-weariness and, as Fen Osler Hampson has remarked, 'a hurting stalemate did exist in the sense that the Cambodian parties found themselves without the foreign support on which their campaigns depended' and had no alternative 'but to agree to the terms of the framework'.[7]

Most outside observers agreed that Cambodia's instability and the country's general underdevelopment, both in an economic and in a civic sense, would require major efforts at reconstruction and peacebuilding. One out of seven Cambodians had lost their lives during the period of violence, civil war and terror from 1975 to 1979. While the UN and other international donors had provided humanitarian assistance throughout that period, Cambodia clearly was in need of more substantive support than just relief.

The country's administrative structure was in a shambles, even though rudimentary forms of a governmental bureaucracy still existed in the form of the 'State of Cambodia' (SOC). Cambodia not only lacked trained staff for essential functions such as policing, health and legal work but, as a consequence of decades of war and genocidal acts, Cambodians were for the most part unable to assume essential responsibilities.[8] The country simply did not have 'a usable bureaucracy' and it was, by many accounts, a 'failed state'.[9]

The four Cambodian factions which had signed the Paris Accords[10] had done so following difficult negotiations in which concessions and trade-offs had often been exacted by their external supporters and international patrons: 'Arguably, the two non-communist groups, the United National Front for an Independent, Neutral, Peaceful and Cooperative Cambodia (FUNCINPEC) and Khmer People's National Liberation Front (KPNLF), stood to gain the most from the settlement itself. All the basic elements of the deal – ending the civil war, opening up the country economically, levelling the playing field politically and implementing widespread disarmament – would tend to cut very heavily in their favour and against the two larger, more heavily-armed, authoritarian factions.'[11]

For the Khmer Rouge, the Paris Accords offered very little; the democratic development of Cambodia would likely lead to an erosion of their military strength and political support. Their hope thus lay in the possibility of an unravelling of the Accords, which might be followed by waning support of the international community for the UN operation. This might, in turn, lead to resumed fighting, a withdrawal of UNTAC and ensuing chaos in Cambodia.

More than two decades of war had already taken a heavy toll on Cambodia's environment and natural resources. This situation was worsened by the continuing exploitation of timber, minerals, gems, fisheries and rubber by both Cambodians and non-Cambodians, particularly Thais.[12]

There were over 360,000 refugees living in camps along the Thai border, two thirds of whom had been engaged in agriculture prior to their flight from Cambodia in the late 1970s. Originally, it was planned to give each returning family a plot of land in their destination of choice. In the spring of 1992 it became clear that most refugees and internally displaced persons desired to settle in north-western Cambodia, which was also that part of the country most heavily mined, and was therefore lacking land suitable for agricultural production. As a result, the UN revised its plans for repatriation by broadening the range of options available to returnees.[13] Thus, 240,000 people had been repatriated by the end of December 1992, and by April 1993 that figure had risen to 365,000.[14]

UNTAC'S MANDATE

The mandate for UNTAC is derived from the Agreement on a Comprehensive Political Settlement of the Cambodian Conflict, those 'Paris Accords' whose signatories agreed to confer upon the United Nations 'all powers necessary to ensure implementation' of the settlement.[15] The Accords outline the proposed mandate for UNTAC in four different sections: a) civil administration, b) military functions, c) elections and d) human rights.

Among the military functions entrusted to UNTAC, mine clearance was the one which contained a major information element, namely mine awareness. This function is listed in the Paris Accords under 'unexploded ordnance devices', which represented a major hazard affecting resettlement of refugees and displaced persons and hindered farming in the country. The Accords called for UNTAC to 'conduct a mass public information programme in the recognition and avoidance of explosive devices'.[16] This task had already been undertaken by UNAMIC which, by November 1991 had established a mine-awareness programme for small teams of UN 'military personnel with experience in training civilian populations on how to avoid injuries from mines or booby-traps'.[17] This very important programme was continued and expanded by UNTAC, which, by the end of 1992, had trained several thousand Cambodians in mine clearance and mine awareness. It led, in April 1992, to the establishment of the Cambodian Mine Action Centre (CMAC), which, with the assistance of non-governmental organizations and several governments continues to perform these vital functions in Cambodia after the transitional period ended.[18]

UNTAC's civil tasks were the most extensive of any UN peacekeeping operation up to that time. They included the following areas: human rights oversight, the organization and conduct of elections, the control of civil administrative agencies in five fields (defence, foreign affairs, finance, public security and information), repatriation and rehabilitation. Among these tasks, human rights and the conduct of the elections were those in which information and education programmes played a very important role. They are thus discussed in detail in the following two sections.

HUMAN RIGHTS

The Paris Accords provided that: 'UNTAC shall be responsible during the transitional period for fostering an environment in which respect for human rights shall be ensured'(Art.16). UNTAC was thus given an authority in the field of human rights which was considered 'enormous'.[19] According to Nassrine Azimi, it was 'the most comprehensive human rights mandate ever entrusted to a United Nations peacekeeping operation'.[20] Its mandate was essentially twofold: 'firstly, to foster an environment in which human rights were respected, essentially for the purpose of free and fair elections, and secondly ... to prevent the return to policies and practices of the past'.[21]

In terms of staffing and overall impact, the human rights component of UNTAC was – with 88 full-time civilian staff, 3,600 civilian police monitors who assisted in human rights investigations and numerous non-governmental organizations and their staff engaged in human rights issues in Cambodia – probably the largest and most influential in the history of human rights in any UN peacekeeping operation.[22] This effort was, in the view of its planners, more than justified by the historical legacy of human rights abuses and genocidal acts perpetrated in Cambodia in the 1970s.

Dennis McNamara, the Director of Human Rights of UNTAC, believed that UNTAC needed to build on the 'inherently positive aspects of Cambodian society and culture'[23] in order to promote human rights in the country. He saw this effort as closely linked with 'respect for a free press and freedom of expression' and, in his post-mission assessment of his experience, 'there were seeds sown in Cambodia in the human rights democratic area which are irreversible and which continue to flourish'.[24] UNTAC's mandate in the human rights field thus clearly extended into the fields of education and of democratic institution-building. When violations occurred and were reported – and there were at least 1,300 complaints or violations reported during UNTAC's time of deployment – UNTAC would take corrective measures.[25]

In January 1993, the Special Representative of the Secretary-General, Yasushi Akashi, 'took the radical step of setting up a Special Prosecutor's Office despite opposition from the State of Cambodia (SOC) and non-SOC parties'.[26] The United Nations publication *The Blue Helmets* summarizes UNTAC's human rights activities in the following manner:

> UNTAC developed a human rights education programme with particular reference to teacher training, dissemination of relevant international instruments, education of health professionals, training of public and political officials and support for local

human rights organizations. Educational materials, posters, leaflets, stickers and other printed materials were disseminated throughout the country. Human rights training was introduced into the Cambodian education system, and human rights studies were incorporated in the curriculum of Phnom Penh University's Law School and Medical Faculty. Collaboration with local human rights organizations was an important aspect of UNTAC's work. UNTAC provided them with materials, training and expertise as well as small grants for basic office expenses.[27]

Once the human rights component's staff was fully deployed, which, according to McNamara, was not until 'six months after the operation landed in Cambodia', ie in September 1992,[28] education programmes were conducted in all Cambodian provinces by mobile teams. In order to implement its human rights education strategy, UNTAC appealed to governments for additional funding. A trust fund was set up which received US$1.85 million and allowed the programme to continue its work in conjunction with non governmental organizations.[29]

ELECTIONS

As in Namibia and in other countries where UN election supervision and monitoring was part of the peace plan, preparing for elections implied a major effort in informing and educating the electorate of its rights. In the case of Cambodia, the United Nations had taken over essential management functions with regard to the electoral process.[30]

Voter registration in Cambodia began on 5 October 1992, initially for a three-month period. It was later extended until 31 January 1993, partly because it was discovered that the electorate was larger than expected,[31] partly because the poor state of the roads in the rainy season made travel for mobile teams more difficult, and partly because of the late enactment of the Electoral Law.

By the time voting rolls closed, 4.6 million Cambodians had registered, a number that far exceeded expectations of UN staff. It reflected not only the courage and determination of the Cambodian voters, but also the skills and experience of UNTAC electoral staff: 'It drew skilfully on previous UN electoral experience in Namibia, the experience of national electoral organizations such as Elections Canada, and the options outlined by the Australian Electoral Commission ... some of which were based on Australian experience in Namibia.' Trevor Findlay concluded: 'This is one case where the UN learned from previous experience, something that cannot be said for other aspects of the Cambodian operation.'[32]

Findlay also gave credit to the 450 UN volunteers who were assigned as district electoral supervisors. They worked, in five-member teams, with 4,000 Cambodian registration personnel, a system Findlay called 'inspired':

> They were able to penetrate remote areas in a non-threatening manner and quietly convince Cambodians of the value of enrolling and voting. Armed with materials produced by UNTAC's Information and Education Division – videos, cassettes, posters, brochures and comic books – civic education teams held community meetings in villages across the country.[33]

However, as Janet Heininger has pointed out, the work of the Information/ Education Division 'was not widely recognized during most of UNTAC's tenure as being critically important'. Heininger considers the work of 'Info-Ed', as the division was commonly called, 'UNTAC's most unqualified success' and questions 'whether free and fair elections could have taken place without the unbiased Khmer-language information provided by the Division throughout the entire country'.[34] James Schear similarly points out that 'it was not until the elections that the full effects of the information campaign were seen'.[35]

Article 6 of the Paris Accords authorized UNTAC 'to ensure a neutral political environment conducive to free and fair elections', which was, indeed, a daunting task. Secretary-General Boutros Boutros-Ghali acknowledged the objective hindrances to creating such an environment in his Introduction to *The United Nations and Cambodia* in 1995. He pointed out that many Cambodians 'were sceptical about the applicability in Cambodia of basic concepts of human rights, including free and fair elections and multiparty political campaigning'. These doubts, according to Boutros-Ghali, were well-founded 'as all the major factions engaged in a certain degree of misleading propaganda and political coercion during the registration/ campaign period'.[36]

The pervasive tactics of intimidation, violence and political coercion of some of the political parties, in particular the Cambodian People's Party (CPP) and Party of Democratic Kampuchea (PDK), the 'Khmer Rouge', are now well documented.[37] The tactics ranged from murder, assassination, arbitrary detention and abduction to extortion and, comparatively 'soft' means of intimidation, such as to the forcible collection of voter registration cards from thousands of people of different political parties and the CPP's coercive membership-drive. With regard to the latter activity by SOC, Judy Ledgerwood wrote:

UNTAC became fully aware of the massiveness of this effort only after it was too late to attempt to prevent it. UNTAC's only recourse was to use the media to inform Cambodians that they did not have to join a political party if they did not want to, and that they did not have to vote for a party they had joined if they did not wish to do so. No one knew until the election what impact, if any, such voter education would have.[38]

At a meeting of the 'Supreme National Council' in Phnom Penh in October 1992, the Secretary-General's Special Representative, Yasushi Akashi, stressed the importance of creating a neutral political environment during the time leading up to the elections:

In order to vote with confidence for the party of their choice, people need to feel secure that they can seek and provide information and exchange views, that they have the right either to openly discuss their choices or remain silent, and that their vote will remain secret unless they themselves choose to divulge it. They must know they have the right to work for, to join and to vote for the party of their choice and that they also have the right not to join or support any party if they choose not to do so. They must feel free from any undue pressure to align themselves with any party or to vote in a certain way.[39]

During the electoral campaign which began on 7 April and ended on 13 May 1993, the UN took the unprecedented step of making its information and broadcasting facilities available to all political parties in order to ensure fair access to the media.[40] As a consequence, according to Findlay, 'Cambodians were swamped with electoral and party political information, including radio and television broadcasts, on a scale never before seen in the country'.[41]

UNTAC's policy during this period is well reflected in an article in the weekly Newsletter issued by the Electoral Component, *Free Choice*:

Developing trust and confidence among Cambodians through direct contact with electoral staff is a key part of UNTAC's civic education programme. Village-level meetings organized by electoral staff are forums for people to ask questions and express their concerns, in addition to receiving information about the election, human rights and other important issues.[42]

THE MANDATE OF INFO/ED

Timothy Carney, who headed the Information/Education Division for the duration of UNTAC, simultaneously functioned as 'Advisor on Information to the Special Representative of the Secretary-General', a novel function in the history of peacekeeping operations. Mr Carney reported about his recruitment to the job:

> My becoming Advisor on Information resulted from an 11 February [1992] interview with Mr Akashi. We discussed the secrecy of the ballot and the vital need to ensure that Cambodians understood that secrecy. I broached an idea that had been gestating for some months, to the effect that secrecy must include not only the individual's own ballot, but that his village must be insulated as well by counting the ballots at a central point and not releasing results for individual polling places. The electoral law subsequently incorporated this notion.[43]

Carney's statement not only reveals his own larger political concerns about the Cambodian situation, but the fact that he, from the outset, considered his function in this mission as a political and policy-setting role. He stated that 'the vital, central role of information received early and complete recognition' by the parties to the Paris Accords and by the United Nations Secretariat. In his post-mission assessment, Carney referred to two documents which he considered as providing his mandate and which, in his view, 'treat information imaginatively'.[44] The first is the above-mentioned Article 6 of the Paris Agreements which reads as follows:

> In order to ensure a neutral political environment conducive to free and fair general elections, administrative agencies, bodies and offices which could directly influence the outcome of the elections will be placed under direct United Nations supervision or control. In that context, special attention will be given to foreign affairs, national defence, finance, public security and information. To reflect the importance of these subjects, UNTAC needs to exercize such control as is necessary to ensure the strict neutrality of the bodies responsible for them. The United Nations, in consultation with the SNC, will identify which agencies, bodies and offices could continue to operate in order to ensure normal day-to-day life in the country.[45]

In addition, Carney considered it important that information be mentioned as one of five 'fields' in Annex 1 to the Accords, which, along with foreign affairs, national defence, finance and public security 'will be placed under the direct control of UNTAC, which will exercize it as necessary to ensure strict neutrality'.[46] This, by United Nations standards, was indeed exceptional in terms of the legal and political authority it could exercize in Cambodia during the transition.

The second important document outlining UNTAC's information mandate was the 'Report of the Secretary-General on Cambodia containing his proposed implementation plan for UNTAC, including administrative and financial aspects' of 19 February 1992. This report described in detail how the United Nations Secretariat, prior to launching UNTAC, envisioned its various functional components. The role of information was mentioned with regard to the human rights component, the civilian police and the electoral components.[47] Paragraph 27 of this report, under the subheading of 'civic education and training', specifically referred to 'the establishment of radio broadcast and print facilities and of distribution networks, including access to community radio and/or television and mobile video units, may be foreseen'.[48]

This report envisaged a far-reaching information mandate for a UN peacekeeping operation. In a special section toward the end, it described UNTAC's particular information needs and elaborated on the difficulties the Cambodian communications infrastructure would pose:

> The rapid and effective flow of information between UNTAC and the grassroots is essential .. Radio appears to be the most efficient method of dissemination of the spoken word, but the radio broadcast facilities inside Cambodia are antiquated and deteriorated and at present the broadcast range covers only about half the Cambodian territory. Television would normally be the most effective means of dissemination, but broadcast facilities in Cambodia have a range of only about 75 kilometres from Phnom Penh. Video parlours are, however, very popular in the country-side. Print media are present, but printing facilities, supplies and distribution networks are inadequate and the impact of the written word is, in any case, hindered by low literacy rates.[49]

This report argued that 'massive civic education campaigns in human rights, mine awareness and electoral matters' will be needed, as well as 'programming to acquaint Cambodians with the Agreement, with UNTAC, its purposes, its activities and goals' in order to 'establish and maintain UNTAC's credibility'.[50] As Carney put it: 'The Information/Education Division took that mandate at its word and ran with it.'[51]

BUDGET AND STAFFING

The overall budget of the Information/Education Division was approximately US$7 million.[52] The largest share of that budget, about US$3 million was spent equipping, installing and operating Radio UNTAC. According to Tim Carney, the Info/Ed Division of UNTAC, had, at its height, 'a staff of 150, with about 45 international staff from 16 nations'.[53] As did other components of UNTAC, Info/Ed suffered from slow recruitment by the United Nations Field Operations Division in New York. As soon as Carney was offered the position of Director of Info/Ed, he began his own recruitment 'of academic specialists on Cambodia who had field experience there and who spoke and read Khmer'. By his own account, he had gained commitments from half a dozen such experts 'to come on board' by the end of March 1992. However, 'it took the Field Operations Division another six months to bring the last one into the country'.[54] In the end, according to Steve Heder, Carney's Deputy Director, the Division 'employed some 45 international staff, of whom 14 spoke and read Khmer and had at least some experience in the country'.[55]

Zhou Mei, Chief of Production of Info/Ed, described the effort in recruiting local staff: 'To get Radio [UNTAC] started, the resourceful Tim Carney literally picked a couple of people off the streets of Phnom Penh' – with mixed results, according to Mei. When she arrived in October 1992, Steve Heder reportedly greeted her: 'Radio is in a mess'. Zhou Mei soon learned this to be the truth, in respect to local and international staff, and she found working with 'that pool of mishmash' exceedingly difficult.[56]

The shortcomings of the international staff, from UN Headquarters in New York and from other duty stations, who were detailed to serve with UNTAC, were also noted by Nassrine Azimi who concluded:

> United Nations reporters who had worked on General Assembly
> and Security Council sessions proved inadequately prepared for
> the mix of news and features needed for Radio UNTAC. Training
> in elementary journalism as well as the mechanics of radio and
> television production could well address this problem.[57]

Steve Heder described another problem, that of varying degrees of loyalty, especially with regard to officials seconded to UNTAC by their respective governments:

> … they included officials from UN member states who wanted
> to work for UNTAC and managed to convince their governments

to let them go. While some of those officials who came to work for UNTAC were clearly still entirely beholden to their governments and exclusively loyal to them, others were just as clearly at loggerheads with their governments or indifferent to whatever policies the latter might have regarding to Cambodia, if any.[58]

Concerning UNTAC's staffing problems throughout, Yasushi Akashi remarked dryly in a post-mission interview with *Time* in November 1993 that 'the quality of personnel was not uniformly outstanding'.[59] Similarly, Trevor Findlay summarized the staffing situation of UNTAC, saying only that: 'The quality of UNTAC's ... civilian personnel varied enormously'.[60]

THE STRUCTURE OF THE INFORMATION/EDUCATION DIVISION

The Info/Ed Division was composed of four units: Production, Control, Analysis and Dissemination, plus the Director's office, as shown in *Figure 1*:

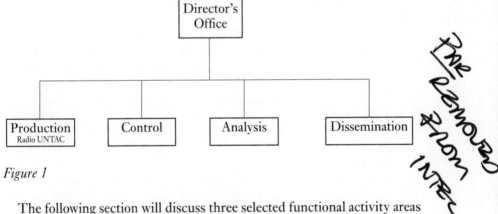

Figure 1

The following section will discuss three selected functional activity areas of Info/Ed that were novel and advanced mission goals in an important way. These were: a) the Analysis Unit; b) Radio UNTAC, which was the part of the Production unit and which probably had the greatest positive effect on the mission; and c) the Control Unit.

a) Analysis Unit

According to Tim Carney, 'the main function of the analysis unit is to determine whether or not our message is getting through to the Cambodian people, and at the same time to look into UNTAC's image and credibility'.[61]

Analysis included assessments of the public positions of the political parties, in particular that 'of the faction of Democratic Kampuchea 'which has its own short-wave radio station to put forth a very specific public position, mainly for use by their own cadre in further efforts to propagandize the Cambodian people'.[62]

The Analysis unit had six staff travelling throughout the country gathering information of this kind for use by the Info/Ed Division in preparing analytical reports of the political situation for the Special Representative of the Secretary-General. In addition, 'the unit provided the necessary expertise to vet the faction's public statements and broadcasts and to explain Cambodia to senior colleagues'.[63] Reports on UNTAC's image were 'used by the components to examine how Cambodians view their component – whether it's good or bad', giving UNTAC the chance to make necessary image corrections.[64] Carney, in retrospect, stated that 'its role ... in assessing UNTAC's image and credibility proved vital, resulting in several focused, confidential memoranda to senior colleagues about areas that needed their attention'.[65] The importance of this function was acknowledged in the Secretary-General's 'Third Progress Report' on UNTAC of 25 January 1993, which stated in paragraph 92:

> Information Officers also conduct regular opinion surveys among Cambodians of all categories and occupations in Phnom Penh and the countryside to assess the impact of UNTAC's information programme and to monitor the attitude of the people towards UNTAC and its implementation of the peace process.[66]

Michael Doyle went further in his evaluation of Info/Ed's analytical capabilities:

> In assessing how well its own message was being received by the Cambodians, Info/Ed developed what may have been the UN's first political intelligence Department. Benefiting from its recruitment of an outstanding group of young Khmer-speaking scholars, the division wrote systematic political reports on the activities of the various factions in each of Cambodia's key provinces.[67]

The assessments and informal 'opinion polls' undertaken by the Analysis Unit also allowed Info/Ed to tailor and refocus its programmes to correct misperceptions or misunderstandings, as well as to identify gaps in understanding among the Cambodians. The Unit's analysis of the Cambodian factions' media enabled UNTAC to adjust its own broadcast messages accordingly.[68] Its focus on the mission's 'credibility' in a country such as Cambodia and its independent assessment capabilities was a major asset to the strategic management of the mission. This was particularly so in times of crisis, such as in March and April 1993 when a series of attacks on UNTAC personnel seriously threatened the mission.[69]

However, in spite of major difficulties with the Khmer Rouge on the ground, Janet Heininger maintained: 'UNTAC had fairly good indications that the rank and file Khmer Rouge were unhappy with their leadership's decision to disrupt the election.'[70] Heininger drew from this the following lesson for future UN peacekeeping operations:

> When considering whether to undertake an operation, the organization should carefully analyse the situation to determine the extent to which the local populace is able to influence the political leaders' views and actions. It should assess whether the populace supports the resolution of the underlying conflict, or whether it would actively undermine a UN operation, and to what extent it is at the mercy of political leaders who control most of the weapons. Obviously, developing accurate assessments may be difficult, if not impossible. To the extent such information is, or can be, made available, however, it should be an integral part of both the design and planning for UN operations.[71]

b) Radio UNTAC

Radio UNTAC was, according to most observers, one of the prime success stories of the UN operation in Cambodia. Nassrine Azimi characterized it as 'a revolutionary innovation',[72] Trevor Findlay called it 'the most popular radio station in the country',[73] while James Schear cited its 'reputation as the most popular and credible radio station in the country and it was widely listened to in Khmer Rouge areas'.[74] Janet Heininger stated that 'radio was an essential tool for getting out UNTAC's message',[75] and General Sanderson, in a post-mission assessment, asserted: ' I do not believe that anyone could now deny the criticality of Radio UNTAC to the whole process.'[76]

In spite of this very positive overall assessment of the first UN–owned and operated radio station in a peacekeeping mission ever, the history of establishing Radio UNTAC was fraught with hindrances and delays. Before it finally broadcast live 15 hours a day, Radio UNTAC went through several earlier phases. In February 1992, pre-mission planning by the Department of Public Information in New York had produced a report which included a possible radio facility. Carney described the recommendations of this report, which was written prior to his recruitment: 'It argued for an FM network to cover all of Cambodia – a notion fatally flawed by the need to have multiple transmitters which would have been vulnerable to sabotage or simple theft.'[77] This proposal was not proceeded with.

While Carney acknowledged that, to many people, 'as of early 1992, a radio broadcast facility seemed excessive', he said that, as soon as they were on the ground in Cambodia and sensed the importance of the faction's radio broadcast, senior UNTAC staff and diplomats became convinced that 'the mission must have its own station'. However, the UN Secretary-General still had doubts about 'the necessity for a broadcast facility' in April 1992 when he, according to Carney, told UNTAC's senior staff during a visit to Phnom Penh that he believed radio broadcasts on factions' transmitters and from neighbouring countries' facilities should suffice. 'It took three months to change his mind, a delay which the UN tendering and procurement process compounded.'[78]

In the meantime, two temporary measures were taken by the Special Representative of the Secretary-General to alleviate UNTAC's radio broadcasting situation. First, arrangements were made through the US Information Agency in Washington to use the *Voice of America* transmitter in Thailand at prime time twice daily. Thai government agreement to this arrangement was secured and, as of 31 July 1992, Radio UNTAC was on the air from Bangkok. These broadcasts which were done through prerecorded tapes, 'concentrated on information regarding the electoral process, human rights and other aspects of the UNTAC mandate'.[79]

Secondly, the Special Representative authorized the Information/ Education Division to negotiate with the 'State of Cambodia' to be able to use an antiquated Phnom Penh-based transmitter. These negotiations, which required Mr Akashi's personal intervention with the authorities, finally succeeded in November 1992: UNTAC had at last found its voice.[80] Zhou Mei, the head of Radio UNTAC from Singapore, described its operation from November 1992 to May 1993:

> When Radio UNTAC finally took over exclusive use of the Philips transmitter along with MW 918kHz on 9 November 1992, a 30-minute programme would be aired thrice a day, at 0530, 1100 and 1800 hours, making a total of 90 minutes a day. (The choice of broadcast time was based on Cambodian lifestyle. We were advised that people got up early, had lunch early and went to bed early.) It was a belated and modest start. But it was a start in the right direction.[81]

In addition to news which was initially largely taken from the Spokesman's daily press briefings (see below), the programmes included materials from the Electoral and the Human Rights components of UNTAC. With the increasing incidents of intimidation and violence in the pre-election period, 'Radio UNTAC needed to be the source of balanced news and information'. According to Zhou Mei, it had to 'reassure the public of UNTAC's determination that the election would take place as scheduled, despite the non-participation of the Khmer Rouge and the unabated acts of violence'.[82] Timeliness was of great importance and, in this connection, Zhou Mei testified to the versatility of Info/Ed's Director, Tim Carney:

> Often, we were able to bring the latest to the listeners with minimal loss of time because Tim Carney would personally hand over relevant hard copies to be used as radio scripts. There were times when Tim Carney wrote the script himself; there were also occasions when he had to do the translation, and at times give 'voice' to the scripts, to slash production time.[83]

Another important issue was the distribution of radios in Cambodia. 'To the average Cambodian household, radios were a luxury they could ill afford.'[84] Fortuitously, donations from Japanese non-governmental organizations and the Japanese government, which totalled 350,000 as well as donations of 800,000 batteries between September 1992 and April 1993, made possible the reception of Radio UNTAC by large numbers of Cambodians.[85] However, these donations also had some unforeseen consequences, according to Zhou Mei: 'The desire for possession was so overpowering that at times, people became ugly. There were incidents of near riots in UNTAC compounds where the radios were stored.'[86]

On 5 April 1993, only seven weeks before the elections, Radio UNTAC moved to its own, well-equipped radio complex, with studios and equipment 'on a par with the best in the world, while surpassing in sophistication that of some internationally renowned stations'.[87] Zhou Mei herself, noting the cost of over US$3 million for Radio UNTAC, asked the question: 'Multimillion Dollar Folly?'

However, the new facilities allowed Radio UNTAC unprecedented programming in a peacekeeping mission: on 19 April 1992, it broadcast nine hours a day, and it also went 'live'. By that time, the 'political' programme – allowing parties 'free and equal access' to the electorate – took up three hours of air-time a day. Zhou Mei thus felt the need for a more 'balanced diet' and decided to focus Radio UNTAC's weekend programmes on non-political developments: 'It was at this stage that Radio UNTAC's occasional health programme became a regular weekend programme while extra time was allotted to feedback obtained from letters sent to Radio UNTAC'.[88] On 12 May 1993 Radio UNTAC launched its 15 hours a day, seven days a week live broadcasts. Zhou Mei exclaimed: 'It was akin to attaining the unreachable.'[89]

In order to fill 15 hours of broadcast time, the producers had to expand the prevalent concept of 'getting news' from the daily press briefings. By election time, this was possible, and according to Zhou Mei had astounding results:

> Radio UNTAC's coverage of the election was multi-frontal: from the field (with reports brought back by radio producers or direct from the provinces via telephone), from the SRSG's [Special Representative of the Secretary-General] spokesperson's press briefings (by then twice a day), from in-house statistical analysis of election returns and live from UNTAC headquarters. Meanwhile, feedback on Radio UNTAC itself had started to come in from the provinces. Already a household name some time before the election, Radio UNTAC, with its election coverage, had the people riveted to MW 918 kHz – boosted by relay transmitters ... to ensure nationwide reach.[90]

In the process of becoming a truly nationwide political force, Radio UNTAC incurred an increased security risk. Several threats to silence the radio station by blowing it up were received, according to Zhou Mei. From 20 April 1993, soldiers of the Ghanaian battalion gave the radio complex 24-hour armed protection.[91]

All of this effort was, in the eyes of UNTAC's observers such as Trevor Findlay, well justified by the outcome: 'Once installed, [UNTAC's radio station] was a powerful tool in familiarizing Cambodians with UN intentions and plans, weaning support away from those opposed to the UN, counteracting anti-UNTAC propaganda and educating the populace in electoral and human rights matters.'[92]

c) The Control Unit

UNTAC's information mandate was, as described above, largely derived from the Paris Accords which gave the UN direct control over the field of information. A 12-person control unit within Info/Ed[93] was tasked to control the information flow and contents from the existing administrative structures governing Cambodia, as well as the information output of the political factions. As Tim Carney described it, 'we control what is produced, so that the neutral political atmosphere is not adversely affected'.[94]

This involved ensuring that newspapers, party bulletins or TV and radio programmes 'did not violate strictures against, say, defamation or incitement to racial hatred', or 'monitoring the loudspeakers in a town market, or sitting in editorial meetings to forestall policies that would result in programmes which could undermine the neutral political environment'.[95] One of the major difficulties was that this control function involved not only the media of the factions, but also other elements of the media in Phnom Penh. Nassrine Azimi described the process established by Info/Ed:

> To ensure transparency and to make absolutely certain the goals of the media and the limits on what might be said or written in the media, the Division created a Working Group which contributed to drafting a set of guidelines for the media. Only the Democratic Kampuchea faction refused to participate in this effort.[96]

The resulting 'media guidelines', published in October 1992, were, according to Carney, the only written documents UNTAC could work with prior to the issue of electoral guidelines by the Special Representative. UNTAC furthermore 'helped launch a Cambodian Media Association of all Cambodian journalists'.[97]

John Marston, who analysed Cambodian news media in the UNTAC period, described how staff of Info/Ed not only monitored the media from their desks at UNTAC headquarters, but 'started making regular visits to the offices of newspapers and radio and television stations':

> While UNTAC in no way actually controlled the media, it did discuss basic journalistic issues with members of the media and attempted to respond to ethical violations that would make a neutral political atmosphere impossible. The fact that the media knew UNTAC was likely to complain about certain things probably limited abuses, it did not eliminate them. UNTAC meetings with the media and its constant emphasis on freedom of the press also helped promote the rise of more independent media.[98]

Nevertheless, difficulties continued, especially with the media controlled by the State of Cambodia which, according to Carney, had the advantage of authorities in power which 'had not yet permitted its own media to be used for political information of the other parties'. This, he said in the interview in March 1993, was one of the main reasons behind Mr Akashi's decision to open UNTAC media to the political parties under the 'Equal Access, Equal Time' formula.[99] Therefore, Carney reflected in a post-mission assessment:

> Control, however, never succeeded in realizing the goal of fair access to the media. Rather, UNTAC used its radio station and TV studio to give the electorate enough information about the political parties and then the political parties produced electoral programming to balance SOC's failure to grant fair access. This party information effort went forward in tandem with imaginative programming to assure voters that their vote would be secret and that the secrecy of the ballot was their shield against intimidation.
>
> Timely, accurate and, above all, transparent programming as censorship-free as possible vitally ensured UNTAC credibility and built its audience. At the same time, a very careful political vetting of drafts, translations and final broadcasts by Khmer-speaking international staff ensured its political appropriateness on the basis of the Khmer-language text of the Paris Agreements.[100]

THE SPOKESMAN'S OFFICE

The Spokesman's Office was separate from the Information/Education Division and directly attached to the Special Representative's Office. There was, however, a close functional relationship between the two. A member of the Spokesman's Office described it as an 'unstructured information-sharing structure' between the two units that had neither 'rules of engagement' nor 'standard operating procedures' which did not, however, 'make either effort less effective'.[101]

Info/Ed would regularly send staff representatives to the daily briefings conducted by the Spokesman's Office and, as discussed above, 'news' would thus be adapted for use by UNTAC Radio or TV. All background papers and statistical updates were regularly sent from the Spokesman's Office to Info/Ed, the Electoral Component and other senior officials. Senior staff from both Info/Ed and the Spokesman's Office attended the daily (later in the mission thrice-weekly) Senior Staff Meetings chaired by the Special Representative, Mr Akashi.

There were three Spokesmen during UNTAC's mandate: the first, Jamel Ben-Yahmed, apparently did not have the confidence of the Special Representative; the second, Eric Falt, who subsequently became Spokesman of UNMIH in Haiti, served at UNTAC through the election period. There was some overlap time between him and Michael Williams who became Coordinator for Press and Media during the last months of the mission.

There were over 2,000 international correspondents accredited by the UNTAC press office. At least a third of them were Japanese. Nassrine Azimi categorized the journalists who covered UNTAC in the following manner: a) the 'war veterans', who had reported on the war in Cambodia since the 1970s; these had a long 'historical memory' and often also definite ideas about the future of the country; b) journalists with an open mind and relatively impartial stand on the issues who were willing to get a clearer picture of the situation; and c) journalists unable to cope with the complexity of a multifaceted peacekeeping operation, who reported bits and pieces to provide basic news stories for their editors.[102]

MILITARY–CIVILIAN RELATIONS IN THE INFORMATION FIELD

Nassrine Azimi and others who have assessed the UN's Cambodia mission have argued that it would have been better to set up a 'unified public information office with sole authority to handle press relations for all of the components'.[103] Instead, separate civilian and military information set-ups were created, following a series of disagreements among senior military and the spokesman as to how best to handle military issues raised by the news media.

These disagreements between the Spokesman's Office and the Force Commander and his staff are documented by Findlay, among others, who reported that General Sanderson complained of 'the UN civilian spokesperson's ignorance of military matters and a tendency to "poor timing and judgement" on the release of military information'.[104] As a consequence 'Sanderson was obliged to recruit an experienced military public relations officer to rectify' this situation.[105] Consequently, in the spring of 1992, Lt. Colonel Richard Palk was appointed Chief of Military Public Information by the Force Commander. Palk had previously worked with Sanderson in Australia and he arrived in Cambodia at the same time as the second civilian Spokesman, Eric Falt. Staff from both the civilian and the military offices reported personality and hierarchical conflicts which, according to several UNTAC staff, were nearly impossible to overcome.[106]

The Military Public Information Office consisted of the Chief and four Information Officers, including the editor of a newsletter for the military component, which, at its peak, had 16,000 members. Lt. Colonel Palk stressed in a letter to the author that his Office 'assisted the UNTAC Information

and Education Division with their education programme in the countryside'
and, leaving aside personality conflicts, characterized 'the relationship
between the UN civilian and military information staff and media
representatives' as 'good'.[107]

The United Nations Institute for Disarmament Research has, over several
years, conducted a very extensive series of interviews with officers who
served with UNTAC in a variety of functions. The results of these interviews
were published in 1996. On the subject of information (collection, public
affairs and the media), the officers surveyed responded in the following
manner when asked if they received 'sufficient relevant information' during
their mission: 'yes': 14 and 'no': 5. When asked whether there was 'a
structured information exchange between headquarters and the units in the
field', 17 responded positively and only 2 negatively. Similarly, when asked
whether public affairs/media were 'essential', 15 of the officers responded
positively, and 2 negatively. When asked whether there was 'a well-funded
and planned communications effort to support and explain your activities
and mission to the local population', 14 responded affirmatively and 5
negatively.[108]

Very important in this regard was the position of the Force Commander,
Lt. General Sanderson, who believed 'that a public information strategy
must be included in the integrated planning' of peacekeeping operations.[109]
Sanderson, according to Palk, saw a need for 'both external and internal target
audiences'[110] and had, on his own account, decided that the central issue in
Cambodia was 'of how to forge an alliance with the Cambodian people which
would convince them of UNTAC's commitment'.[111]

Sanderson's recognition of the importance of mission-internal
information efforts, particularly in the face of mounting pressures on
UNTAC by the Khmer Rouge and the Phnom Penh government, who
attempted, through 'vicious propaganda', to classify some of UNTAC's
nationalities as 'good UNTAC' and others as 'bad UNTAC'. Sanderson,
in retrospect: 'These difficulties were overcome by involving everyone
in the planning, by conducting regular briefings and by clear directives and
orders' and 'This is perhaps the central lesson of UNTAC – it is the lesson
of unity.'[112]

In assessing UNTAC's 'unity of effort' in the information field it must be
stated that the problems that occurred between military and civilian
spokespersons in dealing with the media, were in part personality-driven
and in part a result of different approaches. However, for the purposes of
this study it is important to note that there appears to have been neither
personality conflicts nor substantial disagreements between the MPIO and
Info/Ed.

COMMUNITY RELATIONS

UNTAC's image in the local population was, as is documented, not uniformly positive: 'Stories of poor morale, incompetence within its civil police ranks, and instances of misconduct by some of its soldiers, contributed grist for press depictions of UNTAC as a bunch of brawling soldiers and disorderly keystone cops.'[113] And: 'As stories of outrageous acts by individual ill-disciplined soldiers piled up and were told and retold, UNTAC was also seen with horror as a horde of drinking, whoring, half-naked drivers who ran over people and couldn't care less.'[114]

Prince Sihanouk himself, for his own political reasons, said in one of several well-publicized interviews: 'I have had enough. UNTAC is a terrible cocktail of races who do not even understand each other, who cannot even agree with each other. There is jealousy within UNTAC. There is anarchy. There are people in UNTAC who behave very badly ...'[115]

In light of these persistent criticisms, UNTAC had to act to counter the allegations, justified or not. The major tool to counter negative publicity about UNTAC among Cambodians was the establishment of a Community Relations Office, with a staff of three, headed by Hiroko Miyamura. According to Findlay, this office 'was established primarily in response to an open letter to Akashi published in the *Phnom Penh Post* of 11 October 1992, signed by 100 men and women from UNTAC, NGOs and the Cambodian community'.[116] This letter listed serious concerns about the behaviour of some male UNTAC personnel, including sexual harassment, prostitution and sexually transmitted diseases. It recommended the appointment of an Ombudsperson and a community liaison office to liaise with Cambodians, and to educate UNTAC personnel on issues of cultural sensitivity and gender awareness.

The Community Relations Office[117] was attached to the office of the Deputy Special Representative of the Secretary-General, Behrooz Sadry. As Hiroko Miyamura saw it in hindsight, 'most of the problems ended up being monetary problems', ie the damages caused by UNTAC drivers to Cambodians and their vehicles. Miyamura felt that many of these difficulties could have been avoided by proper training of UNTAC's military and police contingents and stricter discipline.

Among the more innovative programmes undertaken by UNTAC to counter negative perceptions in the Cambodian community were a traffic accident fund, which helped speed up the process of compensating victims, a safe-driving campaign, a 'condom campaign' which was launched in cooperation with the military medical officers, and training videos about 'do's and don't's in Cambodia.

Once Radio UNTAC was fully operational and had set up its network of relay stations all over the country, it was probably the most effective tool in allaying misperceptions about UNTAC because it, as John Marston put it, 'consciously cultivated a sense of connection with the audience by, among other things, reading letters from listeners on the air and playing request songs'.[118]

Also, as Jan Arnesen, the graphic designer seconded from UN headquarters in New York, reported on her experience in Cambodia, UNTAC made creative use of visual information materials to get its message across by using communication tools typically in use in Cambodia:

> Giant billboards were already being used to advertize the local cinema's new movie every few weeks, so it was possible to locate billboard artists who could construct and paint several 20-foot signs telling people to vote. At a very reasonable price, the UN message was everywhere in the main urban capital and hard to miss. Large colourful cloth and vinyl banners were used for similar impact and were widely distributed outside the capital city as well.[119]

PERSISTENT COMMUNICATION PROBLEMS

In addition to the problems that gave rise to public criticism, there were numerous issues where language and cultural misperceptions negatively affected UNTAC's work internally and, as a consequence, its image in Cambodia and internationally. There were, to be sure, the problems of language and interpretation encountered in most other UN peacekeeping missions. Zhou Mei has described her difficulties in screening and training interpreters and language staff for Radio UNTAC.[120] Generally speaking, 'foreign officials with no experience of the country, denied direct contact by the language barrier, found it impossible to comprehend the complex patterns of family, patronage, and political relationships that made up Cambodian society'.[121]

Commentators on 'cultural aspects' of peacekeeping have noted that 'one of the most immediate problems facing the institution of peacekeeping is the need to integrate individuals with diverse backgrounds, understandings and agendas into a quasi-corporate entity – 'the mission'.[122] The use of symbols, flags and other items of 'corporate identity' were extremely important in this regard. A further unifying concept was that of political impartiality. As in Namibia, this concept had to be explained carefully and repeatedly to

UNTAC's local and international staff, particularly in the period leading up to the elections. This process led to the adoption of a code of conduct for UNTAC staff which stipulated strict impartiality and appears to have served its purpose well.

The UNTAC publication *Free Choice* was initially intended for internal mission communication but, after its fourth issue, was also used for external distribution. It helped greatly in increasing the knowledge of field staff, who were often facing similar problems, in how their colleagues in other provinces handled such problems. *Free Choice* kept channels of communication open between the different parts of UNTAC and contributed to the cohesiveness of the operation.

As far as international staff was concerned, there was also the issue of a national (country-of-origin) versus an international, ie a UN, perspective. Dennis McNamara referred to this difficulty in his human rights work: 'We were also concerned that some staff in UNTAC who were government appointees very much reflected the fact that they came from and were returning to governments',[123] that is to say, a nascent national perspective would too often supplant the desired international outlook required. A similar point was made by Marrack Goulding, the former Under-Secretary General for Peacekeeping Operations, who, in an interview about information in peacekeeping operations, said: 'The message required for all the audiences is a United Nations message. National messages will lack that spin and will obviously have a national flavour. This can be helpful with troop-contributing countries, but they will always be a second best.'[124]

Inevitably, there were language problems within the mission. Some members of the police and military contingents simply did not speak either French or English, a requirement tirelessly promulgated by the Department of Peacekeeping Operations in New York, along with the requirement to have a valid driver's licence.[125] Nevertheless, many members of military and police contingents arrived in the mission area having neither qualification, as UNTAC's Civilian Police Commissioner, Klaas Roos, reported in a post-mission assessment:

> Language problems, although in most cases not as life-threatening as a lack of driving skills, nevertheless seriously downgrade the effectiveness of a police mission. UN police personnel, by the nature of their mandate, communicate directly with their local counterparts and with the local population. Language should be taken into account in the selection of potential police-contributing countries. If the UN requests, for example, a South American country to contribute to a mission

where English is spoken, the chances are that language could present a problem, particularly among junior personnel.[126]

ASSESSMENT AND CONCLUSIONS

Cambodia in 1992 posed a very fragile environment for one of the most ambitious peacekeeping operations ever launched. Under these circumstances, information gathering and dissemination would be decisive in the delicate balance between success and failure of the United Nations operation on the ground. UNTAC proved unusually effective in the strategic management of information.

The Paris Accords provided that the mission included 'fostering an environment' for this 'most comprehensive human rights mandate ever entrusted to a UN peacekeeping operation'. That mandate was from the outset seen by the leadership of the mission as an education and institution-building function, to which the timely and accurate dissemination of information would be critical.

This function came to be known in the mission as 'Info/ Ed', and has been credited with having been one of UNTAC's major successes, contributing directly to high voter participation, and this despite a very threatening security environment. Also, the Info/Ed campaign was instrumental in ensuring that the elections were fair and free, and were widely so perceived, both inside Cambodia and by the international community.

It was especially significant that in UNTAC the need for this information process was appreciated by the political and military leadership from the very outset. Public information had been described as an essential function in the Paris Agreements, and this was reiterated in the first report by the UN Secretary General, containing his proposals for the implementation of the mandate. Thus there was a formal mission statement, which in turn called up a budget, a staff and an organisational structure. It may be observed that, however obvious these features might seem, this continuity, from mandate to operational capability, cannot be assumed a norm, especially immediately upon start-up.

The subsequent execution of the Info/Ed function was not without problems. These resulted principally from the enormity of the task, including a media environment strongly affected by propaganda and intimidation. UNTAC's information mandate was a novel undertaking for a peacekeeping operation, both in the magnitude and substance of its information work. It is clear that the early, persistent and high-level guidance Info/Ed received, combined with an exceptional outlay of resources, did result in a unanimity and consistency of effort quite rare in the history of peacekeeping operations.

This Cambodia case study therefore manifests all six of the operational principles presented in Chapter 1, even though principle 5, which refers to cultural sensitivities, was observable principally in the effects of its omission. The results of the elections, and the development of Cambodian civil society since then, speak clearly: despite widely apprehended signals of very real dangers to the process and to the participants, the elections were fair, free and secret. They took place among a people whose recent history might logically have presaged only further disaster. Nevertheless, important seeds were planted by UNTAC, showing the Cambodian people that human rights could be fostered and maintained, and that these elections were their best chance at democratic self-determination. Despite the pitfalls of Cambodian politics, Julio Jeldres's assessment of the long term impact of the UN's operation in Cambodia appears to be pertinent: 'The most hopeful signs for the future are found in the realm of civil society, where new groups of students, women, human rights activists and others friendly to democracy are working to guard the liberties and improve the lives of all Cambodians'.[127]

The fight for democracy and the maintenance of human rights in Cambodia received a major setback in July 1997 when a coup by Hun Sen took place which endangered not only the lives of many political opponents and human rights activists, but also affected press freedom and called into question the future of democratic institutions and values in that country. These developments show that even the best-funded and widely supported peace operation is no guarantee for an automatic peaceful resolution of underlying conflicts, especially in countries without a democratic tradition and with a history of human tragedies.

NOTES

1. See Part VII: Cambodia, *The Blue Helmets – A Review of United Nations Peace-keeping* (3rd edn) New York: United Nations, 1996), and *The United Nations and Cambodia, 1991–1995*, The United Nations Blue Book Series, Vol.II, New York: United Nations, 1995.
2. For a full account of the period leading up to and immediately following the elections, see William Shawcross, *Cambodia's New Deal*, Washington, DC: Carnegie, 1994. A more recent analysis of Cambodia's continuing difficulties is given by Julio A. Jeldres, 'Cambodia's Fading Hopes', *Journal of Democracy*, Vol.7, No.1, Jan. 1996.
3. *The Blue Helmets* (n.1 above), p.741 cites combined expenditures for UNAMIC and UNTAC as US$1.62 billion, excluding the cost of repatriation and resettlement of refugees, as well as rehabilitation assistance which were funded from voluntary contributions. UNTAC thus, just as the United Nations Mission in Namibia described

above, came in under the amount originally budgeted for (US$1.8 billion). By comparison, the UN operation in Somalia (UNOSOM II), which lasted for two years, also cost a total of US$1.6 billion. Ibid., p.722.

4. UN Under Secretary-General Rafeeuddin Ahmed to the author in June 1991. Much support came also from countries in the region, such as Australia which felt a strong commitment to the success of the peace process in Cambodia. See, for example, Senator Graham Maguire, 'Public and Parliamentary Perceptions of United Nations Peacekeeping Operations', in Kevin Clements and Christine Wilson (eds), *UN Peacekeeping at the Crossroads*, Canberra: Australian National University, 1994.

5. Press reporting from Cambodia, as far as international media from Europe and North America were concerned, was predominantly sceptical and negative, up to and even well past the time the elections were held in May 1993. Trevor Findlay, *Cambodia – The Legacy and Lessons of UNTAC*, SIPRI Research Report No.9, Oxford: Oxford University Press, 1995, p.151 reports that 'both Akashi and Sanderson complained of the attitude of the press in covering the Cambodia operation'. James A. Schear, one of the most consistent observers of the situation in Cambodia, argued against the critics who maintained that conditions did not exist for the holding of elections in 1993, that, in hindsight, 'UNTAC's decision to proceed with the elections, despite Cambodia's instability, was the right choice'. James A. Schear, 'Riding the Tiger: The United Nations and Cambodia's Struggle for Peace', in William J. Durch (ed.), *UN Peacekeeping, American Policy, and the Uncivil Wars of the 1990s*, New York: St Martin's Press, 1996, p.173.

6. *The United Nations and Cambodia* (n.1 above), p.54.

7. Fen Osler Hampson, *Nurturing Peace – Why Peace Settlements Succeed or Fail*, Washington DC: Institute of Peace Press, 1996, pp.190–1.

8. United Nations staff, some of whom lived in the country for a year or longer, repeatedly commented to the author during her visit to the country in Sept. 1992 on how dependent Cambodians were on them. Taking initiatives and assuming responsibility were apparently only slowly relearned by the citizens of this war-ravaged country.

9. Juan J. Liz and Alfred Sterna, 'Toward Consolidated Democracies', *Journal of Democracy*, April 1996, pp.20–1, have called into question the usability of the state bureaucracy in former communist countries 'where the distinction between the communist party and the state had been virtually obliterated'. See also the discussion of failing or failed states by Leslie Gelb, 'Quelling the Teacup Wars: The New World's Constant Challenges', *Foreign Affairs*, 73/6, Nov./Dec. 1994 and Chapter 8 of this book.

10. These were: the two non-communist groups, FUNCINPEC and KPNLF; the 'State of Cambodia' SOC-faction, and the Khmer Rouge.

11. Schear (n.5 above), p.139.

12. *The United Nations and Cambodia* (n.1 above), p.27, refers to the support, by the Security Council, in Sept. 1992, for a countrywide moratorium on the export of logs.

13. Ibid., pp.19–20.

14. Ibid., pp.263 and 296: 'Though the great bulk of the returnees came from Thailand, some 2,000 were also repatriated from Indonesia, Viet Nam and Malaysia.'

15. The text of the agreement is contained in *The United Nations and Cambodia*, ibid., pp.97–111.

16. Ibid., p.105.

17. *Report of the Secretary-General on the expansion of UNAMIC's mandate*, S/23331,

reprinted in *The United Nations and Cambodia*, p.152.

18. *The Blue Helmets* (n.1 above), p.477 states: 'By August 1993 ... more than 4 million square metres of Cambodian territory had been cleared of mines. About 37,000 mines and other unexploded ordinances had been destroyed, and some 2,300 Cambodians trained in mine clearance techniques.'

19. Dennis McNamara, 'The Protection and Promotion of Human Rights', in Nassrine Azimi (ed.), *The United Nations Transitional Authority in Cambodia: Debriefing and Lessons*, Netherlands: Kluwer Academic Publishers, 1994, p.165.

20. Azimi (n.19 above), p.23.

21. MacNamara (n.19 above), p.164.

22. However, within UNTAC, it was the smallest component which led Dennis McNamara to complain about 'inadequate staffing.' MacNamara, ibid., p.166.

23. Dennis MacNamara, during the author's visit to UNTAC headquarters in Sept. 1992.

24. McNamara (n.19 above), pp.167 and 168.

25. Azimi (n.19 above), pp.24–5.

26. Ibid., p.24.

27. *The Blue Helmets* (n.1 above), p.474.

28. McNamara (n.19 above), p.166. See also Dennis McNamara, 'UN Human Rights Activities in Cambodia: An Evaluation', in Alice H. Heineken (ed.), *Honoring Human Rights and Keeping the Peace: Lessons from El Salvador, Cambodia and Haiti*, Queenstown, MD: The Aspen Institute, 1995.

29. Azimi (n.19 above), p.26.

30. For a detailed account of the work of the electoral component of UNTAC, see Michael Maley, 'Reflections on the Electoral Process in Cambodia', in Hugh Smith (ed.), *International Peacekeeping – Building on the Cambodia Experience*, Canberra: Australian Defense Studies Centre, 1994. Maley concluded: 'The Cambodian election certainly gave rise to more complex practical difficulties than any previous election with which the UN had been involved. The Organization had full responsibility for the conduct of the poll, which was not the case for example in Namibia, and also had to cope with major language difficulties, an absence of infrastructure, and a much less settled political environment than had been contemplated in the Paris Agreements.' (p.45).

31. See Findlay (n.5 above), pp.54–6 for an explanation of the different reasons.

32. Ibid., pp.55 and 56.

33. Ibid., p.56.

34. Janet Heininger, *Peacekeeping in Transition – The United Nations in Cambodia*, New York: Twentieth Century Fund, 1994, p.116.

35. Schear (n.5 above), p.169.

36. *The United Nations and Cambodia* (n.1 above), p.29.

37. See, in particular, the articles by Judy Ledgerwood, 'Patterns of CPP Political Repression and Violence During the UNTAC Period' and David Ashley, 'The Nature and Causes of Human Rights Violations in Battambang Province', in Steven Heder and Judy Ledgerwood (eds), *Propaganda, Politics, and Violence in Cambodia – Democratic Transition under United Nations Peace-Keeping*, New York: M.E. Sharpe, 1996.

38. Ledgerwood (n.37 above), p.118.

39. Yasushi Akashi, as quoted by Lyndall McLean, 'Civil Administration in Transition: Public Information and the Neutral Political/Electoral Environment', in Smith (n.30 above), p.57.

40. *The Blue Helmets* (n.1 above), p.480.

41. Findlay (n.5 above), p.76.

42. *Free Choice: Electoral Component Newsletter*, Issue No.16, 26 March 1993, p.2.

43. Timothy M. Carney, 'UNTAC's Information/Education Programme', in Azimi (n.19 above), pp.171–2. The author was present at part of the meeting between Mr Akashi and Mr Carney in Washington, DC in Feb. 1992. Mr Akashi was very much impressed by Mr Carney's credentials, in the diplomatic and information field, as well as by his fluency in Khmer.

44. Carney (n.43 above), p.171.

45. Article 6 of Part I, Paris Accords, as reproduced in *The United Nations and Cambodia, 1991–1995* (n.1 above), p.98.

46. Annex 1: 'Proposed mandate for UNTAC', para.4, reproduced ibid., p.101.

47. See 'Report of the Secretary-General on Cambodia containing his proposed implementation plan for UNTAC, including administrative and financial aspects', S//23613, dated 19 Feb. 1992, reproduced as Document 30 in *The United Nations and Cambodia, 1991–1995*, pp.158–84.

48. Ibid., p.161.

49. Ibid., para.159, p.177.

50. Ibid., para.160, p.177.

51. Carney (n.43 above), p.171.

52. Ibid.

53. Ibid., p.171. Jim Schear, 'Riding the Tiger', in Durch (n.5 above), p.149, puts the total number of Info/Ed staff at 160.

54. Carney (n.43 above), p.172. According to Zhou Mei, it was not until Aug. 1992 that most radio officers from Headquarters started to arrive. Zhou Mei, *Radio UNTAC of Cambodia – Winning Ears, Hearts and Minds*, Bangkok: White Lotus, 1994, p.2.

55. Steve Heder and Judy Ledgerwood, 'Politics of Violence: An Introduction', in Heder and Ledgerwood (n.33 above), p.27.

56. See Mei's vivid description of the international mix of personalities and their short-comings, from a professional and personal point of view (n.54 above), pp.2–12.

57. Azimi (n.19 above), p.43.

58. Heder, 'Politics of Violence', in Heder and Ledgerwood (n.37 above), p.28.

59. As quoted by M. Michaels, 'Blue-helmet blues', *Time*, 15 Nov. 1993, p.56.

60. Findlay (n.5 above), p.147.

61. 'Interview: Timothy Carney', in *Free Choice – Electoral Component Newsletter*, 26 March 1993, p.14.

62. Ibid.

63. Carney, 'UNTAC's Information/Education programme', in Azimi (n.43 above), p.172.

64. 'Interview: Timothy Carney' (n.61 above), p.14.

65. Carney, 'UNTAC's Information/Education programme' (n.43 above), p.172.

66. 'Third Progress Report of the Secretary-General on UNTAC', in: *The United Nations and Cambodia, 1991–1995* (n.1 above), p.264.

67. Michael W. Doyle, *UN Peacekeeping in Cambodia – UNTAC's Civil Mandate*, International Peace Academy Occasional Paper, Boulder, CO; Lynne Rienner, 1995, p.55.

68. See a handout on 'Information/Education Division' dated Nov. 1992 issued by the Spokesman's Office of UNTAC and the discussion below on Radio UNTAC. A member of the UNTAC Spokesman's Office told the author that there was criticism in the Special Representative's Office that Info/Ed focused too much on the political analysis of the factions and not enough on 'hearts and minds' activities.

69. See 'Fourth progress report of the Secretary-General on UNTAC' of 3 May 1993, paras.39–41 'Attacks on UNTAC personnel', in *The United Nations and Cambodia, 1991–1995* (n.1 above), p.290, which stated that 'since the beginning of UNTAC, 11 UNTAC civilians and military personnel have been killed as a result of hostile action'. With regard to intimidation in the pre-election period in general, Schear (n.5 above), p.184, quotes from a press statement by Dennis McNamara, the Director of UNTAC's Human Rights Component, on 23 May 1993, according to which between March and mid-May 1993 'UNTAC confirmed 200 deaths, 338 injuries and 114 abductions' among the population of Cambodia. The seriousness of the situation in the theatre of operations from March to May 1993 is well described by Findlay (n.5 above), pp.76–81. Findlay also outlines diplomatic efforts to rescue the mission when both the Australian and the Japanese contingents were in danger of being withdrawn.

70. Heininger (n.34 above), p.111. During the author's visit to Cambodia in Sept. 1992 and in subsequent discussions, UNTAC staff pointed to the high defection rate among Khmer Rouge followers. However, reliable statistics on the actual defection rate have not been found.

71. Heininger (n.34 above), pp.131–2.

72. Azimi (n.19 above), p.42.

73. Findlay (n.5 above), p.76.

74. Schear (n.5 above), p.169.

75. Heininger (n.34 above), p.110.

76. Lieutenant General John M. Sanderson, 'UNTAC: The Military Component View', in Azimi (n.19 above), p.133.

77. Carney, 'UNTAC's Information/Education Programme', in Azimi (n.43 above), p.172. This proposal was, in the projected context, an absurdity due to the limited range of FM broadcasts and the requirements for line-of-sight transmission. Radio UNTAC eventually broadcast on the AM band (see below).

78. Ibid., p.173.

79. *The Blue Helmets*, Part VII, p.479. These broadcasts, according to Zhou Mei, cost US $ 610 per hour. This arrangement lasted until 31 July 1993. Mei (n.54 above), p.19.

80. See Carney (n.43 above), p.173. For a vivid description of the continuing technical difficulties surrounding the operation of this antiquated 120kW Philips radio transmitter, including generator problems, see Mei (n.54 above), pp.14–19.

81. Ibid., p.30.

82. Ibid., p.43.

83. Ibid., p.44.

84. Ibid., p.20.

85. This fact is acknowledged in the 'Fourth Progress Report of the Secretary-General on UNTAC', para.106, in *The United Nations and Cambodia, 1991–1995* (n.1 above), p.298.

86. Mei (n.54 above), p.21.

87. Ibid., p.22.

88. Ibid., p.35.

89. Ibid., p.28.

90. Ibid., p.53.

91. Ibid., p.27 and pp.58–9.

92. Findlay (n.5 above), p.152.

93. Carney said about the Control Unit team; 'Control Unit staffing succeeded in mixing working journalists and Cambodia specialists. The resulting synthesis provided an

informed, sophisticated combination of experience and knowledge.' Memorandum dated 29 July 1993 from Timothy Carney to Behrooz Sadry, the Deputy Special Representative of the Secretary-General.

94. 'Interview: Timothy Carney' (n.61 above), p.13.
95. Ibid.
96. Azimi (n.19 above), p.40.
97. 'Third progress report of the Secretary-General on UNTAC', 25 Jan. 1993, para.70, in *The United Nations and Cambodia, 1991–1995* (n.1 above), p.262. The difficulties in creating an independent journalists' association are described by John Marston, 'Cambodian News Media in the UNTAC Period and After', in Heder and Ledgerwood (n.37 above), pp.213–18.
98. John Marston, in Heder and Ledgerwood (n.37 above), p.218.
99. 'Interview: Timothy Carney' (n.61 above), p.14.
100. Carney, 'UNTAC's Information/Education Programme', in Azimi (n.43 above), pp.174–5.
101. Eric Berman, Deputy Spokesman of UNTAC, information relayed to the author on 27 Aug. 1996.
102. Azimi (n.43 above), p.41.
103. Ibid.
104. Quoted by Findlay (n.5 above), p.151.
105. Ibid.
106. It is of interest to note that most former UNTAC-staff interviewed on the subject of personality problems did not wish to be quoted in this context.
107. Richard Palk in a letter to the author of 23 July 1996.
108. *Managing Arms in Peace Processes: Cambodia*, United Nations Disarmament and Conflict Resolution Project, United Nations, New York and Geneva: 1996, pp.172–85.
109. Lieutenant General J.M. Sanderson, 'UNTAC: Success and Failures', in Smith (n.30 above), p.29.
110. Palk to the author, 23 July 1996.
111. Sanderson in Smith (n.30 above), p.20.
112. Ibid., pp.26 and 31.
113. Schear (n.5 above), p.162.
114. Heder and Ledgerwood (n.37 above), p.32.
115. Prince Sihanouk as quoted by Nayan Chanda and Nate Thayer, 'I Want to Retake Power,' *Far Eastern Economic Review*, 4 Feb. 1993, p.21.
116. Findlay (n.5 above), p.151.
117. The following account of the activities of the Community Liaison Office is based on replies to interview questions received from Hiroko Miyamura on 9 and 10 Sept. 1996.
118. Marston in Heder and Ledgerwood (n.37 above), p.227.
119. Jan Arnesen, letter to the author, 25 Jan. 1997. Arnesen considers her work with local graphic artists, both in Namibia and in Cambodia, the most rewarding part of her work in peacekeeping missions. She reports that her graphic studio at UNTAC became 'a sort of training ground' for local staff, most of them returnees from refugee camps in Thailand (Arnesen, letter to the author of 2 Feb. 1997).
120. Zhou Mei (n.54 above), pp.8–12.
121. Shawcross (n.2 above), p.13.
122. Robert Rubinstein, 'Cultural Aspects of Peacekeeping', in *Millennium*, Vol.22, No.3, Winter 1993, p.554.

123. McNamara, in Azimi (n.19 above), p.166.

124. Marrack Goulding, Under-Secretary General for Political Affairs, United Nations, Interview with author, 29 May 1996.

125. *Managing Arms in Peace Processes: Cambodia* (n.108 above), pp.145–7 surveyed officers who served with UNTAC. They listed, among the most frequently cited 'disadvantages' of a multilateral force: language problems, different operational standards, different cultural backgrounds and differences in skills and equipment.

126. Klaas Roos, 'UNTAC's Civilian Police Operation', in Azimi (n.19 above), p.143.

127. Jeldres (n.2 above), p.156. Another example of the lasting effect of human rights training and education came to light in Rwanda, when, in Feb. 1997 a group of UN human rights workers was ambushed and killed. One of them was Chim-Chan Sastra, a survivor of the Cambodian killing fields who 'felt Cambodia owed the world for all the help it had received from other countries'. *New York Times*, 12 Feb. 1997, 'UN Aide Left Legacy of Asia Role on Rights'.

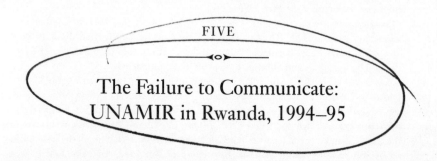

FIVE

The Failure to Communicate:
UNAMIR in Rwanda, 1994–95

RWANDA PRIOR TO 1994

Rwanda is one of the most densely populated countries of Africa. Its population of about seven million people in 1994 was divided into three ethnic groups, the Hutu (about 85 per cent), the Tutsi (about 14 per cent) and the Twa (about one per cent). These three groups speak the same language and share the same culture. During the colonial period, Belgian authorities established a system of identity cards specifying ethnic group, which is still used today. Ethnic identity, combined with rigid social structures imposed by colonial authorities allowed Tutsi domination of the country's politics and economics. This lasted until 1959, when a Hutu peasant revolt overthrew the Tutsi king of Rwanda, thus unleashing the first of several waves of Tutsi refugees, 200,000 of whom fled between 1959 and 1963.[1]

Rwanda became independent in 1962. Along its southern borders was created the Kingdom of Burundi, which became a republic in 1965. While Rwanda became an exclusive Hutu state, in Burundi the Tutsi majority was dominant: 'Each country thus came to mirror in reverse the ethnic composition of the other. Each nation used the other to justify policies of discrimination and control. Ethnically related frictions and, in extreme cases, massacres in one nation raised levels of political and social tension in the other.'[2] In fact, the social and political tensions emanating from Rwanda became a source of instability for the entire Great Lakes region of Africa.

In 1973, General Habyarimana took power in a military coup in Rwanda. He institutionalized previous practices of ethnic discrimination through a policy of 'establishing ethnic and regional balance', which determined the posts and resources allocated to each ethnic group, giving the Tutsi ten per cent.[3] Meanwhile, Tutsi exile groups based in Uganda, Burundi, Tanzania

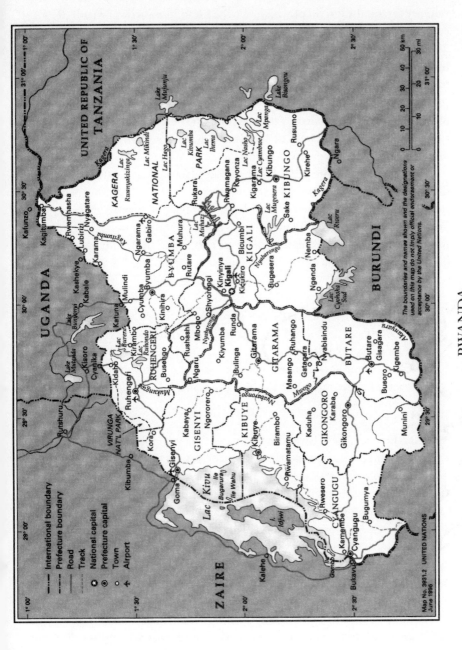

RWANDA

(map no. 3931.2 (Rwanda) reproduced with the permission of the Cartographic Section, Department of Public Information, United Nations) and Zaire – the 'Banyarwanda' – had organized into political parties and military forces, the largest of which was the Rwandese Patriotic Front (RPF), consisting mainly of Tutsi refugees living in Uganda.[4]

The existence of a Rwanda diaspora was used for political purposes by both sides. The RPF became a strong advocate of the right of refugees to return, while Hutu ideologists depicted the RPF as a foreign-inspired reactionary political force. Ethnic differences were also magnified by Hutu ideologists close to President Habyarimana, who described the RPF as a Tutsi party, Tutsis in exile enemies of the Rwandan state, and Hutu participation in the Tutsi-dominated RPF as cosmetic.[5]

In October 1990, the RPF launched an offensive across the Rwanda–Uganda border against the Rwandan government. As a consequence of the fighting, famine broke out and large numbers of displaced Rwandese fled to Kigali. Some 10,000 Tutsis and political opponents were arrested and some of the groups were murdered. France and Belgium intervened militarily, but fighting recurred throughout 1991. *Human Rights Watch* reports:

> Foreign governments and other suppliers were more than willing to fuel this arms race. This small, impoverished nation, which was already unable to meet its own human needs, devoted its scarce resources to an unprecedented accumulation of a wide variety of arms, including the introduction of heavier, long-range weapons systems.[6]

Nevertheless, a new Rwandese constitution was adopted, and in April 1992 a coalition government was formed which included the Hutu *Mouvement republicain national pour le développement* (MRND). This movement's youth branch organized its own militia, called the *Interahamwe* (Those who attack together), which became a major perpetrator of violence. Since 1991, the Hutu government had been distributing weapons to civilians to create 'self-defense forces'; by February 1993, 'there was increasing interaction and overlapping of these forces and the abusive militia'. Assassinations and bombings had plagued Rwanda since the beginning of the war; 'they were carried out quickly and professionally, sometimes by uniformed men'.[7]

A number of attempts were made to negotiate a ceasefire. In July 1992, an agreement was reached to deploy a 50-member military observer group furnished by the Organisation of African Unity (OAU). However, tensions mounted between Rwanda and Uganda, both of whom asked the United

Nations to lend its good offices in 1993. Following further negotiations, the Security Council authorized the establishment of the United Nations Observer Mission Uganda-Rwanda (UNOMUR) on the Uganda side of the common border. UNOMUR, headed by Brigadier-General Romeo Dallaire of Canada as Chief Military Observer, became operational in September 1993 with 81 military observers.[8]

Meanwhile, negotiations continued in Arusha, Tanzania, for an international force to assist in the maintenance of public security and in the delivery of humanitarian aid in Rwanda itself. The talks in Arusha were concluded in August 1993, a UN reconnaissance mission visited Rwanda that month, and the Secretary-General recommended the establishment of the United Nations Assistance Mission for Rwanda (UNAMIR). The mission was to have the following functions:

- Assist in ensuring the security of the capital city of Kigali;
- Monitor the ceasefire agreement, including establishment of an expanded demilitarized zone and demobilization procedures;
- Monitor the security situation during the governmental transition leading up to elections;
- Assist with mine clearance; and
- Provide security for the repatriation of Rwandese refugees and displaced persons.

The Secretary-General proposed that the operation be conducted in four phases: phase one would see the installation of a transitional government; phase two would begin the disengagement, demobilization and integration of the armed forces and gendarmerie; phase three would establish, supervise and monitor a new demilitarized zone, and phase four would ensure the secure environment required for the conduct of elections. The Secretary-General also proposed to place UNOMUR observers under the command of the new force, as well as incorporate OAU observers and deploy a small UN civilian police unit.[9]

UNAMIR was established by the Security Council on 5 October 1993 (SCR 872) for an initial period of six months. It was to end no later than December 1995, following national elections and the installation of a new government in Rwanda. General Dallaire arrived in Kigali on 22 October and succeeded in negotiating a 'status of forces agreement' with the government in November, to which the RPF also agreed. The Secretary-General's Special Representative for Rwanda, Mr Jacques-Roger Booh-Booh of Cameroon arrived in Kigali at the end of November 1993. The first

UNAMIR battalion was deployed in Kigali in early December and many of the projected tasks of phase one of the implementation plan were accomplished by 30 December 1993.[10]

MASS MURDER AND CIVIL WAR

According to the Arusha Peace Agreement, General Habyarimana was supposed to remain in office as President of Rwanda for the transitional period. However, the transitional government and National Assembly were not installed because the parties could not agree on several key issues. Hard-line Hutu parties mobilized opposition to following the process specified in the agreement and the RPF was also reluctant to enter into any power-sharing arrangements while military victory appeared achievable to them.[11]

Phase one of the peace agreement could therefore not be completed, which contributed to a deterioration of the security situation: 'January and February 1994 saw increasingly violent demonstrations, roadblocks, assassination of political leaders and assaults on and murders of civilians', even though the ceasefire still held.[12] The Secretary-General thus recommended the extension of UNAMIR's mandate on 30 March 1994 which the Security Council approved for another three-month period.

On 6 April 1994, President Habyarimana and President Ntaryamira of Burundi were killed when their plane crashed at Kigali airport.[13] According to Minear and Guillot, 'selected and pre-planned murders of Tutsis and moderate Hutus began within hours. Prime Minister Agathe Uwillingiyimana was assassinated by the Presidential Guard. The speaker of the National Assembly and the President of the Supreme Court, both Hutus, were killed. Many moderate government ministers and democratic opposition party members were also murdered, creating a political vacuum.'[14] The killers were drawn from the youth militias, the *Interahamwe* and the *Impuzamugambi*, ('those who have only one goal – which was to prevent a return to Tutsi dominance).[15] Extremist Hutu power ideology, developed in prior years, which some have described as 'tropical nazism', was at the base of the massacres that followed, claiming between 500,000 and one million victims.

Who were the perpetrators of this massive racially-motivated violence, which is now commonly referred to as genocide? According to Matthew Vaccaro, 'the term militias implies greater organization than these groups had ... [they] proved capable only of mob-type tactics against unarmed civilians'.[17] The militias are estimated to have numbered between 30,000 and 50,000. They were spurred on by a vicious propaganda campaign conducted through *Radio-Télévision Libre des Milles Collines* (RTML), a station created in July 1993 and operated by members of President Habyarimana's inner circle. It will be analysed in greater detail in conjunction with the UN's information efforts below.

THE INTERNATIONAL ENVIRONMENT – CONSTRAINTS FOR EFFECTIVE INTERVENTION

It is evident that there were strong forces within Rwanda in 1993 opposed to the Arusha accords, and that those forces became increasingly violent in their opposition to the peace process in early 1994.[18] These were tragically matched by a fatal confluence of external factors which prevented effective international action to stop the carnage in April 1994.

Following the outbreak of violence in Kigali on 6 April the Security Council was deeply divided on the best course of action. Nigeria, speaking on behalf of the non-aligned nations, favoured expanding UNAMIR's mandate and ranks, as did Russia, the OAU and France. The United Kingdom favoured reducing UNAMIR's presence, maintaining the minimum which would encourage dialogue. The United States initially favoured evacuating UNAMIR troops, although they eventually came round to the UK position, and finally supported expansion. Argentina suggested temporarily relocating UNAMIR to a nearby country. Awaiting additional information from the scene, the Security Council did not act until two weeks later, on 21 April.[19]

In an important report on the lessons learned from the Rwanda crisis prepared by the UN Department of Peacekeeping Operations in 1996, the Security Council's attitude to the situation is described as having viewed it 'as a small-scale civil war' and having 'ignored or not explored' mounting evidence of large-scale human rights violations.[20] While some journalists and non-governmental observers have called this miscalculation one of the most 'shameful' episodes in the Security Council's history,[21] it must be remembered that the Rwanda crisis came at a time when the Council was preoccupied simultaneously with the situations in Bosnia, Somalia, Iraq and Haiti. In 1994, the international community was clearly stretched beyond its capacity to respond adequately to a multitude of simultaneous humanitarian crises in different parts of the world.

The Somalia experience had a particularly negative impact on decision-making by the Security Council. Two days before the Council established UNAMIR in October 1993, 18 American soldiers were killed in Somalia, leading to the withdrawal of US forces from the United Nations Operation in Somalia (UNOSOM), to be followed by most Western states shortly thereafter. Secretary-General Boutros-Ghali, in his farewell address to the General Assembly, recalled the events of 1994: 'Disillusion set in. Where peacekeepers were asked to deal with warfare, serious setbacks occurred. The first came in Somalia, and weakened the will of the world community to act against genocide in Rwanda.'[22]

The United States had begun a major review of its peacekeeping policy in February 1993 which culminated in Presidential Decision Directive 25 (PDD 25), announced on 3 May 1994. This directive set strict criteria for any future involvement of the United States in peace operations.[23] In October 1993, President Clinton, addressing the UN General Assembly, said that the United Nations must learn to say 'no' to peacekeeping operations that were not feasible.

There was a great reluctance by most countries to become part of a UN peacekeeping operation in Rwanda. Many were prepared only to assist the Rwandese 'as cheaply as possible, without being drawn into a protracted conflict'.[24] As General Dallaire said in an interview in 1995: 'I don't blame the UN – I believe the UN's effectiveness is the responsibility of the member states. And sometimes I wonder if there are certain member states who want the UN to be ineffective and to be the easy target.'[25] As a consequence, even UNAMIR's authorized force of 2,545, which it reached only by the end of February 1994 (with the arrival of a second battalion from Ghana), was inadequate to cope with the situation it was to face in April:

> The Mission had neither the appropriate mandate nor the means to take any effective action. Senior military officials are in agreement that the force level of 2,545 was too small for any military action to protect victims of the slaughter, even in self-defence, and the force's capabilities had not been put together with a conflict situation in mind. With an extremely weak logistics base, UNAMIR was also rapidly running out of food and medical supplies, even sandbags to protect its accommodation.[26]

The murder on 6 April of ten UNAMIR soldiers of Belgian nationality, who had been tasked to protect the Prime Minister, had a devastating effect on the willingness of UN members to contribute forces for UNAMIR. On 9 and 10 April, several countries began to evacuate their nationals:

> The slowness of the Security Council to respond to the widening vortex of violence was in sharp contrast to the dispatch with which individual member governments acted to evacuate their nationals. The first of 600 French troops landed in Kigali on 8 April, without

prior consultation with the United Nations, evacuating in the next week 1 361 persons, including 450 French nationals. Responding to the execution by the Presidential Guard of 10 Belgian soldiers who had been seeking to protect Rwanda's Prime Minister, some 700 Belgian troops began arriving 10 April to evacuate Belgian nationals, including UNAMIR's Belgian contingent.[27]

On 20 April, the Secretary-General presented three options for the future of UNAMIR to the Security Council: immediate and massive reinforcement of UNAMIR with a mandate that would allow it to coerce the parties into a ceasefire and to attempt to restore law and order; a drawdown of the mission to a small group headed by the Force Commander who would remain in Kigali with the Special Representative, trying to mediate a ceasefire; or the complete withdrawal of UNAMIR. The following day the Security Council adopted resolution 912 (1994) in which it decided to accept the second option, by reducing UNAMIR's troop strength to 270: 'It was obvious that with that force level, as well as the revised mandate, there was no effective action UNAMIR could take to halt the genocide. In fact, there was a certain reluctance among Council members to acknowledge that the problem in Rwanda was one of genocide.'[28]

UNAMIR'S HUMANITARIAN TASKS

UNAMIR's mandate was changed three times and, as some observers have commented, in each case the new mandate was rendered inadequate by rapidly changing circumstances.[29] The Security Council continued to vacillate during the crucial weeks of April and May. On 29 April 1994, it reviewed a proposal by the Secretary-General for more forceful action, on 30 April 1994 it 'demanded that the interim government of Rwanda and the RPF take effective measures to prevent any attacks on civilians under their control'. On 4 May 1994, Secretary-General Boutros-Ghali 'publicly called the situation genocide and warned that the United Nations, if it did not act quickly, might later be accused of passivity'.[30]

By early May, UNAMIR's strength stood at 444 all ranks in Rwanda. Under these circumstances, it is surprising that it was able to function at all. As General Dallaire commented, 'at a time when the situation in fact called for more troops, and when the UN was debating over a new mandate and the number of personnel required to implement it, the UNAMIR force found itself in dire straits; it had little or no ammunition, only a few days of food, a limited supply of potable water, and few medical supplies'.[31]

In spite of this, UNAMIR did manage to gather and protect 8,000 civilians in the Kigali stadium and 2,000 in the hospital compound on 11 April. Two days later, the International Committee of the Red Cross stopped transporting wounded after six civilians had been taken from an ICRC vehicle and shot. There were, predictably, many accusations by survivors of the massacres, by relatives of some of the victims (including the ten Belgian paratroopers), and by aid and human rights groups, that UNAMIR should have done more to assist. Minear and Guillot conclude: 'Some UNAMIR troops acted with heroism. Senegalese Captain M.B.E. Diagne lost his life protecting others. General Dallaire played an active personal role in saving lives … UN troops were clearly overmatched by the situation and altogether unable to head off the blood bath.'[32]

On 23 April, UN Under-Secretary-General for Humanitarian Affairs Peter Hansen led an Inter-Agency Advance Humanitarian team into Kigali. As head of the UN Department of Humanitarian Affairs which was created only two years earlier to coordinate the international response to humanitarian emergencies effectively, Hansen established several sub-offices of the United Nations Rwanda Emergency Office (UNREO) in Nairobi, Kenya and Kabale, Uganda. The advance humanitarian team worked closely with UNAMIR in Kigali, which 'served as a back-up resource for the few remaining humanitarian agencies, numbering only seven … With only a handful of NGOs on the scene, UNAMIR responded to their various requests quickly and effectively, constrained only by the deteriorating circumstances in Kigali and limited resources.'[33]

Within ten days of the outbreak of violence, UNAMIR created a 'humanitarian assistance cell', composed of about six military staff. Major Don MacNeil, a Canadian who served as Operations Officer of that cell, estimated that, during the early phase of the crisis, 25 per cent of UNAMIR's total budget was directed to providing support for humanitarian organizations.[34]

EXPANSION OF MANDATE

On 17 May 1994, the Security Council adopted Resolution 918 and decided to expand UNAMIR's force level to 5,500. Its mandate was also expanded 'to enable it to contribute to the security and protection of refugees and civilians at risk, through means including the establishment and maintenance of secure humanitarian areas, and the provision of security for relief operations to the degree possible'.[35] It also imposed an arms embargo on Rwanda, something that had long been demanded by non-governmental organizations and others concerned with Rwanda.

Still, UNAMIR's strength, on 25 May, was just 471. The reasons were the following: 'When it came to finding the troops for the expanded operation, problems arose. Only African countries and four non-African countries were willing to provide the troops. Logistical support for the ill-equipped African troops was hard to come by and, when offered, required long and tedious negotiations on the conditions under which it was being contributed.'[36]

On 31 May 1994 the Secretary-General informed the Security Council 'that the repercussions of the massacres in Rwanda were enormous, with displaced persons in the range of 1.5 million and an additional 400,000 refugees in bordering countries'.[37] On 3 June major ethnic massacres took place in government-held territory, followed by reprisals in RPF areas. The International Committee of the Red Cross recovered 40,000 bodies from Lake Victoria, and Kigali authorities at that time reportedly buried 67,000.[38] General Dallaire later said that the atrocities were often committed 'after lunch, with the use of light drugs and booze', to hurt and make the enemy suffer, not necessarily with the intention to kill. 'They were hacked and left in puddles of blood to die.'[39]

By mid-June, heavy fighting continued, and advances by the RPF forced the interim government of Rwanda to flee from Kigali to Gizenyi. At that time, the French government decided to intervene unilaterally. The Security Council, in Resolution 929, endorsed Operation Turquoise under Chapter VII of the UN Charter for humanitarian purposes. 'That force was on the ground in the space of a few days, while troops and logistical support for the expanded UNAMIR could not be found.'[40]

On 3 July, France began to set up a 'humanitarian protected zone' in south-western Rwanda covering about one fifth of the country's territory. While the RPF expressed its strong opposition to the French move, it did not interfere with the French operation. According to General Dallaire and other observers, the French intervention achieved its goals, namely to stabilize the area. However, because of the close cooperation between UNAMIR, UNREO and the French, the operation undermined the UN's position of impartiality. Its credibility with the RPF, which declared a unilateral ceasefire on 18 July and formed a government on 19 July, was severely damaged. This became a major problem for UNAMIR for the duration of its mandate.

General Dallaire, in retrospect, also questioned the wisdom of injecting a mission, such as Operation Turquoise, which had been authorized under Chapter VII, into a Chapter VI operation such as UNAMIR.[41] UNAMIR thus found itself deployed between the French forces and one of the belligerents. Furthermore, some of the UNAMIR military who were of the same nationality as some of the troops used in Operation Turquoise, later had to be repatriated.[42]

As Larry Minear and Philippe Guillot have demonstrated, Operation Turquoise, like the US intervention Operation Support Hope of July–August 1994, as well as the military support operations of at least eight other countries,[43] took place parallel to UNAMIR's operations. These other operations were not under the command and control of UNAMIR, but were bilateral responses to the unprecedented humanitarian crisis in Rwanda and, increasingly, in Zaire. In July, the situation was the following:

> Of a total population of approximately seven million, three million persons had been displaced internally and more than two million Hutus had fled to neighbouring countries. Among those who had fled Rwanda, an outbreak of cholera had already claimed as many as 20,000 lives – and would eventually claim some 50,000. UNAMIR had already deployed a company along the border near Goma, as well as a number of observers in that region and in the zone controlled by Operation Turquoise.[44]

As the French government was keen to withdraw from Rwanda by the second half of August, it was important for UNAMIR to redeploy to the south-west, 'where armed elements of the Rwandese government forces had sought refuge in the French-protected zone'.[45] By 10 August 1994, UNAMIR's strength was at 1,257 when it began to deploy in the south-west; on 21 August, it assumed responsibility from Operation Turquoise for the protected zone.

The new 'Government of National Unity' made concerted efforts to normalize the situation, putting in place civilian structures. Longstanding Tutsi refugees returned from Burundi and Uganda, as did some Hutus, who found their property occupied by others. Inflammatory radio broadcasts continued, intended to prevent the return of Hutu refugees in Zaire. Hutus suspected as perpetrators of the April–May massacres were mingled with innocent civilians in the refugee camps in Zaire and, by some accounts, held them hostage. A UN Commission of Experts proposed a plan of action to examine grave violations of humanitarian law at the end of August. This eventually led to the establishment of an international tribunal to prosecute alleged genocide perpetrators.[46]

UNAMIR also assisted the government of Rwanda in establishing a new, integrated national police force, and began a training programme under the guidance of the UN Civilian Police (UNCIVPOL) administration. In October 1994 UNAMIR reached its authorized strength of 5,500, which was to be its maximum.

THE MEDIA ENVIRONMENT: INJURIOUS PROPAGANDA

In Rwanda, the printed press only had limited circulation. The newspapers rarely printed more than a few thousand copies of an issue, they were expensive and circulated mainly in Kigali. Literacy was approximately 50 per cent of those over the age of 15. There was relatively good access to radio in Rwanda, with about 25 per 100 persons owning a radio.[47] 'With 400,000 to 500,000 AM/FM short-wave radio receivers in homes and offices, and seven FM radio relay transmitters providing regular radio service to most of the country, it was radio that reached a broad public audience, especially the 90 per cent of the population which lived in rural areas.'[48]

According to Frank Chalk, who extensively studied the role of radio in the Rwandan genocide, the 'message of hate spread to the airwaves on 3 March 1992, when Radio Rwanda broadcast false news reports all day long stating that a leaflet issued by the Tutsi-based *Parti Libéral* had been discovered in Nairobi advocating the terrorist killing of 22 leading Hutu politicians, army officers, civil servants, priests, businessmen and lawyers.'[49] These broadcasts, according to Chalk, started another wave of killings of Tutsis.

In the summer of 1993, Radio Rwanda staff helped found the privately-owned RTML, ostensibly to counter Radio Muhabura, the RPF radio station, even though, according to Chalk, no evidence was found that the RPF station was spreading propaganda against the Hutu of Rwanda. 'Indeed, with the benefit of hindsight, it seems likely that RTML was founded to evade key clauses of the Arusha peace accords of 1993 which barred the government of Rwanda, as well as the RPF, from incitements to violence, promoting discrimination based on ethnicity, and issuing propaganda inciting the people to hate.'[50] By the end of 1993 RTML named individual Tutsi and Hutu opposed to President Habyarimana as 'enemies' or 'traitors' who deserved death. By March 1994, Radio Rwanda attributed to the RPF an ideology of 'ethnic purification' and misleadingly described the Hutu extremist party CDR (Coalition pour la Défense de la République) 'as pacifist and realistic because it recognized the ethnic problem which had been eating away at Rwanda for centuries'.[51]

The role of the local media in spreading rumours and exacerbating ethnic problems was well known to outside observers of the situation in Rwanda. The Report by the 'Special Rapporteur on extrajudicial, summary or arbitrary executions' of April 1993, for example, noted that Radio Rwanda 'has played a pernicious role in instigating several massacres' and mentioned 'certain broadcasts in Kinyarwanda which differ markedly in content from news programmes broadcast in French, which is understood only by a small part of the population'.[52] The Rapporteur, in 1993, proposed 'a reform of the role and structure of the media', including the adoption of a code of ethics and professional training for journalists.[53] Other observers of the human rights situation in Rwanda also noted that 'the encouragement of ethnic hatred on the radio, together with the creation and arming of militias, was one of the clearest early warning signs of an imminent genocide'.[54]

INTERNATIONAL MEDIA COVERAGE

International reporting of the humanitarian crisis in Rwanda between 1993 and 1994 has been the subject of a number of studies of the media's role in uncovering or preventing massacres and genocide by non-governmental organizations, concerned journalists and others dealing with the international response to humanitarian emergencies.[55] While many of them maintain that 'the presence or absence of media attention may mean life or death for affected populations',[56] detailed analyses of the impact of media reporting on policymakers by Steve Livingston, Nik Gowing and others have shown that media coverage in these crises is 'ambiguous, unclear and often misconstrued'.[57]

The situation in Rwanda in the spring and summer of 1994 is a case in point. A report published by the Danish Foreign Ministry came to the following conclusion:

> The international media played a mixed role in the Rwanda crisis. While the media were a major factor in generating worldwide humanitarian relief support for the refugees, distorted reporting on events leading to the genocide itself was a contributing factor to the failure of the international community to take more effective action to stem the genocide.[58]

While the same could be said for media reporting of other conflicts, coverage of the Rwanda crisis in the spring of 1994 was also encumbered by what some have called 'saturation reporting'. This arose from the fact that Rwanda, on the one hand, was literally in competition with the simultaneous crises in other parts of Africa (eg Sudan, Angola, Liberia and the elections in South Africa) and, on the other, that the 'shock content' of reporting on Rwanda with its powerful imagery of decomposing bodies and mass graves did not elicit the kind of response that might have led to appropriate international intervention:

TV pictures showing the slaughter of at least half a million Rwandans between April and July 1994 produced the opposite political response. Horrifying, intermittent TV images of people being hacked to death, piles of bodies and cadavers floating down rivers shocked ministers of major western governments ... But they did not lead to any *major* or *fundamental* policy change, even though senior officials – especially in the US government – like to believe it did. The international community virtually ignored the terror of Rwanda just as it chose to overlook a series of apocalyptic warnings via the UN and NGO's in late 1993 and early 1994.[59]

It was not until 800,000 Rwandans crossed the border to Zaire in July 1994 that international attention was finally focused on the situation: 'The broadcast by the world's television media of so many suffering people crammed into unliveable space, many dying from cholera due to lack of clean water, finally created the critical mass in the public consciousness.'[60] However, critics of media reporting on the Rwandan crisis such as Steve Livingston have argued that journalists only covered the 'safer medical story' in the refugee camps, two months after genocidal acts had been committed.[61] Livingston has conducted public opinion surveys of US television viewers and comes to the conclusion that only one per cent of the Americans polled in May 1994 were aware of the Rwandan crisis, while 12 per cent showed concern over the death of Richard Nixon.[62]

John Eriksson, who is the principal author of the *Synthesis Report* of the above-mentioned Danish-sponsored 'Joint Evaluation of Emergency Assistance to Rwanda', concludes that 'the overall failure of the media to report accurately and adequately on a crime against humanity significantly contributed to international disinterest in the genocide and the consequent inadequate response'.[63] At a conference in Boston assessing the role of media in covering and preventing humanitarian emergencies, Eriksson stated that Rwanda leads one to the conclusion that 'it is time for the international media to examine itself and its responsibilities'.[64]

Hammock and Charny go even further in their negative assessment of the second phase of the Rwanda relief operation (ie July–August 1994): 'The bitter irony in the case of Rwanda, however, is that the relief effort, generally portrayed as a noble success, has had the effect of strengthening the political control over the refugees of the militant Hutu faction responsible for the genocide that created the emergency.'[65] And Eriksson, who acknowledges that media attention in the second phase of the operation generated unprecedented funds for the refugees in the camps in Zaire, criticizes that 'neglect of the survivors and some instances of sub-optimal placement of relief resources reflected, in part, unbalanced and inaccurate reporting by the international media'.[66]

UNAMIR'S INFORMATION EFFORT

As in the two prior case studies on Namibia and Cambodia, the United Nations sent a survey team to the area of operations following the signing of the Arusha accords. This survey mission was led by the Force Commander-designate and it included political, military and humanitarian desk officers, and staff from the Field Administration and Logistics Division, as well as UNHCR. However, the team did not include a public information officer who might have developed a public relations strategy for the operation. 'In retrospect, the team, though well constituted, was not adequately prepared for the intricacies of the political situation in the country, a factor that contributed to a naive optimism about the entire operation.'[67] The *Synthesis Report*, too, makes the criticism that 'UNAMIR's presence contributed to a false sense of security in Rwanda'.[68]

Although a spokesman did join General Dallaire's team once it was deployed, 'the lack of an effective public information programme was a serious weakness for UNAMIR from the outset'.[69] When the violence began in April, the spokesman, Pierre Mehu, was evacuated with most other civilians. The various spokesmen sent to the mission at later stages were never able to develop an effective information programme.

There were various attempts by the UN Department of Peacekeeping Operations (DPKO) to overcome the technical and financial issues involved during the summer of 1994. A mission was dispatched by DPKO from 17–23 August 1994 to assess the requirements for radio broadcasting in support of UNAMIR operations. Both the United States and the United Kingdom missions to the UN were asked about the availability of radio transmitters and mobile audio production equipment, discussions which continued through September and October 1994.[70]

UNAMIR did not acquire a capacity to communicate the mission's mandate or, for that matter, its constraints, until February 1995, when it finally set up its own radio station. By then, the information team was composed of three professional journalists, one UN volunteer and local staff. It broadcast for four hours daily and in three languages.[71] Its operation, according to the then Special Representative of the Secretary-General, was 'a great success' and it continued until UNAMIR ceased operations.[72]

Apparently it had great credibility with international radio broadcasters who cited it as a source in their newscasts. While based in Kigali and operating in a minimally equipped production and broadcast studio, the station had five FM transmitters and was able to reach the refugee camps in the border region. Programmes included international and local news, interviews, reports on conditions in the country and features touching on the work of UNAMIR and other UN agencies. Topics covered included refugee security, human rights, the justice system, health and education.[73]

The subject of UNAMIR's radio programme had, from the autumn of 1994 onwards, become an area of concern for the Security Council. It was mentioned in statements by the President of the Council in October 1994 and February 1995, as well as in Security Council Resolution 965 of 30 November 1994.[74] At that time, RTLM was still operating and reaching Hutu refugees in the camps, effectively discouraging them from returning to their homes, while the Security Council's main concern was the return of just those refugees. By the time the UN was finally able to set up its own radio programme 15 months after the mission was deployed and ten months after the genocide had been perpetrated, the damage had already been done.[75]

Hate broadcasts continued in 1995 and 1996. So influential were they, that they became a subject of discussion by the Conference of Heads of State of the Great Lakes Region who, on 29 November 1995, declared in Cairo that they 'viewed with deep concern the use of radio broadcasts to spread hate and fear in the region'. They pledged 'to take all possible action to terminate the illegal and inflammatory broadcasts from one country into another'.[76]

THE ISSUE OF JAMMING HATE RADIO

UNAMIR's first Force Commander (who served in Rwanda from 1993 until August 1994) has publicly stated that UNAMIR should have been given the capacity to jam the radio frequencies of RTLM to prevent Hutu extremists from further inciting violence, massacres and genocide. In fact, General Dallaire said that, had he had such a capability, he would have been able to prevent some of the crimes against humanity perpetrated by the Hutu extremists.[77] This argument has been taken up by a number of commentators, human rights activists and students of genocide. The Canadian historian Frank Chalk, in a series of studies on hate radio, has stated that, when General Dallaire asked for the capability to jam RTML hate broadcasts, he was denied it by both the UN Secretariat and the Canadian government.[78]

Another position on jamming is that of Jeffery Heyman, UNPROFOR Radio Unit Head, who visited UNAMIR in August 1994:

> The jamming of broadcasts of Radio Mille Collines, or any other radio station no matter how offensive the broadcasts, should not be undertaken by the United Nations. The jamming option was considered for use in Cambodia against a Khmer Rouge clandestine radio station which was calling for violence against ethnic Vietnamese. Wisely, jamming was rejected as being too politically explosive.[79]

Elsewhere in that report, Heyman recommends that 'establishing a UN radio station in Rwanda ... is much preferable to ... jamming Radio Mille Collines, which could be interpreted as political censorship ...'[80] Heyman, however, questioned the very legality of an UNAMIR radio, even though UNAMIR was by then operating under a Chapter Vll mandate: 'This alone may not be sufficient to mandate radio broadcasting in Rwanda'.[81] Another consultant visitor to UNAMIR, Nicholas Harman, advised just a few months later that 'UN peacekeeping mandates provide in many ways for overriding national laws ... peacekeeping mandates should incorporate the right to install and use broadcasting equipment. ... The UN must control its own broadcasting resources, and protect them against political or criminal interference'.[82]

While these reports may or may not reflect policy, they do show that there was a recognition of the need for a policy, and that the issue was and is possibly more complex and far reaching than a singular reaction to a given emergency, no matter how severe. It is also appropriate in this regard to recall the UN's historical experience in the Congo, as it, too, has a clear bearing on the organization's general approach to peacekeeping radio operations. The 'Congo-legacy' is well described by Brian Urquhart, who was political adviser to four Secretaries-General of the UN. Urquhart, in his biography *Hammarskjold*, relates the serious consequences of the decision of Hammarskjold's Special Representative in the Congo operation in September 1960 to close the airfields, and the Leopoldville radio station, to stop 'incitements of the population, especially of rival youth groups'.[83] Among the political consequences of this step, which, incidentally, did not have the prior approval of the Secretary-General or the Security Council, was a rupture in the relationship between the Secretary-General and the Permanent Delegation of the USSR, which marred Hammarskjold's last year in office. The effect of the 'Congo legacy' on the decisionmakers in the UN Secretariat in the mid-90s cannot be under-estimated.

It will be recalled that one of the main findings of the case studies on Namibia and Cambodia was the importance of cohesive, consistent political leadership by the Special Representative of the Secretary-General (SRSG) and, related to that, a minimum of friction between the top political and military staff.

UNAMIR had two Special Representatives of the Secretary-General between 1993 and 1995. The first one was Jaques-Roger Booh-Booh of Cameroon, a former Foreign Minister and personal friend of the Secretary-General, while the second was Shaharyar Khan of Pakistan, who arrived in Kigali on 4 July 1994. Mr Booh-Booh clearly did not make his presence felt in the Rwandan peace process. First of all, he arrived in the mission area in November 1993, one month after the advance team led by the Force Commander was deployed. The 'Lessons Learned Unit' of DPKO, in its 1996 assessment, stated: 'Consequently, unnecessary tensions impaired coordination efforts at the beginning.'[84] Once the Arusha accords had begun to unravel, the SRSG's position eroded even further, as a 'Lessons Learned Report' of the UN Department of Humanitarian Affairs noted:

> In the Rwandan context the impotence, or perceived impotence, of the SRSG's office is compounded by a lack of understanding of how the UN operates (ie in the sense of the real limitations inherent in the role of a SRSG who tries to act but cannot operate as a Pro-Consul or Lord Viceroy) and by the obvious need to quickly forge ahead and generate the conditions vital for peace.[85]

Mr Booh-Booh was in no position to do either, and he was further hampered by a lack of experience in the UN system. Donini and Niland recommend: 'The Rwandan experience highlights the importance of the SRSG having clearly defined Terms of Reference and being fully familiar with UN system mandates and capabilities.'[86]

The Department of Peacekeeping Operations report addresses the issue of coordination from a different vantage point:

> In a situation as fluid and chaotic as Rwanda during the civil war in 1994, coordination between the peacekeeping mission and the

United Nations agencies in a mission area is perhaps the greatest information challenge. There is no easy solution to the problem of proliferating 'spokesmen' cited by the press. The starting point must be an understanding among all United Nations agencies and offices of the central role of the SRSG and his information staff in managing any public information that has political implications. This is equally true for military public information personnel. Agency and military spokesmen can be relied upon for information about their particular area of expertise, while the SRSG and the mission's civilian spokesman should be at the centre of the United Nations system's public information efforts in the field.[87]

This role, while performed without difficulty in Namibia by Mr Ahtisaari and with few areas of disagreement between the civilian and military leadership in Cambodia by Mr Akashi, was clearly not performed by Mr Booh-Booh at the height of the crisis in Rwanda. As described above, the most forceful personality in the mission area in the spring of 1994 was General Romeo Dallaire, who has, on many occasions, made his own devastating assessment of forces beyond his control.[88] When Shaharyar Khan arrived in Kigali in July 1994, the worst was over. He cooperated well with the military component of UNAMIR and received high praise from the civilian staff working with him in this mission.[89]

ASSESSMENT AND CONCLUSIONS

The sheer number of post-mission evaluations and 'lessons-learned' reports that have been prepared on the UN Rwanda mission indicate that this was an operation fraught with problems. The primary problem was geopolitical, in that the community of states, as assembled in the UN Security Council at that time – in the winter and spring of 1993–94 – was preoccupied with other, more pressing issues, foremost among them Bosnia.[90] While there was no lack of 'early warning' from human rights and humanitarian aid organizations about this looming African disaster, Rwanda occupied a very low priority on the agenda of states.

Another factor was that some countries, in particular the United States, had learned lessons from Somalia and had, with Presidential Decision Directive 25, decided on a form of disengagement from conflicts in Africa in particular, and from peacekeeping in civil war environments in general.[91] The role of the international media was, as we have seen, also unfortunate, in that it gave the wrong messages to the world public in reporting the nature of the Rwandan conflict.

UNAMIR was, as General Dallaire has argued, a mission done on the cheap, with all the unfortunate consequences so often attendant on half-hearted measures. Furthermore, events in early April 1994 and the unilateral withdrawal of the Belgian contingent also illustrated Fen Osler Hampson's argument about the importance of 'the staying power of third parties'. This was, in the case of Rwanda, strikingly absent. Both the regional and the international support for the Arusha accords was ephemeral, and as soon as lives of peacekeepers were lost, the military component of UNAMIR was reduced to the point of inoperability.

The information programme of UNAMIR finally came into being in the form of Radio UNAMIR, fully 15 months after the mission was first launched. The information challenge on the other hand, was greater than any other encountered by the UN in a peacekeeping environment, due to the pernicious effect of the hate radio RTML.

It appears that political, military and legal considerations prevailed in the United Nations when considering the possibility of jamming the radio broadcasts. The issue was given consideration by a number of countries with the necessary capabilities in the summer and autumn of 1994 and again, two years later, by members of the Security Council when confronted with similar problems in Burundi.[92] However, the issues of 'Propaganda for Peace' raised by the more interventionist advocates of jamming,[93] are countermanded by the arguments of those who either fear the infringement of freedom of the press or are concerned about other adverse consequences of using Chapter VII [of the UN Charter] radio.[94]

The Congo legacy notwithstanding, the more robust rules of engagement in a peace enforcement mission still deserve consideration. UNAMIR was compelled always to operate in a 'Chapter VI' mode, while confronted with a situation more complex and dangerous than anything the UN had encountered since the Congo. That discrepancy contributed greatly to the tragedy of UNAMIR. It was also a major source of unrealistic expectations at that time, and gave rise also to numerous *post-facto* criticisms of the operation.

In summary, the six operational principles identified in Chapter 1 above were not applied in the crucial early months of UNAMIR: it was a mission without a voice of its own at the crisis point. Especially the second principle, that international and local opinion will interact to create images which will influence the process, is particularly powerfully demonstrated in this case study. The discussion of the significance and the legitimacy of radio in peacekeeping missions has been stimulated beyond the heretofore accepted dogma by the UNAMIR experience. The proactive use of radio by peacekeepers in a hostile environment is a theme which will certainly be much discussed in future operations.

NOTES

1. See Larry Minear and Philippe Guillot, *Soldiers to the Rescue – Humanitarian Lessons from Rwanda*, Paris: Development Centre of the Organization for Economic Cooperation and Development, 1996, Chapter 3: The Rwanda Context.
2. Ibid., p.54.
3. *The Blue Helmets – A Review of United Nations Peacekeeping* (3rd edn), New York: United Nations, 1996, Chapter 16, p.341.
4. Among the exiles, only those Banyarwanda living in Zaire formed a single group, regardless of the Hutu/Tutsi divide. 'Throughout these years, Rwandan refugees across the Great Lakes diaspora constituted a major threat to regional security.' Minear/Guillot (n.1 above), p.55. A report by the 'Human Rights Watch Arms Project', *Arming Rwanda – The Arms Trade and Human Rights Abuses in the Rwandan War* (New York, Jan. 1994) argues that Banyarwanda living in North America and Europe funded arms acquisitions for the Rwandese Patriotic Front in Uganda (p.21).
5. Minear and Guillot (n.1 above), p.56.
6. *Arming Rwanda* (n.4 above), p.5. This report by 'Human Rights Watch' presents documents concerning a $6 million arms sale to Rwanda by Egypt, a $5.9 million arms purchase from South Africa, as well as arms purchases from France. The investigators also found 'a high degree of institutional complicity between Uganda and the RPF', and 'credible evidence that the Ugandan government allowed the RPF to move arms, logistical supplies and troops across Ugandan soil, and provided direct military support to the RPF in the form of arms, ammunition, and military equipment' (p.21).
7. Ibid., pp.27 and 28.
8. *The Blue Helmets* (n.3 above), p.342.
9. Ibid., p.343.
10. Ibid., p.345.
11. Minear and Guillot (n.1 above), p.58.
12. *The Blue Helmets* (n.3 above), p.345.
13. *The Blue Helmets* (n.3 above), p.346 maintains that the causes of the crash were unknown; Minear and Guillot state that the plane 'was shot down by ground-to-air missile' (n.1 above, p.58). Matthew Vaccaro, based on a report by Francois Misser, maintains that the Presidential airplane 'was hit by two missiles fired from the military camp at Kanombe, which was controlled by the Presidential Guard'. The Presidential Guard then established road blocks that prevented UNAMIR from reaching the airport to investigate the crash. J. Matthew Vaccaro, 'The Politics of Genocide: Peacekeeping and Disaster Relief in Rwanda', in William J. Durch (ed.), *UN Peacekeeping, American Policy, and the Uncivil Wars of the 1990s*, New York: St Martin's Press, 1996, p.373.
14. Minear and Guillot (n.1 above), p.58.
15. Ibid., p.60.
16. J.-P. Chretien, 'Un nazisme tropical', *Libération*, 26 April 1994. Hutu ideologues and activists believed Tutsis to be Hamitic invaders who had reduced Hutus to slavery several

centuries ago and whose return to power had to be prevented by any means.

17. Vaccaro (n.13 above), p.371.
18. *Arming Rwanda* (n.4 above), and *The United Nations and Rwanda, 1993–1996*, the United Nations Blue Book series, Vol.X, New York: United Nations.
19. Minear and Guillot (n.1 above), p.75.
20. *Comprehensive Report on Lessons Learned from United Nations Assistance Mission for Rwanda (UNAMIR), Oct. 1993–April 1996*, Lessons Learned Unit, Department of Peacekeeping Operations, United Nations, New York, Dec. 1996.
21. See Nik Gowing, 'Media Coverage: Help or Hindrance for Conflict Prevention', Carnegie Commission on Preventing Deadly Conflict, New York, 1996, pp.20–1.
22. Secretary-General Boutros Boutros-Ghali, Farewell Address to the General Assembly, UN Press Release SG/SM/6133, 17 Dec. 1996.
23. Victoria K. Holt, *Briefing Book on Peacekeeping – The US Role in United Nations Peace Operations*, Washington, DC: Council for a Livable World Education Fund, 1995, pp.17–19. 'When the conflict in Rwanda escalated in the spring of 1994 and the ongoing peace operation there was expanded, some critics blamed the long delay in organizing a UN response on an American hesitancy to endorse the mission or commit troops to the operation' (p.19).
24. *Comprehensive Report on Lessons Learned from UNAMIR* (n.20 above), p.22.
25. Major-General Romeo Dallaire, *Jane's Defence Weekly*, 15 April 1995.
26. *Comprehensive Report on Lessons Learned from UNAMIR* (n.20 above), p.23.
27. Minear and Guillot (n.1 above), p.76.
28. *Comprehensive Report on Lessons Learned from UNAMIR* (n.20 above), pp.24–5.
29. Minear and Guillot (n.1 above), pp 74–82.
30. *The Blue Helmets* (n.3 above), p.348.
31. Major-General Romeo Dallaire and Captain Bruce Poulin, 'Rwanda: From Peace Agreement to Genocide', *Canadian Defence Quarterly*, 24/3, March 1995, p.9.
32. Minear and Guillot (n.1 above), p.78.
33. Ibid., p.82.
34. Ibid., based on 1993 interview with MacNeil.
35. *The Blue Helmets* (n.3 above), p.350.
36. *Comprehensive Report on Lessons Learned from UNAMIR* (n.20 above), p.25.
37. Ibid., p.351.
38. Minear and Guillot (n.1 above), p.181.
39. Romeo Dallaire, in a presentation to the Pearson Peacekeeping Training Centre in Nova Scotia on 23 Oct. 1995.
40. *Comprehensive Report on Lessons Learned from UNAMIR* (n.20 above), p.25.
41. An enforcement mission, authorized under Chapter VII of the Charter of the UN, will have a different structure and Rules of Engagement, and a different concept of the consent issue, than will a peacekeeping mission, authorized under Chapter VI of the Charter. The two forces are not interchangeable and a given force cannot exchange its roles. This point was made very forcefully by Lt. Gen. Sir Michael Rose when, as UN Commander in Bosnia Hercegovina, he coined the term 'mission creep'.
42. General Dallaire, in *Canadian Defence Quarterly* (n.31 above), p.11, said that 90 staff officers whose countries had joined the French coalition, had to be released.
43. Minear and Guillot (n.1 above), pp.111–44, describe the US operation, as well as other countries' supportive military activities, many of them associated with requests from the UN High Commissioner for Refugees: Canada, the Netherlands, Japan,

Germany, New Zealand, Australia, Israel, Ireland, and the European Community. As Minear and Guillot mention, 'their point of contact with the UN system was UNHCR rather than UNAMIR' (p.142).

44. *The Blue Helmets* (n.3 above), p.353.
45. Ibid., p.354.
46. Ibid., p.359.
47. United States Information Agency, Bureau of Broadcasting, Office of Strategic Planning, *Report on the Mass Media Climate in Sub-Saharan Africa*, Washington, DC: USIA, 1995, pp.111–12.
48. Frank Chalk, 'Hate Radio in Rwanda'. Unpublished manuscript made available by Prof. Chalk, Montreal Institute for Genocide and Human Rights and Dept. of History, Concordia University, Montreal, Canada, p.3.
49. Ibid.
50. Ibid., p.4. According to Chalk, RTML's broadcasting studios were connected to the electric generators of the Presidential Palace. RTML programmes were relayed to all parts of the country via a network of transmitters owned and operated by the government-owned Radio Rwanda.
51. Ibid., p.5. According to Chalk, broadcasts of Radio Rwanda and RTML were monitored 'sporadically' by the BBC and the US Foreign Broadcast Information Service, but 'no one has published complete transcripts of RTML's and Radio Rwanda's broadcasts'. The excerpts from RTML and Radio Rwanda are cited by Chalk.
52. 'Report by the Special Rapporteur on extrajudicial, summary or arbitrary executions on his mission to Rwanda', 8–17 April 1993, reproduced in *The United Nations and Rwanda* (n.18 above), p.210. The Rapporteur also found that 'the two different language versions of reports of the press conference he had given in order to put an end to rumours concerning the objectives of his mission contradicted each other'.
53. Ibid., p.211.
54. Frank Chalk, 'Hate Radio versus Democracy Radio: Lessons from United Nations and United States Experiences in Cambodia, Mozambique, Rwanda, and Somalia' (n.48 above), p.9, based on testimony by Alison DesForges, Human Rights Watch/Africa, in US Congress, second session, 1994.
55. Among the leaders in these efforts are the International Centre for Humanitarian reporting (Boston/Geneva) and its publication *Crosslines-Global Report*, the 'Humanitarianism and War Project' at Brown University, Providence, Rhode Island, the Carnegie Commission on Preventing Deadly Conflict in New York, and analyses done by staff of the UN Department of Humanitarian Affairs in New York, in particular, Antonio Donini and Norah Niland, 'Rwanda: Lessons Learned. A Report on the Coordination of Humanitarian Activities', DHA, New York, 1994.
56. Fred Cate, 'Communications, Policy-Making, and Humanitarian Crises', in Robert I. Rotberg and Thomas G. Weiss (eds), *From Massacres to Genocide, The Media, Public Policy and Humanitarian Crises*, Washington, DC: Brookings, 1996, p.18.
57. Gowing (n.21 above), p.1. See also the excellent empirical/analytical articles by Steve Livingston, in particular Steven Livingston, *US Television Coverage of Rwanda*, Washington DC: The George Washington School of Media and Public Affairs, 1996 (unpublished manuscript).
58. *The International Response to Conflict and Genocide: Lessons Learned from the Rwanda Experience* (Steering Committee of Emergency Assistance to Rwanda, Ministry of Foreign Affairs, Denmark, 1996), Vol.2, p.66.

59. Gowing (n.21 above), pp.20–1 (emphasis in original).
60. John C. Hammock and Joel R. Charny, 'Emergency Response as Morality Play: The Media, the Relief Agencies, and the Need for Capacity Building', in Rotberg and Weiss (n.56 above), p.122.
61. Steve Livingston, 'Media and policy decisions in Rwanda', presentation at a conference in Boston, Massachusetts: 'Lifeline Media: Weapons of War, Tools of Peace', organized by the *International Centre for Humanitarian Reporting*, 4–6 April 1997.
62. Ibid.
63. *The International Response to Conflict and Genocide* (n.58 above), Vol.5: *Synthesis Report*, p.20.
64. John Eriksson, in his presentation at the Conference 'Lifeline Media', referred to in n.61, on 5 April 1997.
65. Hammock and Charny (n.60 above), p.123.
66. *Synthesis Report* (n.63 above), p.66.
67. *Comprehensive Report on Lessons Learned from UNAMIR* (n.20 above), p.5.
68. *Synthesis Report* (n.63 above), pp.19–20. The report adds that UNAMIR lacked a 'formal capacity for collecting intelligence; nevertheless, UNAMIR, through the initiatives of both the Canadian Force Commander and the Belgian Kigali-sector Commander, succeeded in running minimalist, if irregular, intelligence operations'. (p.21).
69. *Comprehensive Report* (n.20 above), p.13.
70. Information received from Mr. Chuck Williamson, OASD, Department of Defence, Washington, DC in June 1996.
71. *The Blue Helmets* (n.3 above), p.357 and information received from Patricia Tome, UNAMIR radio officer in June 1996. Patricia Tome, who had been instrumental in getting Radio UNTAC going, had also had a brief stint in Bosnia and is, as of March 1997, Spokeswoman of UNMIH in Haiti. She has written an assessment of her experience in Rwanda, 'Radio MINUAR, un pari difficile, un succes inachevée' (unpublished manuscript, DPI, New York) The languages in which UNAMIR Radio broadcast were Kinyarwanda, French and English.
72. Information received from Lena Yamacopoulou of the UN Radio Section, UN New York, in March 1997 and from Fred Schottler of the Peace and Security Programmes section, DPI/UN on 10 April 1997.
73. Information received from Fred Schottler on 21 April 1997.
74. S/PRST/1994/59 of 14 Oct. 1994, states: 'The Security Council stresses the importance it attaches to UNAMIR having an effective broadcasting service to provide objective information. It hopes that the Government of Rwanda will assist in enabling the proposed United Nations radio station to come into operation as soon as possible.' Security Council Resolution of 30 Nov. 1994 (S/RES/965) in para.5, 'welcomes UNAMIR's efforts to increase its radio broadcasting capabilities so as to reach the refugee camps in neighbouring countries and expresses the hope that it will soon be possible for the Government of Rwanda to conclude appropriate arrangements with UNAMIR in this regard, including the allocation of a radio frequency.' As late as 10 Feb. 1995, the President of the Council felt it necessary to stress 'the importance of UNAMIR Radio commencing its broadcasts as soon as possible' (S/PRST/1995/7, para.4).
75. This is not underestimate the importance of Radio UNAMIR during its 13 months of operation. In fact, UNAMIR, in its second phase, continued to encounter many difficulties, including the denial of freedom of movement by the RPA, searches and seizures of its vehicles, and anti-UNAMIR demonstrations. *The Blue Helmets* (n.3 above),

p.360 reports that in March 1995, 'Radio Rwanda initiated a virulent propaganda campaign against UNAMIR'. UNAMIR radio during this period was an important 'force multiplier'.

76. 'Declaration of the Conference on the Great Lakes Region', signed in Cairo on 29 Nov. 1995, by the Heads of State of Burundi, Rwanda, Uganda, the United Republic of Tanzania and Zaire, with the former President Jimmy Carter as facilitator (S/1995/1001) reproduced in *The United Nations and Rwanda* (n.18 above), p.601.

77. General Romeo Dallaire, Interview in *Jane's Defence Weekly*, 15 April 1995, and in presentations at the Pearson Peacekeeping Centre, Oct. 1995.

78. Chalk (n.48 above), pp.10–11. I have, however, been unable to corroborate this statement, as no further information was received from the UN Secretariat or the office of General Dallaire in response to my requests.

79. Jeffery Heyman, *Report on a mission to UNAMIR concerning the establishment of a United Nations radio station in Rwanda*, 1994 (unpublished report), p.25.

80. Ibid., p.11.

81. Ibid., p.13. Heyman goes on to say that 'although UNPROFOR operates under Chapter VII, there is nothing in its mandate allowing radio broadcasting'. He cites UNTAC as having a mandate from the Security Council which specifically directed the establishment of a radio broadcast facility.

82. Nicholas Harman, *Information in Rwanda*, (unpublished consultant's report), New York, 31 Oct. 1994. Harman also had some interesting observations on the value of openness and trust, citing the 'remarkable relationship established with the media by the military spokesman: ... his ... presence, ... familiarity with the local situation, and his apparent frankness, won him trust; his policy of helping journalists ... won him gratitude'. The officer referred to is Major Jean-Guy Plante, a Canadian Military Police officer, who had no training or experience as an information or press staff officer.

83. Brian Urquhart, *Hammarskjold*, New York: Harper and Row, 1972, p.445.

84. *Comprehensive Report on Lessons Learned from UNAMIR* (n.20 above), p.8.

85. 'Rwanda: Lessons Learned: A Report on the Coordination of Humanitarian Activities' prepared for the United Nations Department of Humanitarian Affairs by Antonio Donini and Norah Niland, New York: Nov. 1994, p.11.

86. Ibid., p.12.

87. *Comprehensive Report* (n.20 above), p.13.

88. General Dallaire, in conversations at the Pearson Peacekeeping Training Centre in 1995, commented to the author that his experience in Rwanda had led him to the general conclusion that there are political forces that do not wish the United Nations to succeed.

89. Information received from Patricia Tome (n.71 above). In Aug. 1994 Major General Dallaire was replaced by Major General Tousignant, also of Canada.

90. For just two examples: The notorious mortar attack on the Markale Market in Sarajevo occurred on 5 Feb. 1994; on 10 April NATO launched the first live attack in its history, which was in support of a United Nations force, with the airstrikes on Bosnian Serb positions around Gorazde.

91. Having said this, the next Chapter, on the US-led mission in Haiti, which was launched only a few months later, namely in Sept. 1994, will be of interest. It has been argued that the reason the US was amenable to the number of short-term non-UN military assistance missions in Rwanda in the summer and fall of 1994 was that it wished to take similar action in Haiti, as did Russia in the case of Georgia (see Minear/Guillot, n.1 above).

92. Information received from a Senior Political Affairs Officer of the UN Department of Peacekeeping Operations in New York in May 1996.

93. See, for example, Keith Spicer, 'Propaganda for Peace', *New York Times*, 10 Dec. 1994.

94. Lena Yacoumopoulou, a thoughtful and experienced UN radio officer, suggests that 'chances are very strong that the warring factions would, in the same manner that they have been blocking humanitarian convoys, attempt to block the transmission of the UN's radio broadcasts'. Lena Yacoumopoulou, in an unpublished reply to Spicer, dated 12 Dec. 1994 and made available to the author.

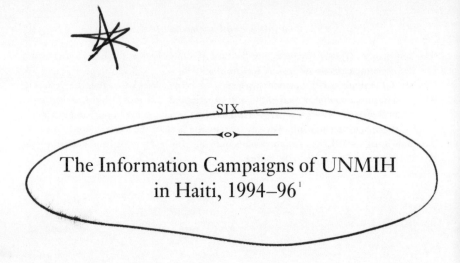

SIX

The Information Campaigns of UNMIH in Haiti, 1994–96[1]

PEACEKEEPING UNDER CONDITIONS OF ANARCHY

In a number of ways, the following case study of three different phases of peacekeeping missions in Haiti provides a testing ground for the principles of communication and information management outlined in Chapter 1. Peacekeeping in Haiti is analysed as a case study of 'peacekeeping under conditions of anarchy'.[2]

As we have seen in the case studies of the operations in Cambodia and Rwanda, both of which might also have been described as 'failed states', operations in such environments require farreaching public information and education campaigns. Given its legacy of the non-intervention in internal affairs of member states, the UN was initially reluctant to use the term 'failed state'. The invocation of such a term would imply a requirement for intrastate intervention, a mode of operation heretofore foreign to UN philosophies and experience.[3]

However, the term 'failed state' has now become accepted in the UN's own publications, such as the 1996 edition of *The Blue Helmets*, which categorizes failed states as 'new dilemmas' and 'challenges' to be met. What has not yet been formally accepted is that operations in such countries bring with them new communication challenges as well. In practice, as we have seen in the last three case studies, information campaigns to support democratic elections, strengthen human rights regimes, curb authoritarian abuses of power, encourage civic responsibility and help legitimize civilian police and legal authorities were included in most recent operations. The case of Haiti will show how such campaigns were vital in supporting emerging democratic structures and helped counteract social disintegration and anarchic violence.

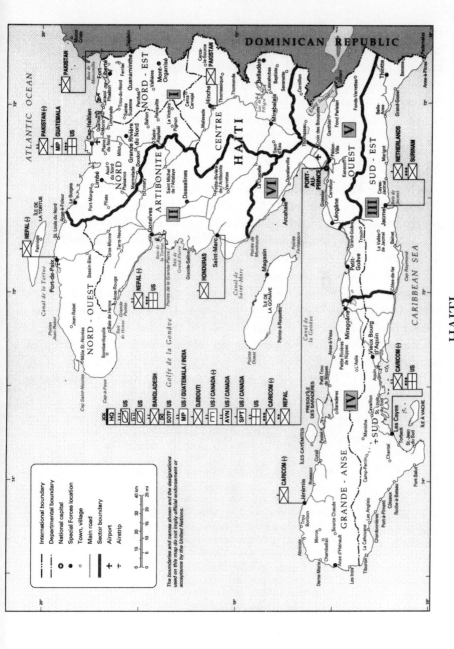

HAITI

UNMIH deployment as of November 1995 (map no. 3952.33 (UNMIH) reproduced with the permission of the Cartographic Section, Department of Public Information, United Nations)

UN'S INFORMATION COMPONENTS

In many respects, the various United Nations Mission in Haiti (UNMIH) information components resembled those of other recent peacekeeping missions in the Western hemisphere, as for example, those in the smaller and not much publicized UN operations in Central America.[5] In UNMIH, they consisted of the office of a civilian Spokesman, military Public Information Officer(s), and a civilian police Public Information Officer (PIO).

The Spokesman

The first UNMIH Spokesman, Eric Falt, was on the ground in Port-au-Prince in 1994 before any of the UN military contingents were deployed and he continued to occupy this post until 1997. He arrived in Haiti after the closure of UNTAC in Cambodia where he also acted as civilian spokesman for the mission. He thus had the advantage of prior peacekeeping and public information experience and worked in the mission during all the three phases analysed. As a French national with excellent English, and his prior experience in Cambodia and New York, he was well prepared for the job. Having been in the country longer than any of the other UN senior staff, he maintained a distinct advantage due to his knowledge of local cultures, traditions and understanding of the media scene.[6] The organisation of the civilian UNMIH 'Integrated Press and Information Office' is contained in *Figure 1* below:

THE INTEGRATED PRESS AND INFORMATION OFFICE

Spokesperson/Head of Public Information*
Deputy Head*
Information Assistant*
Research Assistant**
Administrative Assistant**
Information Assistant for radio and print media**
Information Assistant for TV**
Clerk/Driver

Military Public Information Officer*
Assistant Military Public Information Officers (2)*

Civilian Police Public Information Officer*

(*International Staff ** Local Hire)

Figure 1

Military Public Information Officers

UNMIH military public information officers changed frequently. In fact, 'the mission had three separate sets of military public information officers in one year'.[7] Until February 1996, they were collocated with the civilian information officers and the CIVPOL PIO. However, as of March 1996, Major Marc Rouleau of Canada, an experienced press officer with prior service in Bosnia, was appointed Military Public Information Officer (MPIO) and moved into the Operations branch of UNMIH. Major Rouleau[8] reported directly to the Force Commander, General Pierre Daigle, although he described his 'division of labour' with the civilian spokesman, Eric Falt, and the civilian police PIO to be quite effective.[9] *Figure 2* shows the organogram provided by Major Rouleau in May 1996:

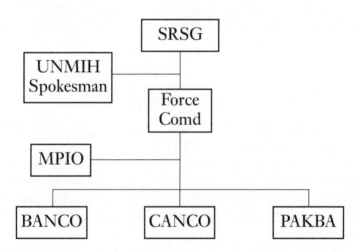

Figure 2

CIVPOL Information Officers

From the outset, the civilian police contingent was a vital part of UNMIH; CIVPOL arrived in Haiti with the UN Advance Team on 5 October 1994. Immediately, a bilingual (French/English) information officer was appointed to work with the Spokesman, Mr Falt. Their main task was to overcome the image of the former Haitian Security Forces as symbols of terror and oppression. The training of the new Haitian police by CIVPOL was accompanied by an information campaign to rebuild the image of the new Haitian National Police officers.[10] Tri-lingual (French, English and Creole) posters and handbills were produced and distributed by UNMIH urging the populace to support the police and the criminal justice system.

MEDIA SERVICES

During the period under review, there were approximately 350 journalists accredited to UNMIH. Only about 30 per cent of them were international correspondents, and many of those were on shortterm assignments. The rest were stringers and local reporters. The UNMIH press office kept track of all media visits, ensured they were *bona fide* and decided which journalists got to see what and with which contingent in the field.[11]

The various information officers provided information on Haiti and UNMIH for members of the press and other official visitors. This included facts and figures on military and police deployments and current activities, the chronology of events related to the UN's tasks, information on electoral and criminal justice issues, the status of civil affairs projects, etc. Once a week, on average, press briefings were held and, in addition, interviews were given by the senior staff of UNMIH on a case-by-case basis. The former Special Representative of the Secretary-General, Mr Lakhdar Brahimi, practised 'judicious media exposure' and favoured 'a policy of openness towards the media'.[12]

NEWS ANALYSIS

The press office routinely analysed the reporting in the local media, and it provided this information to UNMIH senior officials and the spokesperson of the Secretary-General in New York. The mission information staff is thus expected to alert UN Headquarters in case of serious incidents reported in the media. In this way, it can provide key off-the-record information that can contribute to a better understanding of the situation in Haiti in New York and elsewhere.

The *UNMIH Journal*, published twice a month in English and French, served primarily mission-internal information needs by giving updates on policy changes and new developments, as well as news stories on civil affairs projects in the country. Its purpose was to encourage an *esprit de corps* and to inform UN personnel of activities within UNMIH and within other Haiti-based UN agencies and non-governmental organizations.

Twice a month, a 30-minute TV programme *Espace Bleu* was broadcast free of charge on five Haitian stations. UNMIH furthermore provided items for inclusion in UN radio programmes in New York for worldwide distribution.

However, as the Mid-Mission Assessment Report of the Lessons-Learned Unit stated, cooperation and communication between the Mission's information staff and the Department of Public Information (DPI) in New York was 'generally poor, despite the fact that UNMIH is of interest to audiences in Latin America, the Caribbean and the United States'.[13] The lack of consultation and cooperation between the information component of UNMIH and DPI in New York was particularly criticized in connection with a video documentary on UNMIH which was not adequately promoted or distributed.[14]

MILITARY INFORMATION SUPPORT TEAMS

The most innovative component of UNMIH's information programme was the evolution of Military Information Support Teams (MIST). The development of MIST through the various stages of UNMIH provides the main body of this case study and is described in detail on p.119 below. Before doing so, we will need to look at the political leadership of the mission at the time of the introduction of MIST.

As in the UN peacekeeping operations in Namibia and Cambodia, effective political leadership was a vital factor in UNMIH. In Haiti, the Special Representative of the Secretary-General, Lakhdar Brahimi, and his Deputy, Christian Ossa, had extensive experience in the United Nations.[15] Mr Brahimi, who previously headed the United Nations Observer Mission in South Africa, was convinced that it is 'essential to establish an integrated and effective public information operation'. As a consequence, the UN's Lessons-Learned Unit concluded that UNMIH succeeded 'in projecting a unified image' and 'has not suffered from conflicting or contradictory pronouncements, or from unauthorized or unattributed off the record comments to the media by mission personnel'.[16] Mission-internal co-operation and the issue of political control of messages emanating from the mission thus appeared to be functioning well in the period under review.

However, this did not mean that the political and the military leadership necessarily always agreed on the conduct of the mission,[17] but the primacy of political leadership in this peacekeeping operation was established. UNMIH did, on the whole, demonstrate that its overall information effort was integrated and that the information components were seen by the leadership of the mission as a vital strategic management function of the operation. For example, it institutionalized a 'product approval process' which required vetting of all print materials by the Special Representative of the Secretary-General, which meant that Mr Brahimi cleared the messages communicated by the Military Information Support Teams.

THE HAITIAN PUBLIC

The terms 'public', 'public opinion' and 'public perceptions' are much debated among political scientists and communications specialists, particularly when dealing with issues of foreign and security policy and the shaping of opinions on international issues.[18] 'Public opinion' is even more elusive when applied to constituencies and audiences in developing nations, such as in Haiti.

A distinction has been made between elite audiences and the mass public, the latter constituting the great majority of the population. These distinctions, even a few years ago, might have been moot in a country such as Haiti which was governed by a series of dictators without constitutional or popular legitimacy. This situation changed when preparations began for free and fair elections in the early 1990s. Suddenly, it began to matter which issues were of concern to the masses.

A large percentage of the Haitian population is illiterate, unemployment figures are as high as 70 per cent and per capita income continues to be the lowest in the Western hemisphere. In 1991, infant mortality was 137 per thousand and only 50 per cent of the population had access to rudimentary health services. Paul Farmer says: 'As is often the case in settings characterized by extreme structural violence, a certain amount of political violence – usually state-sponsored – was part of the picture for decades.'[19]

The situation is further compounded by the fact that opinion in Haiti is formed rapidly, through a system of word-of-mouth – in Creole, *tele-guele*;[20] rumours are given more credence than in other countries and are more difficult to dispel once they take hold. For a number of historic reasons,[21] public officials in general do not enjoy a high degree of respect, a fact that has impeded the creation of a trustworthy, and trusted, police force.

These factors made the tasks for multinational personnel charged with helping 'to maintain a safe and secure environment', and sustaining confidence in the democratic process, exceedingly difficult. There was a distinct lack of trust in international organizations and in the United States which had, in the eyes of many Haitians, failed to respond adequately to the overthrow of its first democratically elected President. This naturally compounded the communication problems with the Haitian 'public' when the multinational force finally was deployed to 'uphold democracy' in September 1994.[22]

OPERATION 'UPHOLD DEMOCRACY'

As authorized by UN Security Council Resolution 940 of 31 July 1994, the US and other multinational forces were deployed in September 1994 under Chapter VII of the UN Charter to 'use all necessary means to facilitate the departure from Haiti of the military leadership, the prompt return of the legitimately elected President and the restoration of the legitimate authorities of the Government of Haiti, and to establish and maintain a secure and stable environment that will permit implementation of the Governors Island Agreement …'[23] This resolution was the cornerstone of subsequent peace-keeping operations in Haiti.

The multinational force under US leadership (MNF) landed in Haiti on 19 September 1994 without encountering any resistance. The military leadership left Haiti on 14 October and President Aristide returned to Haiti, and to his office, the next day. The multinational force contained a significant information component in the Military Information Support Teams (MIST).

As mentioned previously, the US army has had significant experience in psychological operations, dating from the Second World War and continuing through the Cold War. Among the major adjustments of the post-Cold War period was and continues to be the issue of how the concept of 'psyops' can, or if indeed should, be adapted to 'operations other than war', which includes the new generation of peacekeeping operations.[24] Major inhibiting factors in this process are seen to be military terminology, appropriate as it may have been in war, but potentially offensive in a peacekeeping setting. More basic is the lingering suspicion of journalists and proponents of freedom of the press that 'psychological operations' necessarily include manipulation and propaganda.[25]

In June 1994, a Military Information Support Team was established in Washington. Its goal was 'to create an information environment in support of US objectives to restore democracy to Haiti, to allow President Aristide to present a message of reconciliation to his constituents, and to outline plans for his return to power'.[26] Its most urgent task was 'to stem the flow of Haitian migrants to the United States'. This was undertaken with loudspeaker broadcasts from US Coast Guard ships, and warning messages from US special envoys. According to its organizers, this 'had tremendous success in arresting the flow of Haitian migrants'.[27]

Planning and training for Operation Uphold Democracy began in 1993 and drew on previous US military operations in Northern Iraq, Somalia and Kuwait. During those operations, 'psyops soldiers displayed unprecedented flexibility and initiative in quickly transforming an invasion information campaign into a non-combat information campaign'.[28] They were well prepared:

> Throughout forced entry planning, PSYOPers were a ready source of information for everyone from commanders and operators to logisticians. Unique experience had been gained form a variety of sources – intensive study of Haitian geography,

society, telecommunications, and culture; daily study and analysis of intelligence message traffic; and on-the-ground experience in migrant relief operations as well as individual training opportunities in Port-au-Prince with the US Country team. From the outset, plans were prepared for both permissive and non-permissive environments.[29]

The information campaigns conducted by the Joint Psychological Operations Task Force of the MNF were designed 'to facilitate civil order and reduce Haitian-on-Haitian violence. President Aristide's messages of peace and reconciliation were used in discouraging revenge and retribution'.[30] The messages also emphasized 'that US soldiers were not part of an occupation force, but were rather conducting a mission to ensure that all Haitians may live in a secure and peaceful environment'.[31] However, there was some opposition to the MNF in some Haitian media, and in order 'to put an end to anti-MNF and disinformation campaigns, multinational force soldiers peacefully secured *Radio and TV Nationale* and turned them over to the control of the new Haitian government'.[32]

This experience was clearly in stark contrast to the situation in which General Dallaire found himself in Rwanda just four months earlier when he asked for a UN capability to counter *Radio/Télévision Mille Collines*' propaganda of hate, as discussed in the previous Chapter.

Operation Uphold Democracy was significant in that it not only achieved its immediate political and military goals – the restoration of the elected President by non-violent means – but, when put into the larger context, it was highly successful in applying a UN Security Council Resolution which authorized 'all necessary means', under Chapter VII with a minimum use of force. It furthermore saw a skilful application of a variety of psychological operations tactics in an 'operation other than war'.

UNMIH UNDER US LEADERSHIP

In retrospect and in comparison with other, similar situations in Rwanda, Bosnia or Somalia, the transition from the multinational forces to a United Nations command in the spring of 1995 looks smooth and uncomplicated.[33] However, there was a larger political connection between events in Somalia and in Haiti, which is well described by Stanley Meisler, a former foreign correspondent of the *Los Angeles Times*:

The American decision to withdraw crippled the Somalia operation and made all UN peacekeeping suspect in the eyes of

Americans. The name Somalia became a buzzword for failure. Whenever the Security Council discussed a new peacekeeping venture, critics raised the spectre of another Somali debacle. The Clinton administration issued stringent new guidelines for American participation or even support of UN peacekeeping. If these guidelines were followed strictly, the United States would never support another peacekeeping operation again. The Americans, in fact, had to close their eyes to their own guidelines in 1994 when they persuaded the Security Council to vote for a new peacekeeping venture in Haiti.'[34]

Security Council Resolution 964 of 29 November 1994 commended 'the efforts made by the MNF in Haiti to establish a secure and stable environment conducive to the deployment of the United Nations Mission in Haiti', welcomed the establishment by the UNMIH advance team and the MNF of a joint working group to prepare for the transition, authorized the Secretary-General to strengthen the advance team of UNMIH and to inform the Security Council on prospective increases. The transfer of responsibilities from the MNF to UNMIH was completed on 31 March 1995. Municipal and legislative elections were held in Haiti on 25 June 1995. Security Council Resolution 1007 of 31 July 1995 decided to extend UNMIH's mandate for a period of seven months; no particular mention of the information programme was made in this resolution.

In the initial phase of transition,[35] a Military Information Support Task Force (MISTF) was established which was under the operational control of the UNMIH Force Commander. MISTF support to UNMIH had the following specified tasks:

• Advise and coordinate information campaign strategy with Special Operations Task Force and UNMIH
• Attend Information Coordination Committee meetings to coordinate and deconflict information issues
• Conduct a coordinated and integrated information programme
• Disseminate Radio/TV broadcasts using Haitian national contract Radio/TV assets
• Produce print materials using organic and Haitian national contract facilities.

The Task Force conducted assessments to determine the 'Haitian population's attitude *vis à vis* UNMIH forces' and to decide which of MIST's information products would be most efficient. Its campaign objectives were to increase public support for UNMIH, set conditions for successful elections, increase popular support for democracy in Haiti, gain support for the Haitian National Police and reduce Haitian-on-Haitian violence.

By 10 October 1995, MIST had, by its own accounts, distributed nearly half a million copies of 55 different posters, disseminated nearly three million handbills, developed nine newsletters and disseminated 145,000 copies thereof. It had developed 88 radio messages and broadcast nearly 10,000 radio spots, a further 8,000 radio spots in support of electoral issues with 14 different messages and developed 15 videos and broadcast 310 minutes of videos on TV.[36]

As mentioned above, it had been established that all MIST products had to be approved by the Special Representative of the Secretary-General. Prior to this final political clearance of the content of MIST messages, the information products were reviewed by the Spokesman, Eric Falt, and his staff who also assisted in verifying contents of MIST products in the Creole language.[37]

In September and October 1995, the security situation had significantly improved in Haiti, which was, according to UN observers, 'a result of the more active role played by the Haitian public security forces and the continued efforts of UNMIH'.[38] However, in November the situation deteriorated again when violent demonstrations erupted in Les Cayes which necessitated the deployment of the Quick Reaction Forces and joint Haitian National Police/UNMIH patrols. On 11 November, President Aristide called for immediate and total disarmament and accused the international community of complacency in this regard. When roadblocks were set up and arson and looting spread throughout the country, the Special Representative of the Secretary-General appealed to the people of Haiti not to take the law into their own hands. With the help of UNMIH, the Haitian police slowly reestablished control.

Throughout this critical period, the MIST teams were very active on the tactical level of UNMIH, and military information support teams were spread out over UNMIH's six zones of deployment. As of August 1995, the MIST teams had a total staff of 104, 21 of them Haitian-language linguists. The large majority of MIST staff was deployed in 'tactical dissemination teams' (TDTs) composed of two to three soldiers equipped with loud-speakers whose main job during this period was crowd dispersal and the prevention of acts of violence. Among the themes promoted by MIST to increase popular support for the justice system were the following messages:

• The new justice system will be fair and efficient;
• Everyone must respect the law and the basic rights of their fellow citizens;

- An effective justice system can guarantee respect for your basic rights and safety; and
- The judicial system will punish criminal offenders and protect law-abiding citizens.

How effective these slogans were in convincing the Haitian populace of the efficiency or fairness of their new system of justice in the long run is difficult to assess. Suffice it to say that visits to the jails in Port-au-Prince and Jacmel, where prisoners lingered for months without trial, often without charges, did not convince foreign visitors of the efficacy or fairness of the Haitian legal institutions.[39]

MIST also targeted 'Haitian-on-Haitian' violence which it sought to reduce by propagating the following themes:

- Citizen violence scares foreign investors and reduces jobs;
- When some people don't respect the law, everyone is threatened;
- Crimes must be reported to the proper authorities so the justice system can work; and
- In a democratic society all citizens have the right to a fair trial.

Among MIST's very varied information programmes were also crime hot-line radio broadcasts, handbills and posters, as well as radio and loudspeaker messages to discourage violence. MIST also actively supported UNMIH's 'Weapons Buy Back Programme'. This programme aimed to persuade Haitians voluntarily to turn in arms, and to report illegal possession of arms by offering money for guns, and by encouraging citizens to use the emergency crimeline to report weapons caches.[40] Begun in October 1995, this had resulted by August 1996 in over 13,000 weapons surrendered, including CS (Chemical/Smoke) and smoke grenades, small arms, explosives and larger calibre, crew-served weapons. Prices paid ranged from $25.00 for grenades, $200.00 for small arms to $600.00 for crew-served weapons. This programme was not specifically mandated by the UN Security Council but was a continuation of MNF practice by UNMIH. Although as of May of 1996 rumours about weapons caches were still rife, senior officers of UNMIH considered such reports invalid.[41]

UNMIH also contributed substantially to democratic institution building in Haiti; electoral assistance was provided in five different national and departmental elections. The electoral process culminated with the election, on 17 December 1995, of President Rene Garcia Preval who nominated a new Prime Minister, Mr Rosny Smarth, who took office on 6 March 1996. By that time, a large measure of public order and confidence had been restored:

By all indications, there was no organized threat to the Government of Haiti. However, concern was expressed in many quarters that growing popular discontent could be used by disgruntled groups to foment trouble once President Aristide had handed over power and UNMIH had left the country. Unemployment and underemployment were widespread, services and infrastructure were inadequate or non-existing and there were other economic hardships. The Government of President Preval faced a number of difficult decisions to stimulate economic development and attract domestic and foreign investment.[42]

Or, as another observer of the situation in Haiti commented in an article in *Foreign Policy* in the spring of 1996:

Haiti is not yet on the road to self-sufficiency, and improvements in the Haitian quality of life have not yet taken place … Only 10 per cent of the land is arable. Human and animal densities are among the highest in the world. Because so many trees have been cut down for charcoal, soil erosion has made a tough situation terrible … National infant mortality rates are among the highest in the world. There is little piped, potable water, and the sanitation, electrical, communications, and transportation infrastructures are grossly inadequate.[43]

UNMIH UNDER CANADIAN LEADERSHIP

UNMIH was due to cease its operations on 29 February 1996. However, the Secretary-General, along with most other international observers felt that UNMIH was needed to assist the government of Haiti for a few more months, even though in reduced numbers. The Security Council decided to extend the mandate for four months, with a decreased military component of 1,200 and a civilian police component of 300 personnel.[44] This represented a severe short fall compared with the number of troops requested by the Secretary-General. The government of Canada decided to contribute, at its own expense, a contingent of 700 military personnel to complement the force. The Department of Foreign Affairs and International Trade explained its decision at the time: 'Canada's participation in UNMIH is one of the most important contributions to global security we are making at this time. It is also one that affects us most directly because Haiti is a close neighbour.' It further explained: 'Canada also has a special interest in Haiti. Haiti is the only other Francophone country in the Americas, and one with which Canadians have developed very close links over the years.'[45]

In March 1996 the boundaries of the operational zones of UNMIH were redrawn to conform to UNMIH's reduced strength. Base camps were closed, some of which led to increased anxiety in the Haitian population over the drawdown of the Mission. However, UNMIH maintained a visible presence throughout Haiti. Its main task continued to be to 'assist the democratic government of Haiti … in fulfilling its responsibilities: … sustaining the secure and stable environment, … and the professionalization of a Haitian police force'.[46] The drawdown of US-led UNMIH and the transition to its new, Canadian-led phase spanned a period of two-and-a-half months. The UNMIH Chief of Staff, Bill Fulton, who had been in the country since September 1994, was a key person in this process.

Concerning the evolution of MIST, at least two 'Lessons-Learned' reports were prepared during the transitional phase, one by UN Headquarters in New York and referred to above, and the other a mission-internal report. The latter stated:

> There was confusion on the role of Military Information Support Teams: commanders and staff at all levels were not completely clear on the role that Military Information Support Teams could play on a nationwide basis and locally in support of all the UNMIH missions. This resulted in less than effective use of this key resource particularly at the Zone level. It is difficult to measure the impact of some MIST programmes to determine effectiveness. However at the tactical level some results were immediately evident when crowds dispersed upon being informed of the facts or when music was played.[47]

The report concluded that a clearer delineation of the role of MIST was needed at all levels, and education and orientation on MIST for commanders and all staff was required. This coincides with the above-cited Mid-Mission Assessment Report of the Lessons Learned Unit of the Department of Peacekeeping Operations in New York.[48]

Given the much reduced size of the military component of UNMIH, it was decided to have MIST II deployed primarily at the tactical level, to act 'as a non-lethal weapon' and allow a commander the flexibility to 'accomplish his mission without necessarily having to resort to weapons'.[49] There was to be a MIST platoon of approximately 25 Canadian soldiers to disseminate information at the tactical level, including to the other two battalions from Pakistan and Bangladesh. An advance group of MIST personnel from

Canada was trained for two weeks in Fort Bragg, North Carolina. Further training was then provided in Valcartier, Quebec, before actual deployment to Haiti. The concept of operations for this MIST platoon was the following:

- that it would act in a 'force protection' role, by providing a capability to respond to immediate operational requirements;
- that it would establish dialogue in dealing with crowds and obtain information;
- that it would disseminate messages with loudspeakers and face-to-face communication; and
- that it would work in teams of three, including one Creole speaker.

While it was originally planned that MIST II would also develop radio messages and print products, it did not have such a capability at the end of May 1996.[50] It had, however, had its baptism of fire when earlier that month UNMIH closed its camp in Gonaive, a traditional hot spot, where fights were breaking out over the contents of the camp. MIST loudspeaker teams defused the tension. However, MIST was 'more than a soldier with a loudspeaker', but provided a capability to 'facilitate communications between security forces and the Haitian people'.[51]

CONCLUSIONS

The experiences of the Multinational Forces Operation in Haiti, followed by UNMIH in two distinct phases of operations, from 1994–96, led to a number of conclusions for peacekeeping operations in fragile environments such as the one in Haiti.

The new requirements for peacekeeping operations in the complex emergencies of the 1990s demand an inclusion of a public information campaign as a strategic management function for these operations. Rebuilding societies fallen into anarchy requires an effort at communicating with individual citizens with varying levels of education. These difficulties are exacerbated by inadequate communications environments and, frequently, also by attempts by one or more of the antagonists to influence public opinion and attitudes by means of propaganda. This necessitates innovative techniques in communicating the mission's mandate and goals.

A highly effective means of communicating with the Haitian people was found in the combination of information strategies used by UNMIH, both civilian and military. It was shown to be extremely important to have an integrated information effort in the mission area, from the top – political and military leadership – to the tactical level. In fact, for an information campaign to be successful, the leadership of the mission area must be positive and cohesive, having agreed and coordinated at all levels the messages to be communicated and on the tactics to be employed. When the political and military leadership jointly agreed on policy goals and communication strategies for the mission area, MIST and the UN Spokesman's information efforts were successful, even though the individuals involved may not always have been in agreement about how best to pursue an information campaign.

Both the military and civilian staff involved in information work of this nature need to be sensitive to the cultural values of the country in which they operate, and must fully appreciate the political, psychological and communications context of their work. They must also be sensitive to media and other information professionals external to the mission, and be open to their information needs. Charges of manipulation have been levelled at UNMIH in its first phase, Operation Uphold Democracy, which worked in the 'enforcement mode'; it will be recalled from the discussion in the Introduction to this book that military enforcement operations are more prone to use propaganda than consensual peacekeeping missions. It is therefore important for missions that straddle the lines between Chapter VI and Chapter VII of the UN Charter, that freedom of the press must be maintained and access to a variety of information sources be respected. This will avoid charges of news management and propagandizing.

The willingness of civil and military staff to cooperate with each other was vitally important to the success of UNMIH. Another important factor was prior experience in other peacekeeping operations and, when that was not available, intensive training in public information techniques prior to deployment. Public relations is a field that requires a high degree of professionalism and the pursuit of common, clearly defined goals.

In UNMIH, all six principles of communication set out in Chapter 1 were creatively applied and refined in three successive phases of the operation. This case study thus demonstrates that a public information campaign, combined with effective leadership and provided with adequate resources, is a vital element for effectiveness of the new generation of peacekeeping operations.

NOTES

1. This chapter represents an abbreviated version of a working paper which has, since it was written, been published as *Public Information Campaigns in Peacekeeping: The UN Experience in Haiti*, The Pearson Papers, No. 1, Clementsport, Nova Scotia: The Canadian Peacekeeping Press, 1998.

2. See Alex Morrison and Dale Anderson (eds), *Peacekeeping and the Coming Anarchy*, Pearson Roundtable Series No.1, Clementsport, NS: Canadian Peacekeeping Press, 1996, defines anarchy as 'the absence of effective, accepted authority in the majority of a country, no rule of law, and, consequently, an absence of security; a lack of control, rule or structure; or social or individual actions in which open disrespect is shown for international, regional or national laws, behavioural norms, or customary, civilized conduct' (p.3).

3. For the extensive debate on this subject, see Thomas Weiss (ed.), *The United Nations and Civil Wars*, Boulder, CO and London: Lynne Rienner, 1995, Lori Fisler Damrosch (ed.), *Enforcing Restraint: Collective Intervention in Internal Conflicts*, New York: Council on Foreign Relations, 1993 and William I. Zartman (ed.), *Collapsed States: The Disintegration and Restoration of Legitimate Authority*, Boulder: Lynne Rienner, 1995.

4. *The Blue Helmets – a Review of United Nations Peacekeeping* (3rd edn, United Nations, New York, 1996), p.4 describes 'failed states' as situations 'where governmental functions were suspended, the police and judiciary had collapsed, infrastructure destroyed and populations uprooted'.

5. In implementing the various Central American peace agreements reached in the late 1980s and early 1990s, the UN established a series of small, but successful peacekeeping operations, namely ONUCA, the United Nations Observer Group in Central America, ONUSAL, the UN Observer Mission in El Salvador, as well as election monitoring and human rights missions. They are described in *The Blue Helmets* (ibid.), part VI.

6. The Lessons-Learned Unit, Department of Peacekeeping Operations, United Nations Mission in Haiti, Mid-Mission Assessment Report, April 1995–Feb. 1996 (United Nations, New York), p.29 states: 'In the six-month lead time between the arrival of the UNMIH advance team and full deployment, the information staff conducted a basic survey to determine the media access and habits of representative segments of the population, compiled media contact lists, and developed detailed plans for the public information structure and programme.'

7. Ibid., p.28.

8. Interview with Major Marc Rouleau in Port-au-Prince, 28 May 1996.

9. The differences between the hierarchical relationships depicted in Figures 1 and 2 reflect the traditional tug-of-war between civilian and military personnel in peacekeeping missions. It is also referred to in the Mid-Mission Assessment Report, para.102: 'The rank-consciousness of military personnel also makes it important that the relative level and professional experience of the civilian head of information be at least equal to, and preferably higher than that of his military colleague' (n.6 above), p.28.

10. Information received from Chief Superintendent Neil Pouliot, RCMP (retd.) who was UNMIH Civilian Police Commissioner during 1994 and 1995.

11. There was occasional disagreement over who should deal with media from particular countries; the UNMIH spokesman insisting that he had to be involved in all media visits. Some national contingents, including the Canadians, seemed to feel that journalists from their countries are primarily their concern. Major Rouleau maintained that Canadian media representatives should visit the Canadian contingent and be briefed by Canadian officers. These differences of opinion are mentioned in the Mid-Mission Assessment Report, which recommends that in order to 'avoid unnecessary friction between and unfulfilled expectations, particularly on the part of military officers who may feel that briefing the press on military aspects of the mission should not be left to a civilian spokesman', terms of reference for all information personnel should be agreed upon in advance (n.6 above, p.28).

12. Ibid., pp.27 and 28.

13. Ibid., p.4.

14. See recommendation 9, ibid., p.5.

15. Mr Brahimi relinquished his post in March 1996. He was succeeded by Mr Enrique ter Horst as Special Representative of the Secretary-General.

16. UNMIH Mid-Mission Assessment Report (n.6 above), p.27.

17. During both my visits to UNMIH headquarters in 1995 and 1996, senior military officers remarked that there had been disagreements between the Special Representative and his military counterparts, but they were unequivocal in their acceptance, even admiration, of Mr Brahimi's leadership.

18. See, *inter alia*, the studies by Bernard Cohen, *The Public's Impact on Foreign Policy*, Boston: Little, Brown and Co., 1973; James Rosenau, *The Scientific Study of Foreign Policy: Essays on the Analysis of World Politics*, New York: Nichols, 1980; Bruce Russett, *Controlling the Sword: the Democratic Governance of National Security*, Cambridge, MA: Harvard University Press, 1990; Philip Powlick, 'The Sources of Public Opinion for American Foreign Policy Officials', *International Studies Quarterly*, 39, 1995, pp.427–51.

19. Paul Farmer, 'Hidden Structural Violence in Agrarian Societies: The Case of Haiti', unpublished manuscript from a lecture delivered at Yale University, Jan. 1997, p.14.

20. According to Sgt. Dan Hefkey, Ontario Provincial Police, who served in UNMIH as an UNCIVPOL Detachment Commander.

21. For a fascinating, albeit fictional account of Haiti's early history, see Madison Smartt Bell, *All Souls' Rising*, New York: Pantheon, 1995.

22. See Greg Chamberlain, 'Haiti's Second Independence: Aristide's Nine Months in Office' and J.P. Slavin, 'The Elite's Revenge: The Military Coup of 1991' in *Haiti – Dangerous Crossroads*, ed. by NACLA (North American Congress on Latin America), Boston: South End, 1995.

23. Security Council Resolution 940 of 31 July 1994. For a comprehensive account of the various 'agreements of national reconciliation' negotiated between 1991 and 1994, see Section B of Chapter XXVIII: United Nations Mission in Haiti (UNMIH) of *The Blue Helmets* (n.4 above).

24. See Brian Cloughley 'Peace in Mind – will the UN give psyops a chance?', *Jane's International Defence Review*, Vol.29, No.3, March 1996, pp.59–61 and the references in footnote 12.

25. The ongoing debate between the media and the military in the United States is well reflected in Jacqueline E. Sharkey, *Under Fire – US Military Restrictions on the Media from Grenada to the Persian Gulf War*, Washington: The Center for Public Integrity, 1991 and Everette E. Dennis (ed.): *The Media at War: The Press and the Persian Gulf Conflict*, New York: Gannett Foundation Media Center, 1991. For the US Army perspective of its information campaign in Haiti see Lt. Gen. Hugh Shelton and Lt. Col. Timothy Vane, 'Winning the Information War in Haiti', *Military Review*, Nov./Dec. 1995.

26. 'PSYOP Support to Operation UPHOLD DEMOCRACY' pamphlet issued by the Joint Psychological Operations Task Force Haiti, Fort Bragg, NC: May 1995, p.6.

27. Ibid., pp.6–8 describe the operation in detail, including radio broadcasts from aircraft, and the setting up of 'Radio and Television Democracy' in the summer of 1994.

28. Ibid., p.17.

29. Ibid., p.14.

30. Ibid., p.18.

31. Ibid., p.19. A different perspective on how Haitians perceived the multinational force

entry is provided by Kim Ives, 'Haiti's Second US Occupation' in *Haiti: Dangerous Crossroads* (n.22 above), pp.107–18.

32. 'PSYOP Support to Operation UPHOLD DEMOCRACY' (n.26 above), p.20 It is reported that 'these stations, and several others throughout the country, were later contracted by PSYOP personnel to broadcast messages in support of different information campaigns'.

33. In Somalia, as is well known, the transitions from UNOSOM I to UNITAF to UNOSOM II where UN and US never appeared to see eye-to-eye, the atmosphere of recrimination became a political factor in itself. See Dirk Kirschten, 'Missions Impossible', in *National Journal*, 30 Oct. 1993. For the United Nations version of these operations, see *The United Nations and Somalia, 1992–1996*, United Nations Blue Book Series, Vol. VIII, New York, 1996.

34. Stanley Meisler, *United Nations – The First Fifty Years*, New York: The Atlantic Monthly Press, 1995, p.309. See also p.333 where Meisler writes that 'the forging of a UN mission to replace the American intervention in Haiti was a good example of assertive multi-lateralism at work'.

35. The following description of MIST operations is based on a presentation by UNMIH Chief Operations Officer, Colonel Keith Huber, at UNMIH headquarters in Oct. 1995 and on information received from Major Roy Thomas, Deputy Chief of Operations in May 1996.

36. Information received at UNMIH headquarters from U-3 (Operations) and the Chief of Staff, Colonel Bill Fulton, in Nov. 1995 and during interviews in May 1996.

37. Information received by the author from Mr Falt on 28 May 1996.

38. See *The Blue Helmets* (n.4 above), pp.629–31.

39. The author visited the National Penitentiary in Port-au-Prince on 31 Oct. 1995 and on 26 May 1996; as well as the jail in Jacmel on 2 Nov. 1995.

40. See *Managing Arms in Peace Processes*, UNIDIR, UN, NY and Geneva, 1996, pp.24–5 and 79–80.

41. Conversation with Colonel Bill Fulton on 23 May 1996 and with Colonel Keith Huber on 27 June 1996.

42. *The Blue Helmets* (n.4 above), p.633.

43. Robert Rotberg, 'Clinton Was Right', *Foreign Policy*, Spring 1996, p.140–41.

44. Security Council Resolution 1048 of 29 Feb. 1996.

45. Department of Foreign Affairs and International Trade, *Canadian Policy towards Haiti* (Ottawa, 1996).

46. See *Report of the Secretary-General on the United Nations Mission in Haiti*, S/1996/416 of 5 June 1996, paras.4–12.

47. UNMIH, 'Lessons Learned – 1 April 95–29 Feb. 96', report received from UNMIH Operations Centre in May 1996, p.6.

48. UNMIH Mid-Mission Assessment Report (n.6 above), pp.31–2.

49. Interview with the UNMIH Deputy Chief Operations Officer, Major Roy Thomas, on 28 May 1996.

50. Interview with Lt. James Lande, platoon-commander, on 27 May 1996.

51. Information received from Major Roy Thomas, Deputy Chief of Operations, UNMIH, on 28 May 1996.

———◄◦►———

SEVEN

Peacekeeping in a Propagandist Environment: From UNPROFOR to UNTAES in the Former Yugoslavia

The only truth in the Yugoslav war is the lie.

Misha Glenny[1]

My advice to anyone who wishes to study the problems of the Balkans is to do so with utmost scrupulousness, with a keen sense and an eye for distortion and misinformation.

Miron Rezun[2]

INTRODUCTION: FORGING THE PROPAGANDA WAR

In his book *Forging War – The Media in Serbia, Croatia and Bosnia-Hercegovina*, Mark Thompson gives a vivid description of the role of the media in those three former Yugoslav republics in the early phases of the war. He analyses the destructive power of incitement to ethnic hatred when the media are controlled by nationalist governments.[3] The importance of the media in the dissolution of Yugoslavia and the unleashing of the most devastating war in Europe since the Second World War has been noted by most analysts of the Yugoslav tragedy.

Susan Woodward has described the manner in which, in particular, the leaders of Serbia and Croatia have used censorship of the press, control of television and radio and the intimidation of independent journalists, terming it 'psychological warfare':[4]

> Military strategists and political leaders chose targets and managed media coverage so as to shape international opinion and local sympathies. The Croatian government, for example, placed sharpshooters on the walls of Dubrovnik to draw fire from the federal armed forces, attracting world attention to that inter-

EASTERN CROATIA

(map no. 4057 (Eastern Croatia) reproduced with the permission of the Cartographic Section, Department of Public Information, United Nations)

nationally protected city that even the total destruction of Vukovar could not obtain. The Croatian and Bosnian governments placed mortars and artillery batteries within the walls of hospitals ... for the same purpose, drawing fire from Serb gunners to gain international reaction. To generate war hysteria, both Serbian and Croatian television stations showed footage of war atrocities by the other side that was as likely to have been taken from their own side, or even from World War II films. All sides used attacks (and mutual recriminations of blame) on cultural monuments, on civilians in breadlines, on wedding and funeral parties, on bus-loads of orphans, and on international troops to mobilize sympathies and hostility at home and abroad.[5]

Astute observers of the Yugoslav drama such as Mihailo Crnobrnja have commented on how they had hoped that, following the death of Tito, ' the media would represent a moderating force and influence, using their increased independence to point the way towards a generally more free, transparent, and democratic society', but that, instead, 'the novelty was the new political direction towards nationalism and the readiness, even eagerness, with which the media accepted this new role, allowing themselves to be instrumentalized in the nationalistic war of words that ultimately led to the war with guns'.[6]

UNPROFOR AS SCAPEGOAT

The United Nations Protection Force (UNPROFOR) in the former Yugoslavia was authorized by UN Security Council Resolution 743 on 21 February 1992. Although the Force was conceived as a classical peacekeeping mission, operating under Chapter VI of the Charter, and 'with the full compliance of all parties',[7] that mandate was subject to repeated changes over the next three years. The operation was expanded into Bosnia Herzegovina with the assumption by the UN of responsibility for the operation of the Sarajevo airport.[8] That role was further expanded and formalized as a humanitarian relief operation and simultaneously transformed into an enforcement operation by UNSCR 770 of 13 August 1992. This latter resolution was enacted under Chapter VII of the Charter, and was the first notable example of the syndrome that would come to be known as 'mission creep', and which would characterize the operations of UNPROFOR for the next three years. Subsequently, UNPROFOR expanded into the 'Pink Zones Croatia',[9] created the 'Safe Areas' in Bosnia Herzegovina,[10] launched a preventive deployment in Macedonia,[11] and ultimately joined, however uneasily, with NATO in an air campaign in Bosnia.[12] With respect to the operations in Bosnia, in two years the Security Council promulgated 11 Resolutions under Chapter VII of the Charter.

As Crnobrnja and others have pointed out, on balance, 'the UN relief and humanitarian efforts will probably be judged as overwhelmingly positive. In the face of many daunting obstacles and problems, some of their own making, the UN officials, officers and troops performed a gallant mission, saving many, many lives and relieving the suffering of hundreds of thousands of civilians on all sides.'[13]

There remains nevertheless imbedded in the public consciousness in most European and North American countries a general perception that UNPROFOR failed: failed to protect the Protected Areas, failed to keep safe the Safe Areas, failed to enforce the enforcement mandate. It is this pervasive perception which recalls the ubiquitous linkage of perceptions, policies and performance figured in Chapter 1 of this book. That UNPROFOR is so widely judged to have 'failed', has led to superficial, but pervasive judgements that peacekeeping has 'failed'. For example, the story behind the gruesome cover of a 1994 issue of *The Economist*, showing a corpse-strewn battlefield with a UN flag at half-mast, was entitled 'Shamed are the peacekeepers'.[14] To observe the extent to which these perceptions influence the formulation of policy, the responses of donors and troop contributors, and even the morale of the members of the mission, serves to underscore the vital importance of information as a strategic function of the leadership of the mission. With regard to UNPROFOR, Crnobrnja has noted:

> The UN troops have often been treated as the enemy; they have been accused of taking sides; their vehicles have been stolen; they have been shot at, wounded, and even killed. On a few occasions the warring sides have masqueraded as UN peacekeepers, driving around in white vehicles with UN flags and opening fire on their opponents in order to draw fire against the UN troops. Boutros Boutros-Ghali was heckled by the citizens of Sarajevo during his brief stopover in January of 1993.[15]

The scapegoating of UNPROFOR began almost immediately the Force was deployed. An officer who worked at UNPROFOR HQ tells of the distribution of leaflets by light aircraft over Zagreb, as part of a Croatian presidential election campaign in the late summer of 1992, which read 'UNPROFOR and other occupiers – Go Home!' He notes that it was at about that time that the UN staff cars began nearly every night to be vandalized in the car park of 'their' hotel.[16] He also reports about demonstrations in Zagreb (and elsewhere in Croatia) by former residents of Osijek who were enraged at UNPROFOR because they were not immediately able to return to their homes. UNPROFOR failed to make the obvious point that in accordance with the Vance Plan (to which the Croatian government had consented), Osijek was not within the United Nations Protected Area in Sector East, and was therefore not covered by the UN mandate.

There are consequently many critics of the UNPROFOR information effort, in particular from within the ranks of former United Nations military. A Public Affairs Officer to the Force Commander criticized the UN operation in 1994 in retrospect as having had 'no communications plan', no strategy, even though it was not suffering from a shortage of funds. UNPROFOR was struggling from day to day in response to ongoing crises.[17]

Ms Yacoumopoulou, a United Nations civilian information officer who was with UNPROFOR from April 1992 to June 1993, agrees that 'a comprehensive and regular multimedia information campaign' was never put into place 'despite the existence of a full information team and a generous budget ... both of which had been expanded five-fold since the mission began, with little increase in productivity'.[18] Ms Yacoumopoulou refers to the fact that 'no information campaign could succeed in what the political process had failed to achieve'.[19]

Early on, political factions launched disinformation campaigns to discredit the United Nations and its staff. A case in point was the character assassination of Lewis Mackenzie, the first Chief of Staff and later the first commander of what was then called Sector Sarajevo. Mackenzie had, in 1992, resisted the stereotyping and demonization of the Serbians and the Bosnian Serbs, noting pointedly that there was always enough blame to go around.[20] This unleashed allegations that he had been bribed by the Serbs. The story that he held orgies with Muslim girls held in Serb captivity was a persistent smear campaign which Miron Rezun has identified as 'misinformation' spread by various Bosnian sources. The story was pervasive enough that the Secretary-General was asked to comment on it during a trip to Japan, and it continues to reappear in various European media.[21]

Mark Thompson has written of the deliberate attempt by the Croatian government to discredit UNPROFOR in his book *A Paper House: The Ending of Yugoslavia*: '... the Croatian authorities at all levels encourage ill-feeling toward ... UNPROFOR because [their] role seems ... so wrongly *impartial*. ... it sees no reason not to exploit popular ignorance and desire ... for restitution ...'[22] In his book *Forging War* Thompson wrote that Croatian Radio 'censored UNPROFOR newscasts at least eight times during the first year of UN deployment in Croatia'.[23] This, according to the head of civilian affairs for UNPROFOR, 'was the first case in his experience of a host country interfering with UN broadcasts'.[24]

The constant campaign against UNPROFOR had obvious negative consequences for much of its work, including in the humanitarian field.[25] An officer posted with UNPROFOR in the early phases of the operation, described the situation aptly: 'Vilified publicly at every convenient occasion with impunity by the very people who were manufacturing incidents and confrontations in violation of signed agreements, UNPROFOR remained, seemingly by design, without a voice.'[26]

Consequently, the Secretary-General reported in September 1993 that 'I have been sorely tempted, in the light of the criticism of UNPROFOR by both sides and the dangers and abuse to which its personnel are exposed, to recommend withdrawal of the Force altogether …'.[27] By early 1995, overtly hostile public opinion in Croatia had made it difficult to renew the UNPROFOR mandate. In March 1995 it was decided to remove the name UNPROFOR from UN operations in Croatia. The successor operations were thus separate, at least separately named, operations in Croatia (United Nations Confidence Restoration Operation in Croatia – UNCRO), in Macedonia (United Nations Preventive Deployment – UNPREDEP), and in Prevlaka (United Nations Military Observers in Prevlaka – UNMOP).

It is not intended here to provide an overall assessment of UNPROFOR. The purpose of this Chapter is rather to analyse what, if anything, the UN learned from the UNPROFOR experience, in particular its unfortunate relations with the media, as well as the outright victimization by the factions. This book specifically addresses the matter of a viable public information programme as a function of a peace operation. It is therefore important to identify the hindrances that prevented UNPROFOR from getting its message across.

Chief among these hindrances were of course the rapidly changing mandates, and the repeated contradictions contained in layers of mandates. It is however unlikely that even if these mandates could have been simplified, or better packaged by successive public information specialists, the effect on the operation would eventually have been different. The forces of war in the former Yugoslavia described by Thompson, Glenny, Woodward, Crnobrnja and others were forces which skilfully used propaganda as a major tool in achieving their ends. UNPROFOR never succeeded in overcoming these odds.

FROM ERDUT TO UNTAES, VIA DAYTON

UNPROFOR's former 'Sector East' became roughly the operational area of its major successor, namely the UN Transitional Administration in Eastern Slavonia, Baranja and Western Sirmium (UNTAES). Although the Basic

Agreement on the region of Eastern Slavonia, Baranja and Western Sirmium, which provides for the peaceful reintegration of the region into Croatia, had been signed at Erdut on 12 November 1995, the region remained, for the time being, under Serb control. Notwithstanding this agreement between Croatia and the former Yugoslavia, the United Nations was extremely hesitant to establish another UN mission in the former Yugoslavia.[28]

This was consistent with Boutros-Ghali's longstanding reluctance for the UN to be involved in this conflict at all. Already in 1992 he had said that Yugoslavia was a 'rich man's war',[29] and he was deeply concerned about mounting financial costs to the UN. In his report to the Security Council in May 1995, the Secretary-General complained that 'Yugoslavia dominated the Organization's agenda ... and distorted its ... efforts. The former Yugoslavia accounted for nearly 70 per cent of peacekeepers worldwide and over two thirds of peacekeeping costs'.[30] There were looming tragedies elsewhere which deserved the attention of the world body, yet, by the end of 1995, the UNHCR was spending 50 per cent of its budget in Bosnia Herzegovina and had 15 per cent of its international staff stationed there.[31]

When faced with mounting pressures from members of the Security Council in December 1995 to establish a transitional administration and peacekeeping force in Eastern Slavonia, Boutros-Ghali warned the Security Council: 'Anything less than a well armed division-sized force would only risk repeating the failures of the recent past. The concept of deterrence by mere presence, as attempted in the 'safe areas' in Bosnia and Herzegovina, would be no likelier to succeed on this occasion.'[32] Boutros-Ghali believed that the Eastern Slavonia force should be entrusted to a coalition of member states, rather than to the United Nations.[33] Nevertheless, the much maligned UN was in 1995 still considered to be a credible engine to resolve peacefully the issue of Eastern Slavonia, which was to remain outside IFOR's area of operation.

Boutros-Ghali's reluctance for the United Nations to continue to exercise responsibility for Eastern Slavonia is said to have been the last straw in the increasingly strained relations between the United States and Secretary-General Boutros Boutros-Ghali. The United States, acting probably not for this reason alone, subsequently vetoed the reelection of Boutros-Ghali,[34] paving the way for the election of Kofi Annan as Secretary-General in December 1996. Annan had headed the Department of Peacekeeping Operations since 1993.

UN Security Council Resolution 1037, adopted on 15 January 1996, provided for the establishment of a transitional administration to govern initially for a period of 12 months, although that might be extended a further 12 months at the request of one of the parties. The agreement and its enabling resolution cover, *inter alia*, demilitarization (to be completed within 30 days after full deployment of the UN Force), establishment of police forces, population movement, restoration of property and assistance in reconstruction. It is also stipulated that regional elections be held within 30 days of the termination of the operation's mandate. These elections were held on 13 and 14 April 1997.

UNTAES' MANDATE AND AREA OF OPERATION

UNTAES was established on 15 January 1996, comprising a military force of 5,000, a UN Civilian Police force, and supporting UN civilian staff, to execute that mandate. An American, Mr Jacques Klein, was appointed the Transitional Administrator, and Major General Schoups of Belgium became the first military commander.[35]

The region's demographic make-up has changed dramatically since 1991. The pre-war population of Eastern Slavonia was approximately 44 per cent Croatian, 36 per cent Serbs and 10 per cent Hungarian. According to figures of the United Nations High Commissioner for Refugees, in 1996, the total population living in the UNTAES area was estimated to be 160,000, including refugees and internally displaced persons.[36] Serbs now make up 90 per cent of the population, with an estimated number of 60,000 to 70,000 displaced Croatians eligible to return.

The economy of Eastern Slavonia was based on its being one of the richest agricultural regions in Croatia prior to the war. However, much of the farming was severely disrupted by the war, and in September 1996, when I visited the area, there was no evidence of agricultural production. There are oil deposits in the area, access to which was contested by the Serbs and Croats, and the oil fields had been heavily mined.

According to Administrator Klein, unemployment in Eastern Slavonia was over 60 per cent in October 1996. Nevertheless, it was difficult to find Serb employees who would be willing to work in Croatian public enterprises,[37] thus severely hindering the reintegration of the Croatian economy. Another difficulty was convincing members of the Serb community to accept Croatian citizenship 'to fill the approximately 700 local positions in the Croatian police force in the post-UNTAES period'.[38] Another major contentious issue is that many of the Serbs who arrived in Eastern Slavonia as displaced persons from other parts of Croatia now live in homes not their own, and frequently are squatters in the homes of Croatian displaced persons. Another contentious issue is that of amnesty for those Croatian Serbs who took part in the fighting in 1991 and since.

COMMUNITY CONFIDENCE

The confidence of the Croatian Serb community in Eastern Slavonia in their future in Croatia was initially not high. This lack of confidence was based in part on hard historical evidence, especially following the Croatian military operations 'Flash' in May 1995, which cleared Western Slavonia of Serb forces within 40 hours, and 'Operation Storm', which drove 170,000 Serbs from the Krajina in August 1995. Many of these refugees, in fact, eventually resettled in Eastern Slavonia.

A public opinion poll conducted in early 1997 by the National Democratic Institute of the United States researched attitudes of Serbian and Croatian displaced persons in Eastern Slavonia and in Osijek (the town in Croatia to which many Croatians fled in 1991). Most of the Serbs polled in the region 'regarded Croatia as their country but did not regard Croatian institutions, even current Serb politicians, as representing them'. Even though they did not show anything more than a cultural affinity with the 'Federal Republic of Yugoslavia' (FRY), they 'most commonly' expected that they would have to move there or elsewhere outside Croatia. 'There was strong anger expressed at FRY/Milosevic as they felt used and manipulated in a game over which they have no control. They saw everyone as being against them – Serbia, Croats, UN.'[39]

Among the Croatian displaced persons polled, 'the most significant concerns were economic – job creation, employment, and compensation for war crime sufferers'. There was no sympathy for Serb displaced persons 'who should all leave the region and the country ... as Serbs created the problems. Those few pre-1991 Serb residents ... envisaged staying (characterized as old people), should, however, be allowed some minority rights.'[40] There were clear expectations among Croat displaced persons that they would get their own homes back; estimates among the displaced in Osijek as to how many would return to Eastern Slavonia, ranged from 30 to 70 per cent.[41] These attitudes persisted up to the elections in mid-April, as reported by Zodan Radosavljevic and Jovan Kovacic, respectively from both Croats and Serbs.[42]

MEDIA ENVIRONMENT

Residents of Eastern Slavonia have access to Croatian, Serb and RSK (Republic of Serb Krajina) television, and these are the main sources of information for most of the people living there.[43] Mark Thompson has described largely successful efforts to control and silence independent voices in Serbian and Croatian media from 1992 onward. Of the Serbian media he says: 'Media could not produce a nationalist society; without the media, however, Serbia's leaders could not have obtained public consent and approval of their extreme nationalist politics.'[44] Consequently, according to one UNTAES staff member who lived with a local Serb family and watched nightly television with them in Vukovar, 'there is 100 per cent support from the people for the current regimes and anyone who dares to dissent is a fascist and/or on the CIA payroll'.[45] As far as Croatian media are concerned, 'the only regional daily, *Glas Slavonie*, as well as the radio and TV are completely in the hands of Glavas',[46] and, according to Zlatko Kovatch, there is only one independent print medium, *Bumerang*, which, in mid-1996 printed approximately 7,000 copies, of which 4,000 were sold.[47]

The predominant tone of media reporting in Croatia about UNTAES activities was consequently not positive, a matter raised by the Transitional Administrator, Mr Klein, in reports to the Secretary-General. The latter subsequently informed the Security Council that UNTAES' 'operational intent' was 'misrepresented in the Croatian media', and 'the orchestrated attack on UNTAES in the Croatian media, [which] appeared to be related to domestic political factors and not to the activities of UNTAES on the ground.'[48]

However, there were several local and international non-governmental organizations, such as the 'Centre for Peace, Non-Violence and Human Rights', in Eastern Slavonia which, with much support from European peace centres, organized family reunions and community-based events of a confidence building nature during the period under review.[49]

UNTAES' EFFORTS AT CONFIDENCE BUILDING

In a press conference held at UN Headquarters in Vukovar, on 10 October 1996, the UNTAES Administrator, Mr Klein, said that UNTAES, which had just concluded the demilitarization of Eastern Slavonia by 'moving 16,000 Serb regular troops with their equipment, including 120 tanks, 100 artillery pieces, and 140 mortars', would now have to turn to the 'psychological demilitarization' of the people of the area.[50] Klein, throughout the period leading up to the elections held on 13 and 14 April 1997, exuded optimism and confidence about the peace process. For example, following a series of attacks and incidents of intimidation by both sides between December 1996 and February 1997,[51] he gave press briefings in which he reassured everyone that the process was on track, and that he did not envisage large population movements by Serbs following the end of the transitional period.[52] Klein used his meetings with President Tudjman of Croatia and other senior Croatian officials as opportunities to give the Serbs living in Eastern Slavonia assurances that their rights would be respected in the territory in the future.[53]

A very successful and important innovation of this UN mission was the organization of a weekly 'market day' in Klisa, on the highway between Osijek and Vukovar, in the 'Zone of Separation' established by UNTAES. This market was accessible to both Serbs and Croats from within the region and from Osijek. It was a very popular venue for family reunions and some trading, and certainly helped to build confidence and trust between the communities. At peak weekends, thousands of visitors appeared, with dozens of vendors offering their wares. Administrator Klein often personally attended the market day. The UNTAES Public Affairs Programme distributed information materials from a tent established for the purpose.[54]

Among UNTAES' many civil affairs projects, notable is the creation of a Transitional Administrator's Award fund which supports 'quick impact small community projects' such as mine marking in graveyards, thus recognizing individual contributions to the reintegration process. In general, the economic and social needs were so great in this war-devastated region, that UNTAES civil affairs projects ranged from the repair of the street lights of Vukovar to assistance in the delivery of sugar beets to the refinery in Osijek.

UNTAES PUBLIC AFFAIRS

The Public Affairs Programme, while different in name from the information components of operations reviewed in earlier Chapters, was similar to the Namibia and Cambodia operations described earlier, a well-funded and professionally-staffed effort at a comprehensive information campaign. Significantly, it was part of UNTAES' operational plan from the outset. The fist wave of UNTAES civilian staff arrived in the mission area in January 1997. The Spokesman, Philip Arnold, arrived in March 1996. Mr Arnold had been Spokesman of the UN in Zagreb since June 1995; he had previously been Spokesman of the US Mission to the UN in New York from 1989 to 1993, and had had an earlier career with the United States Information Agency in Washington, DC, and as a journalist.

In October 1996, the UNTAES Public Affairs budget was about $125,000 per six months, plus the salaries for 11 international and 17 local staff, ie a total of about $850,000 a year.[55] At that time, UNTAES broadcast on Radio Vukovar three hours a day, from Monday to Friday. Mr Arnold, as a professional radio broadcaster, produced many of the radio programmes himself, following the establishment of a small studio at UNTAES headquarters. But there had been difficult negotiations with local authorities before UNTAES radio programming could be extended to those three hours daily.[56] Describing UNTAES information activities, the Secretary-General reported to the Security Council in February 1997:

> A priority theme of UNTAES public affairs is to explain the political, ethnic and civil rights which have been guaranteed to residents of the region. The deep fear and mistrust of Croatian authority among local Serb residents is difficult to overcome. Psychological harassment from the Croatian side in the form of television and media propaganda, telephone calls and hate mail undermines confidence. The Croatian media covering the mission, however, have reduced their negative reporting and commentary in recent weeks. UNTAES local language bulletins continue to be circulated three times a month ...[57]

In March 1997, this situation changed drastically. UNTAES had by now entered the crucial pre-election period during which access by the political parties to all available information channels was essential to the conduct of a free and fair election. UNTAES now controlled the radio transmitters in the region and managed to broadcast 11–12 hours a day.

Furthermore, on 5 March 1997, it was reported that UNTAES had begun transmission of its own daily television programme, having secured access to the Belje transmission tower in Eastern Slavonia.[58] Following a personal request from Administrator Klein, a UN television producer from New York was seconded to the mission for a month to help produce UNTAES daily television programmes in Serbo-Croat. Steve Whitehouse, an experienced UN information hand, considered his work in UNTAES a 'unique experience', due to the fact that, by the time he got to the area, 'UNTAES had complete access to the air waves'.[59] The one-hour television programmes he produced were a mix of news reports, electoral education, statements by the UNTAES Administrator and other officials. While he lauded this 'ambitious attempt' at information, Whitehouse doubts whether the UNTAES experience can be seen as typical for information efforts of future UN missions, as it would be unlikely that so much political control by the UN could be achieved in the future.[60]

In the post-election period, UNTAES still produced a 30 minute weekly show three times a week 'on key subjects'. As of the last week of April 1997, the radio broadcasts were reduced to seven hours a day. The UNTAES *Bulletin*, its main voice in print, was published three times a month, in an edition of 60,000 copies. Its main message in the post-election period was 'Look to your future here in the region'.[61]

As this case shows, cooperation between UN information officers at Headquarters and the field need not pose serious problems. Mr Arnold reported having received 'crucial' support from the UN Department of Public Information in New York from the start. In fact, a survey mission was conducted by a senior radio officer from DPI/New York in January 1996, who recommended that 'the start up phase be devoted to developing and sharpening the basic messages, preparation of background information and scouting for staff'.[62] A further positive factor was, as in the case of Cambodia, that many of the local and international staff of UNTAES Public Affairs were recruited from other UN missions in the former Yugoslavia. Prior experience and knowledge of local conditions was clearly an asset for the UNTAES information team.

POLITICAL LEADERSHIP

As noted in the case studies on Namibia, Cambodia and Haiti, the importance of the political leadership of the mission and the priority the top person in the mission area gave to information as a strategic management function, was vital in the case of UNTAES. Administrator Klein, nicknamed by some UNTAES staff 'King Klein', stated, for the record: 'Everything we do, all the progress we expect, will depend on public understanding and support. Our public information programme must be robust, tireless and extensive'.[63]

Mr Klein himself, as described above, spared no efforts at building trust and confidence among the two hostile local communities. He personally negotiated major agreements to assert UNTAES' role in all fields of operation, including the operation of radio and television transmitters, and he intervened when necessary with UN Headquarters in New York to secure additional support for the information programme of his mission. He personally chose an experienced spokesman and information specialist, Philip Arnold, who sought to set up a 'robust press and public information programme employing radio, print, press liaison and community relations activities',[64] and in turn recruited staff from among experienced information professionals in the region.

INTERNATIONAL MEDIA REPORTING

When my colleague and I from the Pearson Peacekeeping Centre visited Eastern Slavonia, many people in the United States and Canada asked: 'Where is that?' A more evocative response was sometimes elicited when we said 'Vukovar – where the war began …' Although international reporting of the shelling of Vukovar in 1991 had been extensive, UNTAES and its area of operations in 1996–97 were only known to those already familiar with the history and current politics of the former Yugoslavia. Even in Zagreb, in September 1996, people often gave us stares of disbelief when we expressed the desire to travel to Vukovar. For many Croatians it is still the symbol of *Schrecklichkeit* or, as Jamie Arbuckle has put it, the 'Croatian Guernica'.[65]

When UNTAES was launched in January–February 1996, it received some coverage in the US media, largely due to the fact that an American with a high media profile was running it. There has been so far very little coverage of this operation, as most of the international media concentrated on developments in Bosnia and the activities of IFOR (and later, SFOR). Even the elections in April 1997 received only passing mention in the US media, and most of that scanty coverage was of irregularities in the electoral process.[66] Among the European media, in Germany reporting also focused predominantly on technical and political difficulties during the elections. Finally, it was widely reported that Administrator Klein had declared the elections as 'free and fair'.[67] Klein also stated that the elections had been, despite some irregularities, 'a victory for reconciliation', and he reported to United Nations Headquarters on 28 April 1997: 'The challenge for the months to come is to find a bridge between Croatian triumphalism and Serb apprehension.'[68]

ASSESSMENT AND CONCLUSIONS

The UNTAES mission was continuing at the time the research for this book was completed. UNTAES' mandate ended on 15 January 1998 and at that time, its key mission objectives, which were 'to accomplish a peaceful, dignified and secure reintegration of the region to the Republic of Croatia' and 'to retain the multiethnic character of the region' were achieved. Much, obviously remains to be done by Croatia and the OSCE follow-up mission to ensure that human rights are fully respected and the conditions for the return of refugees and displaced persons are achieved. Much remains to be done in the field of economic development and the rebuilding of war-ravaged Eastern Slavonia. As in previous case studies, there is no guarantee for sustained and durable peace.

However, as far as UNTAES performance during the transitional period is concerned, it must be given high marks for performing according to the management criteria identified at the outset. In contrast to UNPROFOR, the UNTAES leadership did recognize from the beginning the importance public perceptions would have on the political and operational process. Its skilful and experienced information team was aware of the interaction between local, regional and international public opinion (principle 2); its public affairs programme was structured to include the mission-internal information process from the outset (principle 3). UNTAES's electoral and human rights campaign built on prior experiences in other successful missions; it was cognizant of Eastern Slavonia's military, political and cultural particulars without compromising international principles. Finally, UNTAES itself not only operated in an open, transparent fashion, but attempted to contribute to the diversification of the media landscape in the region through its own broadcasts, and by encouraging independent local journalists in the area.

There thus appears to have taken place an institutional learning process in the transition from UNPROFOR to UNTAES. UNTAES information programme was better planned, designed, staffed and guided by its operational-level leadership and information teams. It clearly was appropriate to the mandate and guided by its mandate, stayed within its budgetary means and adapted them creatively. UNTAES showed an effort well worth emulating by other operations in this region and elsewhere in the future.

NOTES

1. Misha Glenny, *The Fall of Yugoslavia – The Third Balkan War*, New York: Penguin, 3rd edn, 1996, p.21.
2. Miron Rezun, *Europe and War in the Balkans – Toward a New Yugoslav Identity*, Westport, CT and London: Praeger, 1996, p.196.
3. Mark Thompson, *Forging War – The Media in Serbia, Croatia and Bosnia-Herzegovina*, Avon, UK: Bath Press, 1994.
4. Susan L. Woodward, *Balkan Tragedy – Chaos and Dissolution after the Cold War*, Washington, DC: Brookings, 1995, pp.225–36.
5. Owen, Lord David, *Balkan Odyssey*, London: Victor Gollancz, 1995, p.236.
6. Mihailo Crnobrnja, *The Yugoslav Drama*, Montreal: McGill-Queen's University Press, 2nd edn, 1996, p.118.
7. UNSCR 721 of 27 Nov. 1991, and 'Report of the Secretary General' (S/23280) of 11 Dec. 1991.
8. UNSCR 758, 8 June 1992.
9. UNSCR 779, 6 Oct. 1992.
10. UNSCRs 819 of 16 April and 824 of 6 May 1993.
11. UNSCR 842 of 18 June 1993.
12. North Atlantic Council (NAC) Declaration 10–11 Jan. 1994, UNSCR 836 of 4 June 1993 and letter from Secretary-General of the UN to the Secretary-General of NATO dated 6 Feb. 1994.
13. Ibid., p.213.

14. *The Economist*, 'Shamed are the peacekeepers', 30 April–6 May 1994, p.15. The article cited 'botched jobs in Bosnia, Somalia, Angola. But never has the shame been sharper than in the past few weeks in Rwanda …'

15. Crnobrinja (n.6 above), p.212.

16. James V. Arbuckle, *The Level Killing Fields of Yugoslavia: An Observer Returns*, Occasional Paper No.2, Lester B. Pearson Canadian International Peacekeeping Training Centre, Cornwallis, Nova Scotia: The Pearson Press, 1998.

17. Major Yvon DesJardins to the author, April 1996.

18. Lena Yacoumopoulou, 'Information Campaigns in Peacekeeping Missions', (unpublished manuscript, Aug. 1994), p.6. This manuscript is cited with permission of the author; the views contained therein are her personal opinions and not necessarily those of the United Nations.

19. Ibid., p.8.

20. Lewis Mackenzie, *Peacekeeper: The Road to Sarajevo*, Toronto: Harper Collins, 1994, p.291.

21. Rezun (n.2 above), p.193; Renate Flottau, 'Ist die Welt Verrueckt?', *Der Spiegel* (10/1996), p.169, which reports allegations against Mackenzie and statement by Andreas Zumach, correspondent of *Die Tageszeitung* at the International Peacekeeping Training Centre in Stadtschlaining, Austria, on 12 Nov. 1996.

22. Mark Thompson, *A Paper House: The Ending of Yugoslavia*, New York: Pantheon Books, 1992, p.333 (emphasis in original).

23. Thompson (n.3 above), pp.169–70.

24. Quoted in ibid., p.170.

25. UNPROFOR's weekly situation reports were replete with instances in which roadblocks, blockades and hijackings hindered UNPROFOR operations throughout this period.

26. Jamie V. Arbuckle, 'UNTAES: The Past that was Prologue', (unpublished manuscript, March 1997) p.2.

27. 'Report of the Secretary General' (S/26470), dated 20 Sept. 1993.

28. Information received from United Nations Secretariat officials and delegates to the UN Security Council in the summer of 1996.

29. Owen (n.5 above), p.29.

30. *The Blue Helmets*, a *Review of United Nations Peacekeeping* (3rd edn, United Nations, New York, 1996), p.563.

31. Age Eknes, 'The United Nations Predicament in the Former Yugoslavia', in Thomas G. Weiss (ed.), *The United Nations and Civil Wars*, Boulder: Lynne Rienner, 1995, p.121.

32. The Secretary General was speaking in an atmosphere of some urgency: Croatian forces had overrun Western Slavonia in May in less than 40 hours, and had done the same in the Krajina in Aug. in four days. The UN Sector East had estimated in Oct. that the Croatians could mount an attack in Eastern Slavonia in 96 hours, that plans to evacuate the UN forces to Hungary and the FRY would be severely hampered by refugee traffic, and that the UN casualties would be significant. See Arbuckle (n.16 above).

33. S/RES/1023 (1995), and *The Blue Helmets*, (n.30 above), p.554: 'In the Secretary-General's view, the minimum strength needed to implement the Basic Agreement and deter attacks … would require a mechanized division of two brigades, with combat capability, air support and a strong armoured reserve, comprising 9,300 combat and 2,000 logistics troops.' In the event, UNTAES had just about that repertoire of capabilities, but with only 5,000 troops.

34. Barbara Crossette, 'Bhoutros-Ghali's Query to Albright: "What Went Wrong?"', *The*

New York Times, 1 Jan. 1997).

35. See International Crisis Group Report 'Bosnia Project – Eastern Slavonia', 27 March 1996, by Major-General (retd.) John-Arch MacInnis (and others), (available at http://www.intl-crisis-group.org).
36. Fact Sheet 6, included in the Information Package on UNTAES provided by the United Nations Department of Public Information, dated 12 July 1996.
37. The Secretary-General's report to the Security Council of 24 Feb. 1997 refers to an affidavit by the Government of Croatia 'in which it guaranteed the continued employment of Serb employees in public enterprises to be reintegrated' (S/1997/148, para 13).
38. Ibid., para.23.
39. Results of public opinion poll conducted by 'Lake Research' on behalf of the NDI/US, as summarized in: Situation report # 14, covering period 1–10 Jan. 1997.
40. Ibid., p.4.
41. Ibid.
42. Reuters reports of 10 April 1997, Zoran Radosavljevic, 'Croat refugees see no life with Serbs after war', and of 11 April 1997, Jovan Kovacic, 'Croatian Serbs want international protection'.
43. This section is based on information gathered while doing research in Eastern Slavonia in Sept. 1996, on information received on the internet from the OMRI daily digest, and from other researchers in the field. I would like to particularly thank Kristof Gostonyi, currently doing research at Yale University, for his help in this regard. I also received valuable information from an article by Frank Hofmann, 'Unabhaengige Medien Ex-Jugoslawien – Pressefreiheit, Ins Aus demonstriert' (3 March 1997, received by e-mail).
44. Thompson (n.3 above), p.128.
45. Gary Collins to author, 9 Feb. 1997.
46. Crnobrnja (n.6 above), p.170. According to Crnobrnja, Branimit Glavas was commander of the 'Glavas Unit' which 'gained fame by ethnically cleansing Serb villages in the vicinity of the front-line town of Osijek'. In 1996 he was the mayor of Osijek.
47. Zlatko Kovach, 'Eastern Slavonia Human Rights Report', June 1996, p.4. *Bumerang*, according to Kavatch, was highly dependent on funds from the Soros-Foundation. An article by the Balkan Peace Team – Croatia, 'New Wave of Media Suppression in Croatia' reported on 9 May 1996 that 'those publications in Croatia which have remained independent have come under repeated attack by the government', and that Croatian Radio-Television 'has on several occasions not broadcast statements made by foreign diplomats in highly public forums on the need to observe human and minority rights' (*balkan-peace-team@bionic.zer.de*).
48. Report of the Secretary-General on the United Nations Transitional Administration for Eastern Slavonia, Baranja and Western Sirmium (S/1996/883) of 26 Oct. 1996, paras.4 and 5.
49. 'Rough Guide to the Humanitarian Situation in Eastern Slavonia' (manuscript dated March 1996), and internet-site for the Centre for Peace.
50. Summary of Press Briefing by UNTAES Administrator, United Nations, New York, 1 Oct. 1996.
51. As reported in *OMRI Daily Digest* of 30 Dec. 1996, 'Serbs Besiege Croats in Eastern Slavonia attending Christmas Mass', of 8 Jan. 1997, '… and Explosion damages Catholic Church in Eastern Slavonia', 29 Jan. 1997, 'Serbian Mob attacks Croatian Officials in Eastern Slavonia' and 3 Feb. 1997, 'Incidents continue in Eastern Slavonia'.
52. See, for example, *OMRI Daily Digest* of 12 June 1996, 'UN Foresees Extension of

Mandate in Eastern Slavonia', 9 Dec. 1996, 'Donors Pledge over $30 million for Eastern Slavonia', of 6 Jan. 1997, 'Croatia makes Offer to Serbs in Eastern Slavonia', and 17 Feb. 1997, 'Klein says most Serbs will stay in Eastern Slavonia'.

53. See *Secretary-General's Reports on UNTAES*, S/1996/883 and S/1997/148. On 12 Dec. 1996, the President of the Security Council issued a statement in which the Council expressed concern 'at continued acts of harassment, looting and physical attacks against Croatian Serbs and, in particular, involvement by Croatian uniformed military and police officers in a number of those incidents'. (S/PRST, 1996/48).

54. My colleague from the Pearson Peacekeeping Centre and I visited the marketplace in Klisa in Sept. 1996. It apparently became a regular, and very popular event throughout the fall of 1996, except for a brief period in Nov. when Croatian officials tried to prevent it from taking place (according to UNTAES weekly report, 19–25 Nov. 1996).

55. The information contained in this section is based on figures provided by Mr Arnold in Oct. 1996.

56. S/1996/821, para.13 of 1 Oct. 1996.

57. S/1997/148 of 24 Feb. 1997, para.25.

58. Press Release DH/2343, p.4.

59. Steve Whitehouse to the author, 19 April 1997. Whitehouse also had experience in half a dozen other UN peacekeeping missions.

60. Whitehouse to the author. He also warned against being over-optimistic regarding television and radio shows produced by outsiders such as the UN to effect attitude change in war-torn populations: 'You don't change people's minds by Mickey Mouse UN radio programmes ...'

61. Information received from Phil Arnold on 21 April 1997. In his letter, he also stated that the expanded information effort required additional funding and that his budget had expanded by $130,000 since Oct. 1996.

62. Memorandum by Ayman El-Amir, Chief Radio Section, DPI 'Mission Report on Eastern Slavonia', dated 5 Feb. 1996.

63. As quoted by Philip Arnold, in a letter to the author, dated Oct. 1996.

64. 'UNTAES Public Affairs Programme', unpublished paper, dated April 1996 and provided by Mr Arnold, p.1.

65. Arbuckle (n.16 above).

66. See *New York Times*, 14 April 1997, 'Voting Mishaps Add to Tension in Serbian Enclave in Croatia' and 15 April 'Croatian Opposition Defeats President's Party in Vote in Capital'.

67. 'UNO:Kroatien-Wahl war frei und fair', *Der Tagespiegel*, 24 April 1997.

68. *RFE News*, 23 April 1997 and 'Elections Report' sent by Jacques Klein to the Under Secretary-General for Peacekeeping at UN Headquarters on 28 April 1997, p.4.

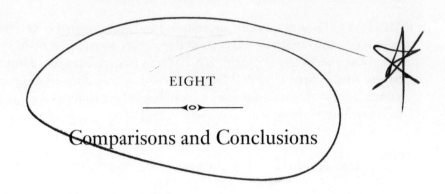

EIGHT

◄◦►

Comparisons and Conclusions

The six principles enunciated in Chapter 1 may now be summarized in their application to the five case studies.

PRINCIPLE 1: THE EFFECT OF PUBLIC PERCEPTIONS

Prior to 1988, peacekeeping operations generally did not reflect an awareness of the direct and dynamic effect that public perceptions could have on operations. All five case studies have shown that this now seemingly self-evident factor has become an essential element in the second-generation peacekeeping operations under review in this book. UNTAG, UNTAC, UNMIH and UNTAES were proactive from the very outset in their determination to manage information effectively and openly. In Rwanda, UNAMIR did not do so and, as was the case with UNPROFOR, was conspicuously prey to unrealistic interpretations of its mandate. UNAMIR suffered as well from false expectations of just what a force of 400 peacekeepers might be able to achieve under conditions of civil war, anarchy and genocide. UNAMIR was, in every sense, 'helpless in the cross-fire'; Principle 1 thus applied, albeit negatively and entirely to the detriment of the operation.

PRINCIPLE 2: INTERNATIONAL AND LOCAL OPINION

UNTAC, UNTAG, UNMIH and UNTAES were concerned, at the operational and tactical levels, with creating a positive climate of public opinion. At the strategic level, this was explicitly expressed only in the Paris Agreements which authorized the Cambodia operation. In Namibia, the information component was effectively added on by the UN Secretariat; it was also quite effectively adapted to the Haiti mission in the creation of the

MISTs. The Rwanda mission, understaffed and overwhelmed in all aspects as it faced one of the great tragedies of the century was, until early in 1995, speechless and largely impotent. UNTAES in Eastern Slavonia, doubtless having learned from UNPROFOR, demonstrated from the very beginning great resolve in communicating with the public in both communities, as well as internally with its own mission members.

PRINCIPLE 3: THE INFORMATION COMPONENT OF THE MISSION

Only UNTAC in Cambodia had positive and specific direction from the strategic (political and diplomatic) level, as contained in the Paris Agreement. Namibia was a case of brilliant, but eleventh-hour, improvisation at the operational level. The operation in Haiti saw a successful, albeit ad hoc, melding of military and civilian capabilities, and showed innovative information techniques in the application of MIST. This was a case of a successful application of new techniques at the tactical level which became an effective operational tool in an anarchic environment. UNTAES, in setting up a strong information component, is a case of a forceful and aware head of mission being allowed to have his own way in executing an effective public affairs programme. As Phil Arnold, the UNTAES Spokesman put it, with pardonable hyperbole: 'You only need three things to set up a peacekeeping mission: an office, some cars and a radio station. Everything else can follow later on.'[1] The Rwanda mission, despite a dynamic and charismatic military leader, was leaderless at the strategic–political level until well after the 1994 crisis had passed.

PRINCIPLE 4: ISSUE-SPECIFIC EDUCATIONAL PROGRAMMES

The Namibia and Cambodia missions were much alike in their overtly political scope, and effectively targeted voter education as a major function of their missions' overall goals. UNMIH in Haiti set out to be an enforcement mission. However, with the early success of the military aspects of the mission, UNMIH swiftly transformed itself to concentrate more on the political tasks in a manner similar to UNTAG and UNTAC. The UNTAES leadership realized early on that commerce, freedom of movement and community confidence were the real challenges, and addressed those issues positively and educationally. It was a signal success of the information campaign of UNTAES, especially when compared to its antecedent, that it managed to foster more positive attitudes in both the Serb and the Croatian communities without jeopardizing its credibility with either group.

PRINCIPLE 5: THE CULTURAL ENVIRONMENT

Missions with highly political goals, such as elections leading to the formation of legitimate governments, have of necessity been sensitive to the cultural environment, as in Namibia, Cambodia and Haiti. Much of their effectiveness has derived from successfully appreciating and even exploiting the cultural environment to their ends. This UNPROFOR most conspicuously failed to do; UNTAES clearly learned from that earlier omission. The continuing cultural and language difficulties of any operation composed of troops from a variety of regions and cultures should not, however, be overlooked as communication challenges for all future peacekeeping missions. UNTAC and UNPROFOR, in particular, faced serious credibility problems as a result of repeated allegations of insensitive, offensive behaviour by some of its military personnel.

PRINCIPLE 6: TRANSPARENCY

The mission, its objectives and its policies must be clear to all: the people, the governments – including those of the contributor states – and the staff of the mission itself. Where this requirement was recognized from the outset, false expectations were avoided or could be curbed, errors could be detected and corrected, and effective communications could be initiated and maintained. While this may appear self-evident to the outside observer, a close analysis of the UN operations in Rwanda in 1994 and in the Former Republics of Yugoslavia before 1996, shows that in such environments in which propaganda has become a tool for conducting war, the peacekeepers themselves will become targets and their efforts become vilified as failure, if not worse.

MAIN RESEARCH QUESTIONS REVIEWED

The four primary research questions which were posed in the Introduction of this study can now be answered in the following manner:

FIRST: Under which conditions did UN peacekeeping operations develop an effective information capacity? The case studies demonstrate that the combination of the application of the six management principles gave each peacekeeping operation where they were positively applied, a good vantage point from which to execute its mandate effectively. Making use of these management tools did not, of itself guarantee the success of these operations, but their contravention sooner or later had severe consequences in the realm of public perceptions. In those latter cases the chances of being caught helplessly in the crossfire increased enormously. Significant omissions condemned those missions to feeble attempts at *ex post facto* damage control in the face of the often ruthless propaganda campaigns of the belligerents.

SECOND: As UNPROFOR and UNAMIR showed, the consequences of not having an information programme were severe, both for the day-to-day operation and for the peace process as a whole. However, as neither one of these operations had a viable peace agreement to implement, it is difficult to judge the relative import of the absence of a strategic information campaign, especially given the overwhelmingly negative political, military and media environment in those countries. It therefore appears that an operation which is saddled with inoperable and contradictory mandates (UNPROFOR), and forced to work with a minimal budget (UNAMIR), is unlikely to have a viable information campaign among its priorities.

THIRD: Bureaucratic constraints continue to be a major lingering impediment to developing effective information campaigns in UN peacekeeping missions. These constraints have their origins both at the strategic level; ie the Security Council and the Secretary-General, and the quality of political analyses which guide their respective actions. Here, it happens that competing interests of states which may have a stake in keeping UN action in a certain conflict weak, divided or ineffectual, are usually the greatest restraining factor. In addition, conflicting interests of UN Departments involved in designing information programmes and uncertain interdepartmental responsibilities which may or may not be politically motivated, are recurrent, unresolved issues which require the assertion of the leadership of the Secretary-General and his office. Secretary-General Annan's July 1997 report *Renewing the United Nations* which, for the first time in the UN's history, describes communications as a strategic management function, is certainly a step in the right direction, but needs to be monitored in its implementation at the operational and tactical levels.

FOURTH: The single most important factor for overcoming bureaucratic constraints at the field level, as the case studies of Namibia, Cambodia and Eastern Slavonia have shown, is the role of political leadership of the mission itself, ie the Special Representative of the Secretary-General and his/her senior political advisers. These studies have shown that, once a mission leadership had decided that strategic communication was important to achieving its goals, issues of funding and recruiting of competent and trained staff were usually resolved without difficulties.

AREAS FOR FUTURE RESEARCH

Among the main issues raised by this book, the overarching one is the future impact of the public dimension on the conduct of international relations. To what extent the United Nations will face issues of legitimacy, similar to those encountered by the European Union,[2] cannot be accurately estimated at this time. Suffice it to say that Secretary-General Annan has in 1997 given the concept of 'civil society' prominence in his reports and public statements. This whole area of study would thus lend itself to further exploration and empirical analysis.

The continuing problems of collaboration between the political and information departments of the United Nations, especially in evolving standards for information components, media strategies and educational campaigns in peacekeeping missions, need to be monitored by scholars and academics of the United Nations.

Whether the issue of communication as a strategic management function will be institutionalized by the UN will also depend on a growing recognition of the importance of communications by delegates to its intergovernmental bodies. Here, further sensitization of diplomats representing their countries on the Security Council, senior managers and field mission staff will be needed. This would appear to be a fruitful area for future research and training.

In areas of conflict where racial, ethnic, religious and political hate propaganda is clearly a tool of the belligerents, the Security Council should take this into account and issue specific information mandates for any mission, civilian or military, which might be deployed in such a scenario. Further study of the role of counterpropaganda in future conflicts is particularly needed. As all case studies have shown, proactive radio programmes by the peacekeepers are desirable in most information environments. Whether jamming of hate radio, which has been advocated by some international observers of conflicts in Central Africa or the Balkans, is either legally acceptable or politically advisable in peacekeeping operations, is a highly sensitive issue, but one which is outside the scope of this book.

FAILED STATE

A larger issue for future peacekeeping operations is the reality of the failed or failing state structures in many areas of the world. As we have seen, proliferating intrastate conflicts have almost entirely replaced traditional interstate conflicts. These internal conflicts are typically accompanied by, where they do not result directly from, a breakdown in governance. The resultant failing states, as manifested in almost all of the cases analysed in this book, pose a growing threat to peace and security. The challenges presented by these failed states, where governmental functions are suspended, the police and judiciary have collapsed, infrastructure has been destroyed and populations have been uprooted, will have immeasurable impact on intervention strategies, and thus on their supporting information programmes. What will be the effect of state failure on the consent issue? How will partnerships be built in conditions of anarchy? How will the mission communicate, as we have seen that it must, and with whom?

Much more consideration needs to be given to the strategic and operational aspects of a mission to a failed state, and how this will impact on information programmes.

CONCLUSIONS

It seems clear from the summary of the case studies depicted in this book that if one management principle is to be identified as primary, it is the third: that field missions must have integral information programmes. These must be installed from the outset in the basic structure of the mission. Eleventh-hour improvisations and add-ons, no matter how brilliant, run just too many risks of being, at the least, too little and too late. At the worst, the mission may be speechless and impotent.

Speechlessness and loss of credibility, as was most evident in the cases of UNPROFOR and UNAMIR, can encourage scapegoating of the UN by the warring parties, based on often deliberately promulgated false expectations, rumours and misinformation. The record which emerges as a result of the case studies is of a conspicuous absence of strategic direction – from the Security Council – to provide for this vital information function in peace-keeping operations. While, on several occasions, inspired juggling and horse-trading by the UN Secretariat and the staff in the field have succeeded in creating viable information components despite rather than because of strategic direction, these ad hoc solutions did not reflect effective manage-ment of highly political and highly visible missions in dangerous crises. It cannot be overstated that, as in all key management functions, the aims, structures and even the budgets of information campaigns must manifest a seamless continuum at the strategic, operational and tactical levels. The United Nations has a message, and it thus has a responsibility no less serious than any other aspect of its operations, to see that message accurately transmitted. No organization as important as the UN in the maintenance of international peace and security can be passive in this regard.

In the new peacekeeping environment of civil and ethnic wars, where hate propaganda is increasingly used as a weapon by the belligerents, ignoring the impact of this information tool is no longer an option. The perils of excluding information components from modern peacekeeping operations are public relations disasters for which the United Nations, due to repeated omissions, has already borne far more than its share of blame.

EPILOGUE: THE CLOSURES OF UNMIH AND UNTAES

As this book was being written, UNMIH and UNTAES completed their mandates, and were wound up, although both have successor missions. It is therefore possible to judge of their efforts with somewhat more definition.

UNMIH

> At the end of June 1996, the mandate for the United Nations Mission in Haiti came to an end, concluding a major phase in the United Nations efforts to help the Haitian people restore democracy, stability and the rule of law in their country. ... Reflecting a request from the Haitian government, the Secretary-General has proposed a new, smaller operation, the United Nations Support Mission in Haiti (UNSMIH). The new mission would help Haiti consolidate the gains already made in professionalizing the Haitian National Police ...[3]

As initially authorized by the Security Council (UNSCR 1063 [1996]), UNSMIH was to consist of 300 civilian police and 600 troops; the initial mandate was to end on 30 November 1996. At the request of the President of Haiti, the Security Council extended the mandate (UNSCR 1086[1996]) to 31 May 1997, and again, at the request of the Secretary-General, for a final time until 31 July, 1997.[4]

There are two significant aspects of this final phase, and both have their origins in a successful information campaign and its effects on the always vital issue of consent. The first point to note is that these extensions were at the request of the Haitian Government who had, despite the obvious stresses of hosting UNMIH, become convinced of its value and of the country's continuing need for this mentoring assistance.

The second point is the very high degree of support for the mission on the part of the international community, who had become convinced of its long term benefits both to the host nation and for the peace and security of the region. One troop contributor continued its military contingent as a unilateral contribution, at no cost to the UN.

UNTAES

UNTAES completed its mandate as scheduled on 15 January 1998. However, at the request of the Croatian government, the Security Council had agreed in its Resolution 1145 (1997) 'to establish a support group of 180 civilian monitors, for a single period of nine months … to continue monitoring the performance of the Croatian police in the Danube region …'. In addition, the OSCE and UNHCR will continue to be active in the area. Two very encouraging developments have been noted: 'there has been no large outflow of refugees from the region and resettlement has been peaceful',[5] and there were no developments in the area which might have impacted unfavourably on operations in Bosnia-Herzegovina. Moreover, 'in the latter part of 1997, some 6,000 Croats and 9,000 Serbs returned to their original homes', and, 'as of 4 December 1997, over 145,000 citizenship papers and 126,000 passports have been issued to residents in the region'.[6]

Peace was given its chance in Eastern Slavonia. Consent was won against some formidable odds, and was maintained amid constant danger of rupture. The tone of the Croatian government was modified by constant pressure from the UN mission, while the initially bleak prospects of the last Serb enclave in Croatia were modified by the constant encouragement and reassurances of the UN personnel. A balance was achieved, invaluable time was won, positive attitudes were built and nurtured. The successful information campaign was a successful peace campaign, and the very government which had vilified the peacekeepers of just a few years earlier, have now requested a form of continuation of this mission, ie its police monitors.

NOTES

1. *1997 Year in Review, United Nations Peace Missions,* Department of Public Information, United Nations, New York, Dec., 1997.
2. Gramberger, *Die Oeffentlichkeitsarbeit der Euroepaeischen Kommission,* Baden-Baden: Nomos Verlagsellschaft, 1997 argues very convincingly that an effective information policy is vital to increasing legitimacy in the European Union.
3. *UN Mission in Haiti (UNMIH),* the Department of Public Information, the United Nations, New York, Sept. 1996; see htpp://www.un.org/Depts/DPKO/Missions/unmih_b.htm.

4. *Haiti (UNSMIH)*, the Department of Public Information, the United Nations, New York, Sept. 1996; see htpp://www.un.org/Depts/DPKO/Missions/unsmih.htm.
5. *Croatia – UNTAES: Recent Developments*, The Department of Public Information, United Nations, New York, 22 Dec. 1997; see http://www.un.org/Depts/DPKO/Missions/untaes_r.htm.
6. Ibid.

Bibliography

A. BOOKS

Abramson, Jeffrey B., Arterton, Christopher and Orren, Gary, *The Electronic Commonwealth: The Impact of New Media on Democratic Politics*, New York: Basic Books, 1988.

Anson, Robert Sam, *War News: A Young Reporter in Indochina*, New York: Simon & Schuster, 1989.

Ansprenger, Franz, *Freie Wahlen in Namibia*, Berliner Studien zur Politik in Afrika, No.10, Frankfurt: Lang, 1991.

Arbuckle, James V., *The Level Killing Fields of Yugoslavia: An Observer Returns*, Occasional Paper 2, Lester B. Pearson Canadian International Peacekeeping Training Centre, Cornwallis, Nova Scotia: The Pearson Press, 1998.

Aukofer, Frank and Lawrence, William P. (eds), *America's Team – A Report on the Relationship Between the Media and the Military*, Nashville, Tennessee: The Freedom Forum First Amendment Center, 1995.

Azimi, Nassrine (ed.), *The United Nations Transitional Authority in Cambodia: Debriefing and Lessons*, Netherlands: Kluwer Academic Publishers, 1994.

Bagdikian, Ben H., *The Media Monopoly*, Boston: Beacon Press, 1983.

Bates, Stephen, *If No News Send Rumours: Anecdotes of American Journalism*, New York: Henry Holt and Company, 1989.

Bloch, Marc, *The Historian's Craft*, New York: Vintage, 1953.

Bonner, Raymond, *Weakness and Deceit: US Policy and El Salvador*, New York: Times Books, 1984.

Booth, Ken and Smith, Steve (eds), *International Relations Theory Today*, University Park, PA: Pennsylvania State University Press, 1995.

Bridgland, Fred, *The War for Africa – Twelve Months That Transformed A Continent*, Gibraltar: Ashanti, 1990.

Brink, Andre, *Imaginings of Sand*, New York: Harcourt, Brace and Jovanovich, 1996.

Bull, Hedley, *The Anarchical Society: A Study of Order in World Politics*, London: Macmillan, 1977.

Cate, Fred, 'Communications, Policy-Making, and Humanitarian Crises', in Rotberg, Robert I. and Weiss, Thomas G. (eds), *From Massacres to Genocide, The Media, Public Policy and Humanitarian Crises*, Washington, DC: Brookings, 1996.

Cohen, Bernard C., *The Public's Impact on Foreign Policy*, Boston: Little Brown & Co, 1973.

Comstock, George, *Public Communication and Behaviour*, Vol.2, Orlando: Academic Press, 1989.

Crnobrnja, Mihailo, *The Yugoslav Drama*, Montreal: McGill-Queen's University Press, 2nd edn, 1996.

Crocker, Chester A., *High Noon in Southern Africa, Making Peace in a Rough Neighborhood*, New York: Norton, 1992.

Dennis, Everette (ed.), *The Media at War: The Press and the Persian Gulf Conflict*, New York: Gannett Foundation Media Center, 1991.

de Sola Pool, Ithiel, 'The Mass Media and Politics in the Modernization Process', in Pye, Lucian W. (ed.), *Communications and Political Development*, Princeton, NJ: Princeton University Press, 1963.

de Sola Pool, Ithiel, *Technologies Without Boundaries: On Telecommunications in a Global Age*, Cambridge: Harvard University Press, 1990.

Der Derian, James (ed.), *International Theory – Critical Investigations*, New York: New York University Press, 1995.

Durch, William E. (ed.), *The Evolution of UN Peacekeeping – Case Studies and Comparative Analysis*, New York: St Martin's Press, 1993.

Elshtain, Jean, *Women and War*, Brighton: Harvester Press, 1987.

Fiske, John, *Reading the Popular*, London: Unwin Hyman, 1989.

Findlay, Trevor, *Cambodia – The Legacy and Lessons of UNTAC*, SIPRI Research Report No.9, Oxford University Press, 1995.

Fisler Damrosch, Lori (ed.), *Enforcing Restraint – Collective Intervention in Internal Conflicts*, New York: Council on Foreign Relations, 1993.

Franck, Thomas M. and Nolte, Georg, 'The Good Offices Function of the United Nations', in Roberts, Adam (ed.), *United Nations, Divided World*, Oxford: Clarendon, 1993.

Ganley, Oscar and Ganley, Gladys, *To Inform or to Control? The New Communications Networks*, Norwood: New Jersey, 1989.

George, Alexander, *Forceful Persuasion: Coercive Diplomacy as an Alternative to War*, Washington, DC: US Institute of Peace Press, 1991.

George, Alexander, *Bridging the Gap: Theory and Practice in Foreign Policy*,

Washington, DC: US Institute of Peace Press, 1993.

Glenny, Misha, *The Fall of Yugoslavia – The Third Balkan War*, New York: Penguin, 3rd edn, 1996.

Goldstein, Judith and Keohane, Robert (eds), *Ideas and Foreign Policy: Beliefs, Institutions and Political Change*, Ithaca, London: Cornell University Press, 1993.

Gramberger, Marc R., *Die Oeffentlichkeitsarbeit der Europaeischen Kommission, 1952–1996 – PR zur Legitimation von Integration?*, Baden-Baden: Nomos Verlagsgesellschaft, 1997.

Gregg, Robert W. and Barkun, Michael, *The United Nations System and Its Functions*, Princeton, NJ: Van Nostrand, 1968.

Gregory, James R., *Marketing Corporate Image – The Company as our Number One Product*, Lincolnwood, Ill: NTC Publishing, 1993.

Grunig, James E., 'Communication, Public Relations, and Effective Organizations', in Grunig, James E. (ed.), *Excellence in Public Relations and Communication Management*, Hillsdale, 1992.

Gurr, Ted Robert, *Minorities at Risk, A Global View of Ethnopolitical Conflicts*, Washington, DC: US Institute of Peace Press, 1993.

Haas, Ernst B., *The United Nations and Collective Management of Conflict*, New York: United Nations Institute for Training and Research, 1986.

Habermas, Juergen, *The Structural Transformation of the Public Sphere*, Cambridge: MIT Press, {1962} 1989.

Halperin, Morton H. and Scheffer, David, *Self-Determination in the New World Order*, Washington, DC: Carnegie Endowment for International Peace, 1992.

Hampson, Fen Osler, *Nurturing Peace – Why Peace Settlements Succeed or Fail*, Washington, DC: US Institute of Peace Press, 1996.

Handy, Charles, *Understanding Organizations*, New York, Oxford: Oxford University Press, 1993.

Heder, Steve and Ledgerwood, Judy, *Propaganda, Politics, and Violence in Cambodia – Democratic Transition under United Nations Peace-keeping*, Armonk, New York: M.E. Sharpe, 1996.

Heininger, Janet, *Peacekeeping in Transition – The United Nations in Cambodia*, New York: Twentieth Century Fund, 1994.

Holt, Victoria, *Briefing Book on Peacekeeping – The US Role in United Nations Peace Operations*, Washington, DC: Council for a Livable World Education Fund, 1995.

Human Rights Watch, *Arming Rwanda – The Arms Trade and Human Rights Abuses in the Rwandan War*, New York: Human Rights Watch, 1994.

Inglehart, Ronald, *The Silent Revolution*, Princeton, NJ: Princeton University Press, 1977.

Innis, Harold, *The Bias of Communication*, Toronto: University of Toronto Press, 1951.

James, Alan, *Peacekeeping in International Politics*, New York: St Martin's Press, 1990.

Kaplan, Robert D., *Balkan Ghosts: A Journey Through History*, New York: Vintage, 1994.

Keohane, Robert, Nye, J. and Hoffmann, S. (eds), *After the Cold War: International Institutions and State Strategies in Europe, 1989–1991*, Cambridge, Mass: Harvard University Press, 1993.

Knightley, Philipp, *The First Casualty*, New York: Harcourt, Brace and Jovanovich, 1975.

Kriesberg, Louis and Thorson, Stuart (eds), *Timing the De-Escalation of International Conflicts*, New York: Syracuse, 1991.

Kunczik, Michael, *Images of Nations and International Public Relations*, Bonn: Friedrich-Ebert-Stiftung, 1990.

Lichter, S. Robert, Rothmann, Stanley and Lichter, Linda, *The Media Elite*, New York: Adler and Adler, 1986.

Lippmann, Walter, *Public Opinion*, New York: Free Press, {1922} 1965.

Lipset, Seymour Martin, *Consensus and Conflict*, New Brunswick, New Jersey: Transaction Books, 1985.

Liu, F.T., *United Nations Peacekeeping and the Non-use of Force*, Boulder, CO: Rienner, 1992.

Luard, Evan, *Peace and Opinion*, London: Oxford University Press, 1962.

MacArthur, John R., *Second Front Censorship and Propaganda in the Gulf War*, Berkeley: University of California Press, 1993.

MacKenzie, Lewis, *Peacekeeper: The Road to Sarajevo*, Toronto: Harper Collins, 1994.

McLuhan, Marshall, *Understanding Media*, New York: American Library, 1964.

Meisler, Stanley, *United Nations – the First Fifty Years*, New York: Atlantic Monthly Press, 1995.

Meyer, Robert S., *Peace Organizations Past and Present: A Survey and Directory*, Jefferson, N.C., London: McFarland, 1988.

Minear, Larry and Guillot, Philippe, *Soldiers to the Rescue – Humanitarian Lessons from Rwanda*, Paris: Development Centre of the OECD, 1996.

Morrison, Alex (ed.), *The New Peacekeeping Partnership*, Clementsport, NS: Pearson Peacekeeping Centre, 1995.

Morrison, Alex and Anderson, Dale (eds), *Peacekeeping and the Coming Anarchy*, Pearson Roundtable Series No.1, Clementsport, NS: Canadian Peacekeeping Press, 1996.

National Atlas of South West Africa (Namibia), Capetown: National Book-printers, 1983.

Neuman, Johanna, *Lights, Camera, War – Is Media Technology Driving International Politics?*, New York: St Martin's Press, 1996.

Neuman, W. Russell, *The Future of the Mass Audience*, Cambridge: Cambridge University Press, 1991.

Newsom, David D., *The Public Dimension of Foreign Policy*, Bloomington and Indianapolis: Indiana University Press, 1996.

Niedermayer, Oscar and Sinnott, Richard (eds), *Public Opinion and International Governance*, London: Oxford University Press, 1995.

Nimmo, Dan D. and Sanders, Keith R., *Handbook of Political Communication*, Beverly Hills/London: Sage, 1981.

Owen, David, *Balkan Odyssey*, New York: Harcourt, Brace and Jovanovich, 1996.

Parenti, Michael, *Inventing Reality: The Politics of the Mass Media*, New York: St Martin's Press, 1986.

Pedelty, Mark, *War Stories, The Culture of Foreign Correspondents*, New York/London: Routledge, 1995.

Postman, Neil, *Amusing Ourselves to Death*, New York: Viking, 1985.

Puetz, Joachim, von Egidy, Heich and Caplan, Perri (eds), *Namibia Handbook and Political Who's Who*, Windhoek: Magus, 1989.

Raevsky, Andrei, *Managing Arms in Peace Processes: Aspects of Psychological Operations and Intelligence*, United Nations, New York and Geneva, 1996.

Rezun, Miron, *Europe and War in the Balkans – Toward a New Yugoslav Identity*, Westport, CT/London: Praeger, 1996.

Riggs, Robert E. and Plano, Jack C., *The United Nations International Organization and World Politics*, Belmont, California: Wadsworth, 1994.

Rikhye, Indar Jit, *The Theory and Practice of Peacekeeping*, London: Hurst, 1984.

Roberts, Adam and Kingsbury, Benedict, *United Nations, Divided World–The UN's Roles in International Relations*, Oxford: Clarendon Press, 1993.

Rosenau, James N., *Public Opinion and Foreign Policy: An Operational Formulation*, New York: Random House, 1961.

Rosenau, James, *The Scientific Study of Foreign Policy: Essays on the Analysis of World Politics*, New York: Nichols, 1980.

Rosenau, James N., *Turbulence in World Politics*, Princeton, NJ: Princeton University Press, 1990.

Rosenau, James, *The United Nations in a Turbulent World*, Occasional Paper, New York: International Peace Academy, 1992.

Rotberg, Robert and Weiss, Thomas G. (eds), *From Massacres to Gencocide – The Media, Public Policy, and the Humanitarian Crises*, Harrisonburg, VA: Donnelley, 1996.

Russett, Bruce, *Power and Community in World Politics*, San Francisco: Freeman, 1974.

Russett, Bruce, *Controlling the Sword: the Democratic Governance of National Security*, Cambridge, MA: Harvard University Press, 1990.

Salmon, Charles T., *Information Campaigns: Balancing Social Values and Social Change*, Newbury Park, CA/London: Sage, 1989.

Schiller, Herbert, *The Mind Managers*, Boston: Beacon Press, 1973.

Schudson, Michael, *Advertising: the Uneasy Persuasion*, New York: Basic Books, 1984.

Sharkey, Jacqueline, *Under Fire – US Military Restrictions on the Media From Grenada to the Persian Gulf*, Washington, DC: The Center for Public Integrity, 1991.

Shawcross, William, *Cambodia's New Deal*, Washington, DC: Carnegie, 1994.

Smartt Bell, Madison, *All Souls' Rising*, New York: Pantheon, 1995.

Tehranian, Majid, *Technologies of Power: Information Machines and Democratic Prospects*, Norwood, NJ: Ablex, 1990.

Thompson, Mark, *Forging War – The Media in Serbia, Croatia and Bosnia-Hercegovina*, Avon, UK: Bath Press, 1994.

United States 4th Psychological Operations Group, *Capabilities Handbook*, 1993.

United States Information Agency, Bureau of Broadcasting, Office of Strategic Planning, *Report on the Mass Media Climate in Sub-Saharan Africa*, Washington, DC: USIA, 1995.

Urqhhart, Brian, *Hammarskjoeld*, New York: Alfred Knopf, 1972.

Urqhhart, Brian, *A Life in Peace and War*, London: Weidenfeld, 1987.

Virilio, Paul, *Speed and Politics*, New York: Columbia University, 1977.

Walzer, Michael, *Just and Unjust Wars: A Moral Argument with Historical Illustrations*, New York: Basic Books, 1977.

Weiss, Thomas (ed.), *The United Nations and Civil Wars*, Boulder, CO: Lynne Rienner, 1995,

Woodward, Susan, *Balkan Tragedy – Chaos and Dissolution after the Cold War*, Washington, DC: Brookings, 1995.

Zartman, William (ed.), *Elusive Peace – Negotiating an End to Civil Wars*, Washington, DC: Brookings, 1995.

Zartman, William (ed.), *Collapsed States: The Disintegration and Restoration of Legitimate Authority*, Boulder, CO: Lynne Rienner, 1995.

B. ARTICLES

Branscomb, Lewis M., 'A Faulty Connection? Technology and International Relations', *Harvard International Review*, 16 (2), 1994.

Chamberlain, Greg, 'Haiti's "Second Independence": Aristide's Nine Months in Office', in *Haiti – Dangerous Crossroads*, by NACLA, North American Congress on Latin America, 1995.

Chanda, Nayan and Thayer, Nate, 'I Want to Retake Power', *Far Eastern Economic Review*, 4 Feb. 1993.

Chretien, J.-P., 'Un nazisme tropical', *Liberation*, 26 April 1994.

Cloughley, Brian, 'Peace in Mind – will the UN give psyops a chance?', *Jane's International Defence Review*, Vol.29, No.3, 1996.

Crocker, Chester and Hampson, Fen Osler, 'Making Peace Settlements Work', *Foreign Policy*, No.104, 1996.

Crossette, Barbara, 'Boutros-Ghali's Query to Albright: "What Went Wrong?"', *New York Times*, 1 Jan. 1997.

Dobbie, Charles, 'A Concept for Post-Cold War Peacekeeping', *Survival*, 36 (6), 1995.

Eldon, Stewart, *From Quillpen to Satellite: Foreign Ministries in the Information Age*, London, 1994.

Everts, Philip, 'NATO, the European Community, and the United Nations', in Niedermayer, Oscar and Sinnott, Richard (eds), *Public Opinion and International Governance*, Oxford: Oxford University Press, 1995.

Goulding, Marrack, 'Case-Study: The United Nations Operation in Namibia', in *The Singapore Symposium – The Changing Role of the United Nations in Conflict Resolution and Peace-Keeping, 13–15 March 1991*, United Nations, New York, 1991.

Goulding, Marrack, 'The Evolution of United Nations Peacekeeping', *International Affairs*, 69 (3), 1993.

Gowing, Nik, 'Real-Time Television Coverage of Armed Conflicts and Diplomatic Crises: Does it Pressure or Distort Foreign Policy Decisions?' *Working Paper Series*, 1, Shorenstein Barone Center on the Press, Politics and Public Policy, Harvard University, 1994.

Gowing, Nik, 'Media Coverage: Help or Hindrance for Conflict Prevention?', *Diagnostic Paper*, Carnegie Commission on Preventing Deadly Conflict, New York, 1996.

Gramberger, Marc and Lehmann, Ingrid, 'UN und EU: Machtlos im Kreuzfeuer der Kritik – Informationspolitik zweier internationaler Organisationen im Vergleich', *Publizistik*, 40 (2), 1995.

Grunig, James E., 'Public Relations and International Affairs', *Journal of International Affairs*, 47 (1), 1993.

Hanning, Hugh, *Peacekeeping and Confidence-Building Measures in the Third World*, New York, International Peace Academy, Report No.20, 1985.

Jeldres, Julio A., 'Cambodia's Fading Hopes', *Journal of Democracy*, Vol.7, No.1, 1996.

Keohane, Robert O., 'Sovereignty, Interdependence, and International Institutions', 1993.

Kirschten, Dick, 'Missions Impossible', *National Journal*, 25 (44), 1993.

Ledgerwood, Judy, 'Patterns of CPP Political Repression and Violence During the UNTAC Period', in Heder, Steven and Ledgerwood, Judy (eds), *Propaganda, Politics, and Violence in Cambodia – Democratic Transition under United Nations Peace-Keeping*, New York: M.E. Sharpe, 1996.

Lehmann, Ingrid, 'United Nations Peace-Keeping Operations in the Seventies', *SIPRI Yearbook*, Ch.15, 1980.

Lehmann, Ingrid, 'Public Perceptions of UN Peacekeeping: A Factor in the Resolution of International Conflicts', *The Fletcher Forum of World Affairs*, 19 (1), 1995.

Lehmann, Ingrid, 'Peacekeeping, Public Perceptions and the Need for Consent', *Canadian Defence Quarterly*, 25 (2), 1995.

Linz, Juan J. and Alfred, Stepan, 'Toward Consolidated Democracies', *Journal of Democracy*, Vol.7, No.2, 1996.

Livingston, Steven, 'US Television Coverage of Rwanda', The George Washington University School of Media and Public Affairs, 1996.

Livingston, Steven and Eachus, Todd, 'Humanitarian Crisis and US Foreign Policy: Somalia and the CNN Effect Reconsidered', *Political Communication*, 12 (4) October–December 1995.

Maguire, Graham, 'Public and Parliamentary Perceptions of United Nations Peacekeeping Operations', in Clements, Kevin and Wilson, Christine (eds), *UN Peacekeeping at the Crossroads*, Canberra, Australian National University, 1994.

Maley, Michael, 'Reflections on the Electoral Process in Cambodia', in Smith, Hugh (ed.), *International Peacekeeping – Building on the Cambodia Experience*, Canberra: Australian Defense Studies Centre, 1994.

McNamara, Dennis, 'UN Human Rights Activities in Cambodia: An Evaluation', in Henkin, Alice H. (ed.), *Honouring Human Rights and Keeping the Peace: Lessons from El Salvador, Cambodia and Haiti*, Queenstown, MD: The Aspen Institute, 1995.

Miller, Linda and Smith, Michael J. (eds), *Ideas and Ideals. Essays in Honour of Stanley Hoffmann*, Boulder, San Francisco, Oxford, 1994.

Page Fortna, Virginia, 'United Nations Transition Assistance Group', in Durch, William J. (ed.), *The Evolution of UN Peacekeeping – Case Studies and Comparative Analysis*, New York: St Martin's Press, 1993.

Perez de Cuellar, Javier, 'The Role of the UN Secretary-General', in Roberts, Adam and Kingsbury, Benedict (eds), *United Nations, Divided World*, Oxford: Clarendon, 1993.

Powlick, Philip, 'The Sources of Public Opinion for American Foreign Policy Officials', *International Studies Quarterly*, 1995.

Roberts, Adam, 'The Crisis in UN Peacekeeping', *Survival*, 36 (3), 1995.

Rose, Michael, 'Bosnia-Herzegovina 1994 – NATO Support for Wider UN Peacekeeping Operations', *Natos's Sixteen Nations*, 3/4, 1994.

Rosenau, James N., 'Governance in the Twenty-first Century', *Global Governance*, 1 (1), 1995.

Rubinstein, Robert, 'Cultural Aspects of Peacekeeping', *Millennium*, 22/3, 1993.

Ruggie, John, 'Territoriality and Beyond: problematizing modernity in international relations', *International Organization*, 7 (1), 1993.

Sanderson, John M., 'UNTAC: Success and Failures', in Hugh Smith (ed.), *International Peacekeeping: Building on the Cambodia Experience*, Canberra: Australian Defense Studies Centre, 1994.

Schear, James, 'Riding the Tiger: The United Nations and Cambodia's Struggle for Peace', in Durch, William (ed.) *UN Peacekeeping – American Policy and the Uncivil Wars of the 1990's*, New York: St Martin's Press, 1996.

Schear, James, 'Bosnia's Post-Dayton Traumas', *Foreign Policy*, No.104, 1996.

Shelton, Hugh and Vane, Timothy, 'Winning the Information War in Haiti', *Military Review*, Nov./Dec. 1995.

Tharoor, Shashi, 'The Future of Peacekeeping', in Whitman, Jim and Pocock, David (eds), *After Rwanda – The Coordination of United Nations Humanitarian Assistance*, London: Macmillan, 1996.

Touval, Saadia, 'Why the UN Fails', *Foreign Affairs*, 73 (5), 1994.

Vaccaro, J. Mathew, 'The Politics of Genocide: Peacekeeping and Disaster Relief in Rwanda', in Durch, William J. (ed.), *UN Peacekeeping, American Policy, and the Uncivil Wars of the 1990s*, New York: St Martin's Press, 1996.

C. UNITED NATIONS DOCUMENTS

Annan, Kofi A., *Renewal amid Transition*, Annual Report on the Work of the Organization, New York, United Nations, 1997.

Boutros-Ghali, Boutros, *An Agenda for Peace*, New York, United Nations, 1992.

Donini, Antonio and Niland, Norah, 'Rwanda: Lessons Learned. A Report on the Coordination of Humanitarian Activities', Department for

Humanitarian Affairs, United Nations, New York, 1994.

Harman, Nicholas, 'Information in Rwanda', unpublished consultant's report submitted to the United Nations Secretariat, New York, 31 Oct., 1994.

Heyman, Jeffrey, Report on a mission to UNAMIR concerning the establishment of a United Nations radio station in Rwanda, unpublished consultant's report submitted to the United Nations Secretariat, 1994.

Paquet-Sevigny, Therese, 'A Plan to Revitalize the Department of Public Information', United Nations internal Document No.87-45565, 1987.

Raevsky, Andrei, 'Aspects of Psychological Operations and Intelligence', United Nations, New York and Geneva, 1996.

This is DPI – The United Nations Department of Public Information and How It Works, United Nations, New York, 1984.

United Nations, *The Blue Helmets – A Review of United Nations Peace-Keeping*, New York, United Nations Department of Public Information (2nd edn), 1990.

United Nations, *The Blue Helmets – A Review of United Nations Peace-Keeping*, New York, United Nations Department of Public Information (3rd edn), 1996.

The United Nations and Cambodia, 1991–1995, The United Nations Blue Book Series, Vol.II, United Nations, New York.

The United Nations and Rwanda, 1993–1996, The United Nations Blue Book Series, Vol.X, United Nations, New York.

United Nations Disarmament and Conflict Resolution Project, *Managing Arms in Peace Processes: Cambodia*, United Nations, New York and Geneva, 1996.

United Nations Department of Peace-keeping Operations, *Comprehensive Report on Lessons Learned from United Nations Assistance Mission for Rwanda (UNAMIR), Oct. 1993–April 1996*, Lessons Learned Unit, DPKO, United Nations, New York, 1996.

United Nations Department of Peace-keeping Operations, United Nations Mission in Haiti, Mid-Mission Assessment Report, April 1995–Feb. 1996, United Nations, New York, 1996.

United Nations Department of Public Information, Fact Sheet 6, Information Package on UNTAES: S/1996/883, 26 Oct. 1996; S/1996/821, 1 Oct. 1996; S/1997/148, 24 Feb. 1997; Secretary-General Boutros Boutros-Ghali, Farewell Address to the General Assembly, UN Press Release SG/SM/6133, 17 Dec. 1996.

D. MANUSCRIPTS

Arbuckle, James V., 'UNTAES: The Past that was Prologue', unpublished manuscript, March 1997.

Doyle, Michael W., *UN Peacekeeping in Cambodia – UNTAC's Civil Mandate*, International Peace Academy Occasional Paper, Boulder, Lynne Rienner, 1995.

Farmer, Paul, 'Hidden Structural Violence in Agrarian Societies: The Case of Haiti', unpublished manuscript from a lecture delivered at Yale University, 1997.

International Crisis Group, Report: 'Bosnia Project – Eastern Slavonia', 27 March 1996.

Kalb, Marvin, 'The Dangers of Patriotic Journalism', unpublished manuscript, Harvard University, 1993.

Kanninen, Tapio, *Organizational Retrenchment and Reorganization: The Case of the United Nations' Response to the Financial Crisis of the Mid-1980s*, Doctoral dissertation, City University of New York, 1990.

Livingston, Steven, 'Beyond the CNN-Effect', Washington, DC, 1997 (manuscript made available by the author).

Yacoumopoulou, Lena, 'Information Campaigns in Peace-Keeping Missions', unpublished manuscript, 1994.

E. PERIODICALS

Crosslines Global Report, The Independent Newsjournal on Humanitarian Action, Development and World Trends, Geneva and Boston.

F. PAMPHLETS

Joint Psychological Operations Task Force Haiti, PSYOP Support to Operation UPHOLD DEMOCRACY, pamphlet, Fort Bragg, North Carolina, 1995.

Index

censorship, 42, 129
Central America, 15, 112, 126 (n.5)
Centre for Peace, Non-Violence and
  Human Rights, 138
Chalk, Frank, 95, 99
Charny, Joel R., 97
Charter, United Nations, 4, 9 (n.10), 22,
  93, 100, 103, 105 (n.41), 116, 125, 131,
  132
Cherif, Anwar, 33
Cisse, Abdou, 40, 49 (n.41)
'civil society', concept of, 151
CIVPOL (civilian police) Information
  Officers, 112, 113
Clinton, President, 90; administration, 119
CMAC (Cambodian Mine Action Centre),
  55
CNN, 2, 24
Coalition pour la Defénse de la République
  (CDR), 95
Cockburn, Alexander, 48 (n.21)
Code of Conduct for Political Parties
  (Namibia), 32, 43
Cold War, 1, 2, 117
Commissioner for Namibia, 30
communication: principles of, 18–19, 77,
  103, 110, 125, 147–9; technology, 1, 2,
  11; towards a theory of political
  communication, 11–21; see also
  information
Communications and Project Management
  Service, 24, 33
Conference of Heads of States of the Great
  Lakes Region (1995), 99
conflict: analysis, 15; resolution theories,
  12; ripeness, 12, 15, 53
Congo legacy, 100–1, 103
consent, 4, 9 (n.10), 15, 17–18
consent divide, 4
Constituent Assembly, Cambodia, 53
constraints: bureaucratic, 150;
  environmental, 14
constraints model, 16
Controller (UN), 40, 49 (n.42)
corporate image-making/identity, 4, 39, 74;
  see also identity programme
correspondents see journalists/
  correspondents
Council for Namibia, 30
counterpropaganda, 151
CPP (Cambodian People's Party), 58
Crnobrnja, Mihailo, 131, 132, 134
Croatia, 129, 131, 132, 133, 134, 135, 136,

137, 138–9, 140, 142, 145 (nn.37, 47),
  154
Croatian Radio, 133
Croats/Croatians, 136, 137, 139, 142, 144
  (n.32), 149, 154
Crocker, Chester, 15
Cuba, 35
Cubans, 30, 32, 47 (n.5)
cultural sensitivities, 19, 45, 74, 77, 125,
  149

Daigle, General Pierre, 113
Dallaire, Brigadier-General Romeo, 87, 90,
  91, 92, 93, 98, 99, 102, 103, 108 (n.88),
  118
Danish Foreign Ministry, 96
Dearth, Doug, 10 (n.17)
demobilization, 51, 53, 87
democracy, 18, 77, 120; Operation Uphold
  Democracy, 116–18, 125; see also
  elections
Department of Humanitarian Affairs
  (United Nations), 92, 101
Department of Peacekeeping Operations
  (United Nations), 22, 25, 26, 26 (n.1),
  75, 89, 98, 101–2, 123, 135; see also
  Lessons Learned Unit
Department of Public Information (United
  Nations), 20 (n.7), 22–5, 26, 32, 33, 39,
  40, 49 (n.42), 65–6, 114, 115, 141
Development Programme (United
  Nations), 24
Diagne, Captain M.B.E., 92
displaced persons, 51, 54–5, 87, 136, 137,
  142; see also refugees
District Centres, 31, 33, 36, 41, 43–4, 50
  (n.54)
Dobbie, Charles, 4, 9 (n.11)
Donini, Antonio, 101
donor fatigue, 2
Doyle, Michael, 64
DPI see Department of Public Information
DPKO see Department of Peacekeeping
  Operations
Dubrovnik, 129

Eastern Slavonia, 6, 7–8, 15, 26, 135, 136,
  137, 138, 139, 140, 141, 142, 143, 144
  (n.32), 148, 150, 154
Eckhard, Fred, 25, 33, 41
Economist, The, 132
education, 4, 7, 19, 35, 56–7, 61, 148
Egypt, 104 (n.6)

Sihanouk, Prince, 73
slogans, 40–1, 121
Smarth, Rosny, 121
SNC, 60
SOC *see* State of Cambodia
SOFA (Status of Forces Agreement), 17
Somalia, 1, 2, 3, 5, 9 (nn5, 10), 10 (n.12),
  14, 78 (n.3), 89–90, 102, 117, 118–19,
  128 (n.33)
South Africa, 28, 30, 32, 34, 35, 37, 44, 48
  (nn.21, 23), 96; Administration in
  Namibia, 31, 34, 42
South African Bureau of Information, 37
Southern Africa, 15; *see also* names of
  countries
South-West Africa, 30, 31, 35
South-West African Broadcasting
  Corporation (SWABC), 31, 38, 41–2, 46,
  49 (nn.33, 35)
South-West African People's Organization
  (SWAPO), 28, 30, 34, 35, 36, 37, 47–8
  (n.21), 48 (n.28)
Soviet Union, 35
Special Operations Task Force, 119
Special Prosecutor's Office (Cambodia), 56
Special Rapporteur on extrajudicial,
  summary or arbitrary executions, 95–6,
  106 (n.52)
Special Representative of the Secretary-
  General, 5, 150; in Cambodia, 56, 64, 66,
  68, 69, 70 (*see also* Akashi, Yasushi); in
  the Congo, 100; in Haiti, 114, 115, 120,
  127 (nn.15, 17) (*see also* Brahimi,
  Lakhdar); in Namibia, 28, 30, 31, 32, 39,
  41, 42, 43, 44 (*see also* Ahtisaari, Martti);
  in Rwanda, 87, 91, 98, 101, 102 (*see also*
  Booh-Booh, Jacques-Roger; Khan,
  Shaharyar)
Spokesman, 67, 70–1, 98, 112, 113, 120,
  125, 139, 148; *see also* names of
  individuals
Spokesman's Office: Cambodia, 70–1;
  Namibia, 41; of the Secretary-General,
  33
Stadtler, Walter, 10 (n.12)
State of Cambodia (SOC), 54, 56, 58–9, 66,
  69, 70
Status of Forces Agreement (SOFA), 17
staying power of third parties, 36, 46, 103
strategic level, definition of, 5
strategic management function,
  communication as, 19, 150, 151
substantive theories, 13–16

Sudan, 2, 96
Supreme National Council of Cambodia,
  51, 59
SWABC *see* South-West African
  Broadcasting Corporation
SWAPO *see* South-West African People's
  Organization
Synthesis Report, 97, 98, 107 (n.68)

tactical dissemination teams, 120
tactical level, definition of, 6
Tanzania, 86
Taroor, Shashi, 1
Task Force on the Reorientation of United
  Nations Public Information Activities,
  24–5
television, 1, 2, 11, 38, 42, 61, 69, 97, 114,
  119, 120, 129, 131, 137, 138, 140, 141
Thailand, 66
Thais, 54
Thomas Watson Institute for International
  Studies, 14
Thompson, Mark, 129, 133, 134, 137
Thornberry, Cedric, 39, 44, 46, 48 (n.23),
  49 (nn.33, 43)
Time, 63
Tome, Patricia, 107 (n.71)
training, 33–4
Training Institute for Namibia, 30
Transitional Administrator's Award fund,
  139
transparency, 19, 149
Tripartite Agreements (1988), 32
Tudjman, President, 138–9
Tutsi, 84, 86, 88, 94, 95, 104 (n.16)
Twa, 84

Uganda, 86, 87, 92, 94, 104 (n.6)
UNAMIC (United Nations Advance
  Mission in Cambodia), 51, 55, 77 (n.3)
UNAMIR (United Nations Assistance
  Mission for Rwanda), 6, 7, 84–109, 147,
  150, 152; assessment, 102–4; expansion
  of mandate, 92–4; historical background,
  84–8; humanitarian tasks, 91–2;
  information effort, 98–9; international
  environment, 89–91; international media
  coverage, 96–8; issue of jamming hate
  radio, 99–101; mass murder and civil
  war, 88–9; media environment, 95–6;
  political leadership, 101–2; and
  principles of communication, 147;
  selected as case study, 6, 7